# WEB DEVELOPER.COM GUIDE TO DYNAMIC HTML

*Steven Holzner*

**WILEY COMPUTER PUBLISHING**

John Wiley & Sons, Inc.
New York • Chichester • Weinheim • Brisbane • Singapore • Toronto

Publisher: Robert Ipsen
Editor: Cary Sullivan
Assistant Editor: Kathryn A. Malm
Managing Editor: Erin Singletary
Electronic Products, Associate Editor: Mike Green
Text Design & Composition: Benchmark Productions

Designations used by companies to distinguish their products are often claimed as trademarks. In all instances where John Wiley & Sons, Inc., is aware of a claim, the product names appear in initial capital or ALL CAPITAL LETTERS. Readers, however, should contact the appropriate companies for more complete information regarding trademarks and registration.

Internet World, Web Week, Web Developer, Internet Shopper, and Mecklermedia are the exclusive trademarks of Mecklermedia Corporation and are used with permission.

*Library of Congress Cataloging-in-Publication Data:*

Holzner, Steven.
    Web developer.com guide to dynamic HTML / Steve Holzner.
        p.   cm.
    Includes index.
    ISBN 0-471-24102-4 (pbk. : alk. paper)
    1. HTML (Document markup language)  2. Web sites--Design.
  I. Title
  QA76.76.H94H65    1997
  005.7'2--dc21                                     97-28342
                                                    CIP

Printed in the United States of America
10 9 8 7 6 5 4 3 2 1

# CONTENTS

# INTRODUCTION

**W**elcome to our book on Dynamic HTML! This book demonstrates some extraordinary, eye-opening things—from Web pages that change themselves as you watch to powerful, layered graphics; from graphics animation that involves the whole Web page to dialog boxes that let us really communicate with the user; from dragging objects around our Web pages using the mouse to "binding" data to a Web page and accessing that data without additional downloads from the Internet server. Much of Dynamic HTML revolutionizes the creation of Web pages, and this book provides a fully guided tour of these powerful new resources.

Dynamic HTML represents a whole new level in Web page creation. Although you have probably heard a lot of hype about Dynamic HTML, the underlying truth is no less impressive. Dynamic HTML really does make Web pages "come alive" in a way that was impossible before. When the Web first started, Web pages were static affairs with text and graphics only. Then a Web page became an arrangement of static elements with some active objects (like Java applets or ActiveX controls) embedded in it. Things have gone to the next logical level now: *Everything* is active. Your page can "watch" and react as the mouse travels over text, graphics, or tables. You can place graphics behind or on top of text—and then make those graphics move. You can fade text in or out as the user moves the mouse near it. In this and other ways, literally every part of your Web page is active, which is an incredible advance in fulfilling the promise of the Web.

This book will take you on a guided tour of Dynamic HTML. Two major implementations of Dynamic HTML are in use today: Netscape's Navigator, and Microsoft's Internet Explorer. If you want to work with Dynamic HTML, you should be familiar with both implementations.

## Two Browsers, Two Dynamic HTML Visions

It would be great if the two major Dynamic HTML implementations were similar, but, unfortunately, they're not, as we'll see. What both browsers refer to as "Dynamic HTML" goes well beyond the World Wide Web Consortium (or WWWC;

www.w3.org) specifications for new tags and style sheets. In fact, there are such major differences between the two that it's almost impossible to get any but the most basic Dynamic HTML Web page working for both browsers (although you can outsmart them by checking what browser your page is running in and actually rewriting your page on the fly, tailoring it to the user's browser, as we'll see later in this book). The differences include such basic mainstays in Dynamic HTML as how to handle mouse and keyboard events, how to handle the new graphics techniques and animation, and the new properties that have been added to the basic HTML tags that were already supported. Nonetheless, we'll cover what both browsers refer to as Dynamic HTML in this book, because HTML programmers should be familiar with both.

Internet Explorer's Dynamic HTML implementation is far larger, as we'll see. Now almost every tag has "come alive" with added properties and events. Netscape Navigator has added new properties and events as well, but fewer of them.

We should note that what Microsoft calls Dynamic HTML is several times larger than what Netscape calls Dynamic HTML, so much of the material in this book will concern Internet Explorer only. Here's a brief overview of the new topics we'll explore for Internet Explorer:

- Rewriting Web pages at any time
- Using the mouse and keyboard
- Style sheets
- Dialog boxes and windows
- Positioning Web page object dynamically
- Graphics animation
- Changing objects' appearances dynamically
- Working with Web pages offline
- Database connections

Here's a brief overview of what we'll see for Netscape Navigator (note that almost every one of these topics is implemented differently than the corresponding Internet Explorer implementation):

- Rewriting Web pages
- Using the mouse and keyboard
- Style sheets
- Dialog boxes and windows
- Using layers in a Web page

- Positioning Web page object dynamically
- Graphics animation
- Dynamic fonts

The text makes it clear which browser we're talking about at any particular time.

There's another difference between these two implementations that we'll see throughout the book as well: scripting languages. Internet Explorer uses both VBScript and JavaScript; Netscape Navigator uses only JavaScript at present. On the other hand, most programmers who program for Internet Explorer seem to prefer VBScript, and in fact, Microsoft itself seems to prefer it as well—all its Dynamic HTML documentation and samples use VBScript, not JavaScript.

This gives us a dilemma: If we stuck to JavaScript, we'd be using a scripting language that both browsers can understand. On the other hand, we wouldn't be serving the majority of Internet Explorer programmers who use VBScript (not to mention the beginners who want to understand Microsoft's documentation and examples, all written in VBScript).

The solution is to use *both* JavaScript and VBScript, which is what this book does. (In fact, this is a good solution, because the implementation of Dynamic HTML is so very different in the two browsers, it's very rare that a Dynamic HTML Web page would work in both browsers, even if it were written in a scripting language both browsers can understand.) In this book, the Internet Explorer examples use mostly VBScript, and the Netscape Navigator examples use JavaScript. In this way, we will learn how to use both JavaScript and VBScript, and that knowledge is an asset to any Web programmer. (The languages are similar enough so switching back and forth between them is common.)

## How This Book Is Organized

This book will help you add skill after skill as you progress through the chapters. For example, we'll start in *Chapter 1: Our Foundation: HTML Itself* by reviewing the elements of a Web page and some of the basic HTML tags.

In *Chapter 2: Scripting Your Web Page*, we'll see how to use a scripting language to connect code to our Web pages elements. This knowledge will be invaluable throughout the book, because much of Dynamic HTML involves using a scripting language.

Then, in *Chapter 3: Changing Your Web Page on the Fly!*, we're ready to start working with Dynamic HTML itself, which we'll do by learning how to change Web pages on the fly. We'll see all kinds of examples here, seeing how Web pages can actually rewrite themselves as you watch. We'll see how to rewrite Web pages under the direction of the user, according to the time of day, and much more.

In the next chapter, *Chapter 4: Powerful Mouse and Text Effects*, we'll see many new text and mouse effects, including how to read the location of the mouse directly in our scripts and how to read keys straight from the keyboard. We'll also see many new Dynamic HTML effects, such as changing the color of hyperlinks as the user brings the mouse near them.

In *Chapter 5: Active HTML Tags*, we'll see that Internet Explorer has gone all out for Dynamic HTML. Now all its HTML tags have become active in a way that only buttons or text boxes were before. We'll see how there's much more to the usual Web page than meets the eye.

The next chapter, *Chapter 6: Amazing Graphics Effects*, is all about new graphics effects. We'll see how to use filters to change graphics on the screen, making them wave or flip around, coloring them, and more. We'll see how to overlap text, draw amazing graphics with the structured graphics control, and use layers.

After we've worked with graphics, we'll see how to create graphics animation in *Chapter 7: Graphics Animation*. This is where our Web pages come alive as we see how to move, rotate, and enlarge images on the fly. We'll also see how to let the user drag and drop images and how to use Web page layers for animation.

In *Chapter 8: Working with Dialog Boxes and Windows*, we'll see how to create dialog boxes that seem to leap out of a Web page. Dialog boxes are a professional touch for any Web page; when they pop up, it can be a very impressive effect.

Finally, in *Chapter 9: Web Pages That Work Offline and with Databases*, we'll see how Internet Explorer supports Web pages that work offline when we investigate data binding. When you bind data to a Web page, the browser will no longer need to make multiple references to the Internet server to work with data in a page; all the data we need will already have been downloaded, and we can sort, filter, or manipulate it as we like.

In addition, you'll find that all the samples in this book are stored on the Web site for this book – that's explained more fully in the Appendix.

All in all, there's a lot coming up in this book!

## Tools You Will Need

In order to use this book, you'll need a few tools—a Web browser, for one. As mentioned, two Web browsers support Dynamic HTML today: Microsoft Internet Explorer 4.0 and Netscape Navigator 4.0. You'll need one of these browsers, and if you want to be a heavy-duty Dynamic HTML programmer, you'll need both. There are big differences in what the two browsers consider Dynamic HTML, as we'll see throughout the book; Internet Explorer's version is far larger than Netscape's. In this book, we'll use Internet Explorer 4.0 Preview 2 and Netscape Navigator 4.02 browsers.

Besides a browser, you'll need a text editor or word processor of some kind so that you can create your own Web pages. As discussed in Chapter 1, this editor must be able to save text in "plain text" format so that your Web browser can read it. (Refer to the discussion in Chapter 1 for more details.) If you have a program specifically devoted to Web page creation, that's fine (but note that we won't make use of the many bells and whistles that often come built into such pages).

You might want a graphics program as well so that you can create and edit graphics files. This is not necessary, however, because all the graphics files that appear in this book are also available on the accompanying Web site. Those are all the tools you'll need to make profitable use of this book.

If you want more information about a specific browser's implementation of Dynamic HTML, you might check out these sites on the Web: www.microsoft .com/workshop/author/dynhtml for Microsoft and developer.netscape.com/library/ documentation for Netscape (look for references to Dynamic HTML).

This book is example based, because it's always easiest to see how something works by seeing an example rather than just talking about it. We'll build up the examples in book incrementally, step by step, for clarity, and then we'll run the example, seeing it in action. When we add new code to a Web page, we'll indicate the new lines like this, with arrows:

```
<HTML>

<HEAD>                                                          ⇐
<TITLE>Textbox Example</TITLE>                                  ⇐
</HEAD>                                                         ⇐
   .
   .
   .
```

Our examples will be short, bite sized, and powerful. There's no use working through page after page of code just to learn one point. And this book has plenty of examples—more than four dozen, in fact.

## What's on the Web Site

You'll find that all the examples for this book are on the Web site. Here's how it works: you can either download the examples zipped in the file named code.zip, or look at the examples individually in your browser by clicking the appropriate link in the Web site — each link corresponds to a Web page from the book.

If you decide to download code.zip and unzip it, a new directory will be created for each example, and each directory will contain the code for that example. To see an example at work, just open the .htm file in the directory with the same name as the example. That's all it takes.

## On Your Mark . . .

We're ready to start! To begin our exploration of Dynamic HTML, we'll need a good foundation in the creation of Web pages, so Chapter 1 reviews the fundamentals. If you already feel confident about your abilities in creating standard Web pages, you can move on to Chapter 2. Because so many elements in a Web page can be active, we need some way of working with the various elements in a Web page. Chapter 2 is an introduction to scripting your Web pages for that purpose.

We'll start our guided tour of Dynamic HTML by creating a standard Web page in Chapter 1. This is intended as a review or brush-up page; if you don't feel comfortable with the level of discussion in that chapter, you might consider taking a look at a good standard (static) HTML book before continuing, such as the *HTML Sourcebook*, third edition, by Ian Graham (John Wiley & Sons, 1995), or something more basic like *The Project Cool Guide to HTML* by Martin and Davis (John Wiley & Sons, 1997). On the other hand, if you already have some experience with HTML, turn to Chapter 1 now to get fully up to speed.

# CHAPTER ONE

# OUR FOUNDATION:

## *HTML Itself*

I n this chapter, we'll take a look at straight HTML (HyperText Markup Language) so that our HTML foundation is firm before we build on it throughout the rest of this book. Web pages are written in HTML and are usually uploaded to an Internet service provider (ISP) for placement on the Web. The details of installing a Web page on an ISP vary from provider to provider. Typically, you will use an FTP (File Transfer Protocol) program of some sort to upload your pages to a specific area set aside by your ISP for that purpose. After that—you're on the Internet! The address of your Web page is called its URL (Universal Resource Locator), and that URL will start with "http:" like Microsoft's site (http://www.microsoft.com) or Netscape's site (http://www.netscape.com).

How basic can Web pages get? Very simple indeed—in fact, you can place files of simple (non-HTML) text on the Web, and users can then download and look at that text in their Web browsers:

```
------------------------------------------------------
|                                                    |
|                    Simple Text                     |
|                                                    |
------------------------------------------------------
```

Of course, if that's all there was to it, this would be a very short book. Simple text appears just as it might in the Windows Notepad or WordPad applications— as nothing special. The first step toward controlling your Web page's appearance is to start using *HTML tags*.

# HTML Tags

Web browsers make use of HTML tags to understand just how you want your Web page to appear. Using HTML tags, you set up colors, headings, tables, images, and, much, much more. To indicate to a Web browser that your Web page uses HTML, you start with the HTML tag. All <HTML> tags are enclosed in angle brackets, < and >:

This is the actual text, "<HTML>," that you enter into the document that is to become your Web page. You can create your Web pages with any standard word processor or editing program that can save text as simple text, without special formatting codes. (If you use a word processor like Microsoft Word that places such codes into documents, you'll have to save your text in plain-text format using the Save As... item in the File menu—for example, in Windows 95 WordPad, select Save As, then select Text Document in the "Save as type" box.) Such files have the extension .html or .htm. To make things easiest for most readers, this book uses the 8.3 file-naming convention (a maximum of eight characters followed by a three-letter extension), so we'll use the extension .htm. We'll call this first Web page, in which we review HTML, html.htm. Here's our first line in that file:

Now that we've started our new Web page, let's take a look the usual method of making what's going on inside a Web page easier to understand: comments.

## Web Page Comments

To keep things straight in a Web page, you may want to add notes to yourself, but you don't want such internal notes to appear to the user. You use *comments* for that purpose. Comments don't appear in Web browsers, but note that their text is downloaded with the rest of the Web page, so they can increase download time. Comments are enclosed in angle brackets, < and >, and begin with an exclamation point like this:

```
<!-- This is a comment. You use comments to add explanatory text to
your Web pages, as we'll see in this Web page. We start the Web page
with the HTML tag, indicating this is a Web page written in HyperText
Markup Language.>
<HTML>
     .
     .
     .
```

In addition, almost every HTML tag like <HTML> needs a closing tag, the text of which begins with a forward slash, like this: </HTML>. So we add that at the end of html.htm:

In our actual Web page file, that looks like this:

```
<!-- This is a comment. You use comments to add explanatory text to
your Web pages, as we'll see in this Web page. We start the Web page
with the HTML tag, indicating this is a Web page written in Hypertext
Markup Language.>
<HTML>
     .
     .
     .
</HTML>                                                         ⇐
```

Although we've used the HTML tag here, most Web browsers don't require it—in fact, Web browsers are very accommodating programs, tolerant of missing HTML tags and other errors. Web browsers are tolerant because the people viewing your Web pages have no way of fixing errors, but of course you should try to make your Web pages as free of error as possible. You can use Web page *validators* to look for errors in your Web page—just search for the word "validator" on the Web; these programs will read in your Web page once you give them its URL, and they will give you a report on any errors.

Now that we've set up the outline of our Web page, let's look at the first element of most Web pages: the Web page heading.

## Web Page Headings

We really begin the Web page with its *heading*. We set up the heading with the HEAD tag this way:

```
 -----------------------------------------------------
|<HTML>                                               |
|                                                     |
|  -------------------------------------------------  |
| |<HEAD>                                           | |    ⇐
| |                                                 | |
| |                                                 | |
| |</HEAD>                                          | |    ⇐
|  -------------------------------------------------  |
|                                                     |
 -----------------------------------------------------
```

The heading used to have a formal structure that contained formatting information about the rest of the page, but now it's become abbreviated and usually holds only the Web page's title.

## The Web Page's Title

A Web page's *title* is quite important (although many Web page programmers don't realize its importance and omit it, to their cost) because the title is the text that will appear in the title bar of the Web browser when that browser is displaying your page. It's also the text that appears in Web page directories like Yahoo or Alta Vista. A Web page's title is set up with the TITLE tag in the header, as shown here. Note that we enclose the title's text itself between the <TITLE> and </TITLE> tags:

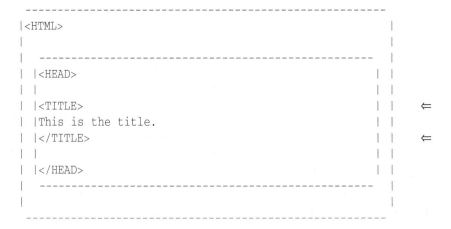

```
 -----------------------------------------------------
|<HTML>                                               |
|                                                     |
|  -------------------------------------------------  |
| |<HEAD>                                           | |
| |                                                 | |
| |<TITLE>                                          | |    ⇐
| |This is the title.                               | |
| |</TITLE>                                         | |    ⇐
| |                                                 | |
| |</HEAD>                                          | |
|  -------------------------------------------------  |
|                                                     |
 -----------------------------------------------------
```

Let's add the title "Welcome to Dynamic HTML!" to our Web page now. That looks like this in our page's HTML:

```
<!-- This is a comment. You use comments to add explanatory text to
your Web pages, as we'll see in this Web page. We start the Web page
with the HTML tag, indicating this is a Web page written in HyperText
Markup Language.>
<HTML>



<!-- The next section is the Web page's header. We place the title of
the Web page here. This title is displayed by Web browsers and WWW
directories.  The header starts with the HEAD tag, and the title
starts with the TITLE tag.>
<HEAD>                                                          ⇐
<TITLE>Welcome to Dynamic HTML!</TITLE>                         ⇐
</HEAD>                                                         ⇐
    .0
    .
    .
```

Now that the Web page's header is set up, we can continue on to the part where all the action is: the Web page's body.

## The Web Page's Body

The Web page's *body* is where things really happen in a Web page. We set up the body with the BODY tag:

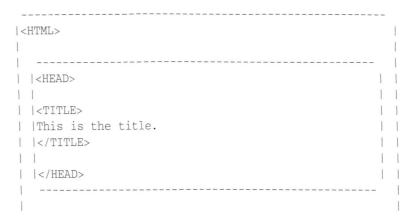

```
 ------------------------------------------------------
|<HTML>                                                 |
|                                                       |
|  --------------------------------------------------   |
| |<HEAD>                                            |  |
| |                                                  |  |
| |<TITLE>                                           |  |
| |This is the title.                                |  |
| |</TITLE>                                          |  |
| |                                                  |  |
| |</HEAD>                                           |  |
|  --------------------------------------------------   |
|                                                       |
```

```
|   ------------------------------------------------   |
|  |<BODY>                                         |   |      ⇐
|  |                                               |   |
|  |                                               |   |
|  |</BODY>                                        |   |      ⇐
|   ------------------------------------------------   |
|                                                      |
|</HTML>
 ------------------------------------------------------
```

We can use several keywords called *attributes* in the BODY tag to set such items as the color of the page's background, the default color of the text, the color of hyperlinks (that is, the underlined items you click to jump to new location), the color of links you've already visited, and more. Here's how to use the <BODY> tag in both Internet Explorer and Netscape Navigator. (When we introduce new HTML tags throughout the book, we'll list them for both browsers this way.)

**Internet Explorer**

```
<BODY
ALIGN=CENTER | LEFT | RIGHT
ALINK=color
BACKGROUND=string
BGCOLOR=color
BGPROPERTIES=FIXED
ID=string
LEFTMARGIN=variant
LINK=color
SCROLL=string
STYLE=string
TEXT=color
TITLE=string
TOPMARGIN=string
VLINK=color
event = script
>
```

**Netscape Navigator**

```
<BODY
ALINK="color"
BACKGROUND="bgURL"
BGCOLOR="color"
LINK="color"
TEXT="color"
ONBLUR="blurJScode"
ONFOCUS="focusJScode"
ONLOAD="loadJScode"
ONUNLOAD="unloadJScode"
VLINK="color"
>
```

In our case, let's set the colors of text, links, active links, and links we've already visited. We set colors by specifying a red, green, and blue color value in *hexadecimal* (base 16) format. Each color value can range from 0 to 255, which is from 00 to ff in hexadecimal. Those color values go together in a six-digit hexadecimal value—red first, then green, then blue. For example, black has all color values set to 0, so black is represented as 000000. White has all color values set to 255 (ff), so white is represented by ffffff. A color like pure, bright red is ff0000, green is 00ff00, and blue is 0000ff. We'll set the colors we want in our Web page's BODY tag this way:

```
<!-- This is a comment. You use comments to add explanatory text to
your Web pages, as we'll see in this Web page. We start the Web page
with the HTML tag, indicating this is a Web page written in HyperText
Markup Language.>
<HTML>


<!-- The next section is the Web page's header. We place the title of
the Web page here. This title is displayed by Web browsers and WWW
directories. The header starts with the HEAD tag, and the title
starts with the TITLE tag.>
<HEAD>
<TITLE>Welcome to Dynamic HTML!</TITLE>
</HEAD>


<!-- Next comes the Web page's body. This is where the Web page proper
is set up, enclosed with the BODY tag.>
<BODY TEXT = ffff00 LINK = ff0000 ALINK = ffffff VLINK = ffff00>       ⇐
    .
    .
    .
```

It's not always easy to figure out the color values for the colors you want, so Web browsers define many colors by a name that you can use in place of the hexadecimal value. These colors appear in Table 1.1 for Internet Explorer; each has a corresponding hexadecimal value. For example, gray is 808080, coral FF7F50, crimson DC143C, and so on. Table 1.2 shows the predefined colors for Netscape Navigator.

**Table 1.1  Predefined Colors in Internet Explorer**

| | | |
|---|---|---|
| aliceblue | darkkhaki | green |
| antiquewhite | darkmagenta | greenyellow |
| aqua | darkolivegreen | honeydew |

*Continued*

## Table 1.1  Continued

| | | |
|---|---|---|
| aquamarine | darkorange | hotpink |
| azure | darkorchid | indianred |
| beige | darkred | indigo |
| bisque | darksalmon | ivory |
| black | darkseagreen | khaki |
| blanchedalmond | darkslateblue | lavender |
| blue | darkslategray | lavenderblush |
| blueviolet | darkturquoise | lawngreen |
| brown | darkviolet | lemonchiffon |
| burlywood | deeppink | lightblue |
| cadetblue | deepskyblue | lightcoral |
| chartreuse | dimgray | lightcyan |
| chocolate | dodgerblue | lime |
| coral | firebrick | maroon |
| cornflowerblue | floralwhite | navy |
| cornsilk | crimson | olive |
| olive | cyan | purple |
| purple | darkblue | red |
| darkcyan | ghostwhite | silver |
| darkgoldenrod | gold | teal |
| darkgray | goldenrod | white |
| | gray | yellow |

## Table 1.2  Predefined Colors in Netscape Navigator

| | | |
|---|---|---|
| aliceblue | antiquewhite | aqua |
| aquamarine | azure | beige |
| black | blanchedalmond | blue |
| blueviolet | brown | burlywood |
| cadetblue | chartreuse | chocolate |
| coral | cornflowerblue | cornsilk |

## Table 1.2  Continued

| | | |
|---|---|---|
| crimson | cyan | darkblue |
| darkcyan | darkgoldenrod | darkgray |
| darkgreen | darkkhaki | darkmagenta |
| darkolivegreen | darkorange | darkorchid |
| darkred | darksalmon | darkseagreen |
| darkslateblue | darkslategray | darkturquoise |
| darkviolet | deeppink | deepskyblue |
| dimgray | dodgerblue | firebrick |
| floralwhite | forestgreen | fuchsia |
| gainsboro | ghostwhite | gold |
| goldenrod | gray | green |
| greenyellow | honeydew | hotpink |
| indianred | indigo | ivory |
| khaki | lavender | lavenderblush |
| lawngreen | lemonchiffon | lightblue |
| lightcoral | lightcyan | lightgoldenrodyellow |
| lightgreen | lightgrey | lightpink |
| lightsalmon | lightseagreen | lightskyblue |
| lightslategray | lightsteelblue | lightyellow |
| lime | limegreen | linen |
| magenta | maroon | mediumaquamarine |
| mediumblue | mediumorchid | mediumpurple |
| mediumseagreen | mediumslateblue | mediumspringgreen |
| mediumturquoise | mediumvioletred | midnightblue |
| mintcream | mistyrose | moccasin |
| navajowhite | navy | oldlace |
| olive | olivedrab | orange |
| orangered | orchid | palegoldenrod |
| palegreen | paleturquoise | palevioletred |
| papayawhip | peach | puffperu |

*Continued*

**Table 1.2 Continued**

| | | |
|---|---|---|
| pink | plum | powderblue |
| purple | red | rosybrown |
| royalblue | saddlebrown | salmon |
| sandybrown | seagreen | seashell |
| sienna | silver | skyblue |
| slateblue | slategray | |
| snow | springgreen | steelblue |
| tan | teal | thistletomato |
| turquoise | violet | wheat |
| white | whitesmoke | yellow |
| yellowgreen | | |

Now we can specify an image to use for our Web page's background. The Web browser will "tile" the background with this image, as we'll see.

## Using a Background Image

To specify an image for the background of our Web page, we can use another BODY tag with the BACKGROUND attribute to set to the name of the image file we want to use to cover the background. (You don't have to use a new BODY tag in the Web page if you don't want to; you can simply add the BACKGROUND attribute to the BODY tag we already have.)

Image files are often stored in subdirectories called "images" or "gif" or "graphics" files. In this case, we'll place the image file we'll use for the background, back.gif, into a subdirectory named gif. The image in back.gif appears in Figure 1.1.

We add the new background image by referring to the image file by path, gif/back.gif:

```
<!-- This is a comment. You use comments to add explanatory text to
your Web pages, as we'll see in this Web page. We start the Web page
with the HTML tag, indicating this is a Web page written in HyperText
Markup Language.>
<HTML>


<!-- The next section is the Web page's header. We place the title of
the Web page here. This title is displayed by Web browsers and WWW
```

**Figure 1.1  Our background image, back.gif.**

```
directories. The header starts with the HEAD tag, and the title
starts with the TITLE tag.>
<HEAD>
<TITLE>Welcome to Dynamic HTML!</TITLE>
</HEAD>


<!-- Next comes the Web page's body. This is where the Web page proper
is set up, enclosed with the BODY tag.>
<BODY TEXT  = fff00 LINK  = ff0000 ALINK = ffffff VLINK = ffff00>


<!-- Using the BACKGROUND keyword, we can tile the Web page's
background with an image of our choosing.>
<BODY BACKGROUND = "gif/back.gif">                              ⇐
        .
        .
        .
```

Now our new background appears, as shown in Figure 1.2. As you can see, the browser used the image file to "tile" its background, giving it a pinstriped appearance.

Now we've set up our Web page's body. The next step is to start displaying some text. In our case, we'll display a visible heading with the text: "Welcome to Dynamic HTML!"

## Visible Headings

Web pages wouldn't be very interesting unless we displayed something in them. We'll begin with a visible heading (as opposed to the Web page's invisible heading,

**Figure 1.2 Our Web page's new background.**

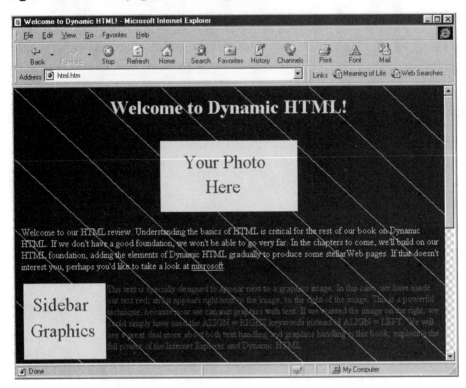

which contains its title). To display a heading, we use the H# tags. There are six of them: H1 to H6. The largest is H1, which we'll use to display our Web page's main heading:

```
|<HTML>                                                            |
|                                                                  |
|   ------------------------------------------------------------   |
|  |<HEAD>                                                      |  |
|  |                                                            |  |
|  |<TITLE>                                                     |  |
|  |This is the title.                                          |  |
|  |</TITLE>                                                    |  |
|  |                                                            |  |
```

```
|  |</HEAD>                                                    |  |
|   ------------------------------------------------           |
|                                                              |
|   ------------------------------------------------           |
|  |<BODY>                                               |  |
|  |                                                     |  |
|  |           <H1>This is our main heading</H1>         |  |    ⇐
|  |                                                     |  |
|  |</BODY>                                              |  |
|   ------------------------------------------------           |
|                                                              |
    -------------------------------------------------------
```

In addition, we'll *center* our Web page's main heading with the **CENTER** tag:

```
<!-- This is a comment. You use comments to add explanatory text to
your Web pages, as we'll see in this Web page. We start the Web page
with the HTML tag, indicating this is a Web page written in HyperText
Markup Language.>
<HTML>


<!-- The next section is the Web page's header. We place the title of
the Web page here. This title is displayed by Web browsers and WWW
directories. The header starts with the HEAD tag, and the title
starts with the TITLE tag.>
<HEAD>
<TITLE>Welcome to Dynamic HTML!</TITLE>
</HEAD>


<!-- Next comes the Web page's body. This is where the Web page proper
is set up, enclosed with the BODY tag.>
<BODY TEXT  = fff00 LINK  = ff0000 ALINK = ffffff VLINK = ffff00>


<!-- Using the BACKGROUND keyword, we can tile the Web page's
background with an image of our choosing.>
<BODY BACKGROUND = "gif/back.gif">


<!-- Now we set up a visible heading for the Web page. We do that with
```

```
the H1 tag, which sets the font size to the largest heading possible.
The CENTER tag makes sure the heading appears centered in the Web
page.>
<CENTER>                                                        ⇐
<H1>Welcome to Dynamic HTML!</H1>                               ⇐
</CENTER>                                                       ⇐
   .
   .
   .
```

The result appears in Figure 1.2. As you can see in that figure, the heading
"Welcome to Dynamic HTML!" appears centered in large type. The other headings get progressively smaller, all the way down to H6, which is the smallest. We've
placed some text into our Web page; next, we'll take a look at the other type of
content in standard Web pages: graphics.

## Web Page Images

Web pages usually contain images called *graphics*.

```
     -----------------------------------------------------
    |<HTML>                                               |
    |                                                     |
    |  ------------------------------------------------   |
    | |<HEAD>                                          |  |
    | |                                                |  |
    | |<TITLE>                                         |  |
    | |This is the title.                              |  |
    | |</TITLE>                                        |  |
    | |                                                |  |
    | |</HEAD>                                         |  |
    |  ------------------------------------------------   |
    |                                                     |
    |  ------------------------------------------------   |
    | |<BODY>                                          |  |
    | |                                                |  |
    | |        <H1>This is our main heading</H1>       |  |
    | |                                                |  |
    | |              ---------------------             |  |
    | |             |                     |            |  |
    | |             |                     |            |  |
    | |             |                     |            |  |
```

We embed images in Web pages with the IMG tag. That tag has become quite complex, with many attributes, as shown here (we'll see what these attributes do throughout the book):

**Internet Explorer**

```
<IMG
ALIGN=ABSBOTTOM | ABSMIDDLE |
BASELINE | BOTTOM | LEFT |
MIDDLE | RIGHT | TEXTTOP | TOP
ALT=string
BORDER=integer
DATAFLD=string
DATASRC=string
DYNSRC=string
HEIGHT=string
HSPACE=variant
ID=string
ISMAP=string
LOOP=string
LOWSRC=string
NAME=string
SRC=string
STYLE=string
TITLE=string
USEMAP=string
VRML=string
VSPACE=string
WIDTH=string
event = script
>
```

**Netscape Navigator**

```
<IMG
ALIGN="LEFT"|"RIGHT"|"TOP"|
"ABSMIDDLE"|"ABSBOTTOM"|"TEXTTOP"|
"MIDDLE"|"BASELINE"|"BOTTOM"
ALT="AlternateText"
BORDER="pixBorder"
HEIGHT="height"
HSPACE="pixHorzMarg"
ISMAP
LOWSRC="Location"
NAME="imgName"
ONABORT="imgLoadJScode"
ONERROR="errorJScode"
ONLOAD="imgLoadJScode"
SRC="Location"
USEMAP="Location#MapName"
VSPACE="pixVertMarg"
WIDTH="width"
>
```

Let's place an image in our Web page. First, though, let's include a little vertical space to separate it from our heading.

## The BR Tag

Before actually placing graphics in our Web page, we'll leave a little vertical space between it and the heading we've just added. We do that with the BR tag, which introduces a line break (like skipping a line in a text document). The BR tag is one of those unique HTML tags that need no closing tag:

```
<!-- This is a comment. You use comments to add explanatory text to
your Web pages, as we'll see in this Web page. We start the Web page
with the HTML tag, indicating this is a Web page written in HyperText
Markup Language.>
<HTML>


<!-- The next section is the Web page's header. We place the title of
the Web page here. This title is displayed by Web browsers and WWW
directories. The header starts with the HEAD tag, and the title
starts with the TITLE tag.>
<HEAD>
<TITLE>Welcome to Dynamic HTML!</TITLE>
</HEAD>


<!-- Next comes the Web page's body. This is where the Web page proper
is set up, enclosed with the BODY tag.>
<BODY TEXT  = fff00 LINK  = ff0000 ALINK = ffffff VLINK = ffff00>


<!-- Using the BACKGROUND keyword, we can tile the Web page's
background with an image of our choosing.>
<BODY BACKGROUND = "gif/back.gif">


<!-- Now we set up a visible heading for the Web page. We do that with
the H1 tag, which sets the font size to the largest heading possible.
The CENTER tag makes sure the heading appears centered in the Web
page.>
<CENTER>
<H1>Welcome to Dynamic HTML!</H1>
</CENTER>


<!-- The BR tag adds a line break, moving us down one line and
```

```
allowing us to space the elements of a Web page as we like.>
<BR>                                                              ⇐
   .
   .
   .
```

Now we're ready to embed our image in the Web page. The first image is often a picture of the Web page's proud author, so we'll call this image yourgif.gif (besides .gif format images, Web browsers can, of course, open other image formats like JPEG—.jpg—not to mention browser-specific support for other formats like .bmp, .tif, and video formats like .avi, .mov, and so on). This image appears in Figure 1.3.

To embed this image in our Web page with the IMG tag, we need to know the image's dimensions. You can find those dimensions with many of the shareware graphics utilities on the Net—in fact, there are even programs on the Net that will read in an image from a URL you give it and indicate that image's dimensions. (If you can convert the image file to .bmp format, you can open it in the Windows Paint program and select the whole image; the dimensions of the image will appear at lower right.) In our case, we add the image to our Web page like this:

```
<!-- This is a comment. You use comments to add explanatory text to
your Web pages, as we'll see in this Web page. We start the Web page
with the HTML tag, indicating this is a Web page written in Hypertext
Markup Language.>
<HTML>
   .
   .
   .
<!-- The BR tag adds a line break, moving us down one line and
allowing us to space the elements of a Web page as we like.>
```

**Figure 1.3 Our yourgif.gif image.**

```
<BR>


<!-- The IMG tag indicates that we want to add a graphic image to our
Web page. In this case, we display the image file yourgif.gif.>
<CENTER>                                                              ⇐
<IMG WIDTH=236 HEIGHT=118 SRC="gif/yourgif.gif"></IMG>               ⇐
</CENTER>                                                            ⇐
      .
      .
      .
```

## Displaying Text

Now we've placed an image into our Web page. So far, the only text we've displayed
is an H1 heading, but we can also display straight text in a Web page this way:

```
   --------------------------------------------------------
  |<HTML>                                                  |
  |                                                        |
  |  ---------------------------------------------------   |
  | |<HEAD>                                             |  |
  | |                                                   |  |
  | |<TITLE>                                            |  |
  | |This is the title.                                 |  |
  | |</TITLE>                                           |  |
  | |                                                   |  |
  | |</HEAD>                                            |  |
  |  ---------------------------------------------------   |
  |                                                        |
  |  ---------------------------------------------------   |
  | |<BODY>                                             |  |
  | |                                                   |  |
  | |      <H1>This is our main heading</H1>            |  |
  | |                                                   |  |
  | |         ---------------------                     |  |
  | |        |                     |                    |  |
  | |        |                     |                    |  |
  | |        |                     |                    |  |
  | |        |       Image         |                    |  |
  | |        |                     |                    |  |
  | |        |                     |                    |  |
  | |         ---------------------                     |  |
```

When we want to display text in a Web page, we just place that text directly into the body of the page. The text will appear in the default color (which we set in the BODY tag) and font. (You can change the font of the text, as well as the font size and style, with the FONT tag, as we'll see soon.) In our case, we'll place this introductory text into the Web page:

```
Welcome to our HTML review. Understanding the basics of HTML
is critical for the rest of our book on Dynamic HTML. If we
don't have a good foundation, we won't be able to go very far.
In the chapters to come, we'll build on our HTML foundation,
adding the elements of Dynamic HTML gradually to produce some
stellar Web pages. If that doesn't interest you, perhaps you'd
like to take a look at <A
HREF="http://www.microsoft.com">microsoft</A>.
```

We'll set aside this text in a paragraph with the P tag so the Web browser (which rejustifies the text by default to fit the browser's window) keeps this text separate from other text in the page:

```
<!-- This is a comment. You use comments to add explanatory text to
your Web pages, as we'll see in this Web page. We start the Web page
with the HTML tag, indicating this is a Web page written in HyperText
Markup Language.>
<HTML>
    .
    .
    .
<!-- The IMG tag indicates that we want to add a graphic image to our
Web page. In this case, we display the image file yourgif.gif.>
<CENTER>
<IMG WIDTH=236 HEIGHT=118 SRC="gif/yourgif.gif"></IMG>
```

```
</CENTER>

<!-- The P tag, which stands for paragraph, lets us format text in a
rudimentary way All the text enclosed in the P tags will appear as
separate paragraphs on the screen.>
<P>        ⇐
    Welcome to our HTML review. Understanding the basics of HTML
    is critical for the rest of our book on Dynamic HTML. If we
    don't have a good foundation, we won't be able to go very far.
    In the chapters to come, we'll build on our HTML foundation,
    adding the elements of Dynamic HTML gradually to produce some
    stellar Web pages. If that doesn't interest you, perhaps you'd
    like to take a look at <A
HREF="http://www.microsoft.com">microsoft</A>.
</P>                                                                    ⇐
<BR>
<BR>
```

The result appears in Figure 1.2. If you want to format text yourself, you can use the PRE (for preformatted) tag to enclose your text. When you do, the Web browser does its best to display the text just as you've formatted it, preserving spacing and carriage returns.

Note that at the end of the text in Figure 1.2, we've included a *hyperlink*. That is, notice that the word "microsoft" is underlined in that figure; when you click that word, the Web browser navigates to the Microsoft Web site, http://www.microsoft.com. (By the way, HTTP stands for HyperText Transfer Protocol, in case you didn't know). We make this happen using the Anchor tag.

## The Anchor Tag and Hyperlinks

The *Anchor tag*, A, is used primarily to establish hyperlinks. Using the Anchor tag, you can set up both hyperlinks to other pages and hyperlink targets (called *anchors*) inside a page. Here are possible attributes of the A tag (and we'll see more about them throughout this book):

| Internet Explorer | Netscape Navigator |
|---|---|
| ```<A``` | ```<A``` |
| ```ACCESSKEY=string``` | ```HREF="Location"``` |
| ```HREF=string``` | ```NAME="AnchorName"``` |
| ```ID=string``` | ```ONCLICK="clickJScode"``` |

**Internet Explorer** *(Continued)*

```
LANGUAGE=JAVASCRIPT | VBSCRIPT
METHODS=string
NAME=string
STYLE=string
TARGET=string
TITLE=string
URN=string
event = script
>
```

**Netscape Navigator** *(Continued)*

```
ONMOUSEOUT="outJScode"
ONMOUSEOVER="overJScode"
TARGET="WindowName"
>
```

We use the HREF attribute to set a hyperlink. For example, in the text we've already placed into our Web page, we set up a hyperlink to the Microsoft Web site this way, making sure that the actual underlined text that appears on the screen is simply "microsoft":

```
Welcome to our HTML review. Understanding the basics of HTML
is critical for the rest of our book on Dynamic HTML. If we
don't have a good foundation, we won't be able to go very far.
In the chapters to come, we'll build on our HTML foundation,
adding the elements of Dynamic HTML gradually to produce some
stellar Web pages. If that doesn't interest you, perhaps you'd
like to take a look at <A
HREF="http://www.microsoft.com">microsoft</A>.                    ⇐
```

When the user clicks this hyperlink, the Web browser jumps to the Microsoft Web site. It's that easy to set up a hyperlink.

Now we've added text to our Web page. In fact, we can mix both text and graphics in our Web pages, as we'll explore next.

## Mixing Text and Graphics

We can *align* images and text in Web pages; for example, let's add a sidebar image, as shown in Figure 1.4, on the left of our Web page, with some text on the right:

```
 --------------------------------------------------------
|<HTML>                                                  |
|                                                        |
|   ----------------------------------------------    |
| |<HEAD>                                          | |
| |                                                | |
```

```
| |<TITLE>                                                |  |
| |This is the title.                                     |  |
| |</TITLE>                                               |  |
| |                                                       | |
| |</HEAD>                                                |  |
|  ------------------------------------------------   |
|                                                        |
|  ------------------------------------------------   |
| |<BODY>                                                 | |
| |                                                       | |
| |        <H1>This is our main heading</H1>              | |
| |                                                       | |
| |              --------------------                     | |
| |             |                    |                    | |
| |             |                    |                    | |
| |             |                    |                    | |
| |             |        Image       |                    | |
| |             |                    |                    | |
| |             |                    |                    | |
| |              --------------------                     | |
| |                                                       | |
| |  ------------------------------------------      | |
| | |                                          |     | | |
| | |                                          |     | | |
| | |              Text                        |     | | |
| | |                                          |     | | |
| |  ------------------------------------------      | |
| |                                                  | |
| |  --------   -------------------------------      | |
| | |       |  |                             |       | | |
| | |       |  |                             |       | | |
| | | Image |  |          Text               |       | | |   ⇐
| | |       |  |                             |       | | |
| | |       |  |                             |       | | |
| |  --------   -------------------------------      | |
| |                                                  | |
|  ------------------------------------------------   |
|                                                        |
 --------------------------------------------------
```

Aligning text and graphics is easier than you might expect. To do so, we simply use the IMG tag's ALIGN attribute to place the image on the left. The Web

**Figure 1.4 Our sidebar image, sidebar.gif.**

Sidebar
Graphics

browser will then place the following text on the right of the image automatically. Here's the text we'll use next to the image:

```
This text is specially designed to appear next to a graphics image.
In this case, we have made our text red, and it appears right next
to the image, to the right of the image. This is a powerful
technique, because now we can mix graphics with text. If we wanted
the image on the right, we could simply have used the ALIGN = RIGHT
keywords instead of ALIGN = LEFT. We will see a great deal more
about both text handling and graphics handling in this book,
exploiting the full power of the Internet Explorer and Dynamic
HTML.
```

Here's how that text looks in html.htm, where we use the keywords ALIGN = LEFT in the IMG tag:

```
<!-- This is a comment. You use comments to add explanatory text to
your Web pages, as we'll see in this Web page. We start the Web page
with the HTML tag, indicating this is a Web page written in HyperText
Markup Language.>
<HTML>
    .
    .
    .

<!-- The P tag, which stands for paragraph, lets us format text in a
rudimentary way. All the text enclosed in the P tags will appear as
separate paragraphs on the screen.>
<P>
    Welcome to our HTML review. Understanding the basics of HTML
    is critical for the rest of our book on Dynamic HTML. If we
```

```
      don't have a good foundation, we won't be able to go very far.
      In the chapters to come, we'll build on our HTML foundation,
      adding the elements of Dynamic HTML gradually to produce some
      stellar Web pages. If that doesn't interest you, perhaps you'd
      like to take a look at <A
HREF="http://www.microsoft.com">microsoft</A>.
<BR>
<BR>
</P>



<!-- Now we'll mix text and graphics. In this case, we'll place a
sidebar image on the left of the Web page, with text on the right. We
do that with the ALIGN keyword. We'll see how to do this better using
the DIV tag later in the book.>
<IMG WIDTH=141 HEIGHT=126 SRC="gif/sidebar.gif" ALIGN=LEFT>         ⇐
      This text is specially designed to appear next to a graphics image.
      In this case, we have made our text red, and it appears right next
      to the image, to the right of the image. This is a powerful
      technique, because now we can mix graphics with text. If we wanted
      the image on the right, we could simply have used the ALIGN = RIGHT
      keywords instead of ALIGN = LEFT. We will see a great deal more
      about both text handling and graphics handling in this book,
      exploiting the full power of the Internet Explorer and Dynamic
      HTML.
</IMG>
<BR>
<BR>
   .
   .
   .
```

The result appears in Figure 1.2. Now we're mixing graphics and text in our Web pages, and we've added a little more power to our HTML arsenal. Besides simply displaying text, we can control *how* we display that text. We'll take a look at that next.

## Changing the Default Font

To alter the way we display text, we use the FONT tag. This tag includes attributes that let us set the font's type, style, size, and color:

| Internet Explorer | Netscape Navigator |
|---|---|
| ```<FONT``` | ```<FONT``` |
| ```COLOR=color``` | ```COLOR="color"``` |
| ```FACE=string``` | ```FACE="fontlist"``` |
| ```ID=string``` | ```SIZE="fontSize"``` |
| ```SIZE=string``` | ```>``` |
| ```STYLE=string``` | |
| ```TITLE=string``` | |
| ```event = script``` | |
| ```>``` | |

For example, to turn to red the text we've just aligned next to the sidebar image, we simply enclose it with FONT tags this way:

```
<!-- This is a comment. You use comments to add explanatory text to
your Web pages, as we'll see in this Web page. We start the Web page
with the HTML tag, indicating this is a Web page written in HyperText
Markup Language.>
<HTML>
    .
    .
    .

<!-- The P tag, which stands for paragraph, lets us format text in a
rudimentary way. All the text enclosed in the P tags will appear as
separate paragraphs on the screen.>
<P>
    Welcome to our HTML review. Understanding the basics of HTML
    is critical for the rest of our book on Dynamic HTML. If we
    don't have a good foundation, we won't be able to go very far.
    In the chapters to come, we'll build on our HTML foundation,
    adding the elements of Dynamic HTML gradually to produce some
    stellar Web pages. If that doesn't interest you, perhaps you'd
    like to take a look at
<A HREF="http://www.microsoft.com">microsoft</A>.
<BR>
<BR>
</P>


<!-- Now we'll mix text and graphics. In this case, we'll place a
sidebar image on the left of the Web page, with text on the right. We
do that with the ALIGN keyword. We'll see how to do this better using
```

```
the DIV tag later in the book.>
<IMG WIDTH=141 HEIGHT=126 SRC="gif/sidebar.gif" ALIGN=LEFT>
<FONT COLOR = "ff0000">                                              ⇐
    This text is specially designed to appear next to a graphics image.
    In this case, we have made our text red, and it appears right next
    to the image, to the right of the image. This is a powerful
    technique, because now we can mix graphics with text. If we wanted
    the image on the right, we could simply have used the ALIGN = RIGHT
    keywords instead of ALIGN = LEFT. We will see a great deal more
    about both text handling and graphics handling in this book,
    exploiting the full power of the Internet Explorer and Dynamic
    HTML.
</FONT>                                                              ⇐
</IMG>
<BR>
<BR>
  .
  .
  .
```

Now the text appears in red. (Note that the text color goes back to the default yellow when we use the </FONT> tag.) Besides changing the text's color, we can also change other aspects of the text, such as its size. For example, we can use the FONT tag to place some enlarged text into our Web page:

```
    ------------------------------------------------------------
    |<HTML>                                                    |
    |                                                          |
    |   ----------------------------------------------------  |
    |   |<HEAD>                                             |  |
    |   |                                                   |  |
    |   |<TITLE>                                            |  |
    |   |This is the title.                                 |  |
    |   |</TITLE>                                           |  |
    |   |                                                   |  |
    |   |</HEAD>                                            |  |
    |   ----------------------------------------------------  |
    |                                                          |
    |   ----------------------------------------------------  |
    |   |<BODY>                                             |  |
    |   |                                                   |  |
    |   |         <H1>This is our main heading</H1>         |  |
```

```
| |                                                         | |
| |           ---------------------                         | |
| |          |                     |                        | |
| |          |                     |                        | |
| |          |                     |                        | |
| |          |         Image       |                        | |
| |          |                     |                        | |
| |          |                     |                        | |
| |          |                     |                        | |
| |           ---------------------                         | |
| |                                                         | |
| |  -------------------------------------------------      | |
| | |                                                 |     | | |
| | |                                                 |     | | |
| | |                    Text                         |     | | |
| | |                                                 |     | | |
| |  -------------------------------------------------      | |
| |                                                         | |
| |  ---------   --------------------------------------     | |
| | |         | |                                      |    | | |
| | |         | |                                      |    | | |
| | |  Image  | |               Text                   |    | | |
| | |         | |                                      |    | | |
| | |         | |                                      |    | | |
| |  ---------   --------------------------------------     | |
| |                                                         | |
| |  -------------------------------------------------      | |
| | | Enlarged Text                                   |     | | |   <==
| |  -------------------------------------------------      | |
| |                                                         | |
|   -------------------------------------------------------   |
|                                                             |
 -------------------------------------------------------------
```

Let's add the enlarged text to html.htm. We simply enclose the text we want ("We can also use the FONT tag this way . . .") in FONT tags setting the font size to 5, which is fairly big (the font size can go from 1 to 7):

```
<!-- This is a comment. You use comments to add explanatory text to
your Web pages, as we'll see in this Web page. We start the Web page
with the HTML tag, indicating this is a Web page written in HyperText
Markup Language.>
<HTML>
```

```
                  .
                  .
                  .
<!-- Now we'll mix text and graphics. In this case, we'll place a
sidebar image on the left of the Web page, with text on the right. We
do that with the ALIGN keyword. We'll see how to do this better using
the DIV tag later in the book.>
<IMG WIDTH=141 HEIGHT=126 SRC="gif/sidebar.gif" ALIGN=LEFT>
<FONT COLOR = "ff0000">
    This text is specially designed to appear next to a graphics image.
    In this case, we have made our text red, and it appears right next
    to the image, to the right of the image. This is a powerful
    technique, because now we can mix graphics with text. If we wanted
    the image on the right, we could simply have used the ALIGN = RIGHT
    keywords instead of ALIGN = LEFT. We will see a great deal more
    about both text handling and graphics handling in this book,
    exploiting the full power of the Internet Explorer and Dynamic
    HTML.
</FONT>
</IMG>
<BR>
<BR>


<!-- The FONT tag lets us adjust the size of the text we display. In
this case, we set the font size to 5 temporarily.>
<FONT SIZE = 5>                                                    ⇐
We can also use the FONT tag this way....
</FONT>                                                            ⇐
<BR>
<BR>
                  .
                  .
                  .
```

The result appears in Figure 1.5. As you can see, the enlarged text appears just
as we want it—in a larger font. Using the FONT tag, you can change a font's size
at any time. (We'll see more powerful ways of creating even larger text later in this
book.)

We've handled both text and graphics in our Web page now, but of course there
are many, many more elements that you can use in Web pages. One of the most
popular and most basic is the Web page table. We'll look at that next.

**Figure 1.5 Our enlarged text.**

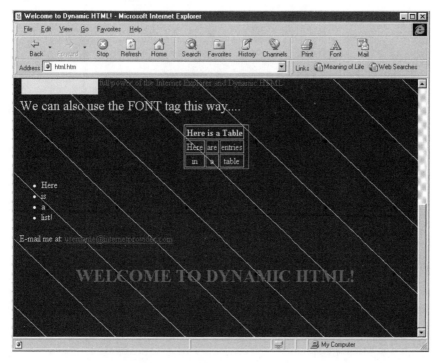

## Using Tables in Web Pages

A Web page *table* helps us to format a Web page. We can place all kinds of entries into the cells of a table: text, images, hyperlinks, and so on. Let's add a new table to our Web page html.htm now:

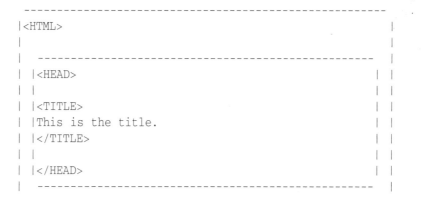

```
-------------------------------------------------------
|<HTML>                                                |
|                                                      |
|   -------------------------------------------------- |
|   |<HEAD>                                          | |
|   |                                                | |
|   |<TITLE>                                         | |
|   |This is the title.                              | |
|   |</TITLE>                                        | |
|   |                                                | |
|   |</HEAD>                                         | |
|   -------------------------------------------------- |
```

```
|                                                                  |
|   --------------------------------------------------------    |
|  |<BODY>                                                  |   |
|  |                                                        |   |
|  |        <H1>This is our main heading</H1>               |   |
|  |                                                        |   |
|  |           ---------------------                        |   |
|  |          |                     |                       |   |
|  |          |                     |                       |   |
|  |          |                     |                       |   |
|  |          |        Image        |                       |   |
|  |          |                     |                       |   |
|  |          |                     |                       |   |
|  |           ---------------------                        |   |
|  |                                                        |   |
|  |   -------------------------------------------------    |   |
|  |  |                                                 |   |   |
|  |  |               Text                              |   |   |
|  |  |                                                 |   |   |
|  |   -------------------------------------------------    |   |
|  |                                                        |   |
|  |   ---------    -------------------------------------   |   |
|  |  |        |  |                                      |  |   |
|  |  |        |  |                                      |  |   |
|  |  | Image  |  |              Text                    |  |   |
|  |   ---------    -------------------------------------   |   |
|  |                                                        |   |
|  |   -------------------------------------------------    |   |
|  |  | Enlarged Text                                   |   |   |
|  |   -------------------------------------------------    |   |
|  |                                                        |   |
|  |               -----------------                        |   |
|  |              |                 |                       |   |
|  |              |-----------------|                       |   |
|  |              |    |       |    |                       |   |
|  |              |-----------------|                       |   |
|  |              |    |       |    |                       |   |
|  |               -----------------                        |   |   ⇐
|  |                                                        |   |
|   --------------------------------------------------------    |
|                                                                  |
 ----------------------------------------------------------------
```

Here are the elements of the table we'll add: three columns, two rows, and a header that spans all the columns this way:

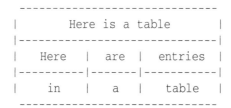

```
 ------------------------------
|           Here is a table    |
|------------------------------|
|   Here  |  are  | entries    |
|---------|-------|----------|
|    in   |   a   |  table     |
 ------------------------------
```

To put this table together, we use the TABLE tag:

**Internet Explorer**

```
<TABLE
ALIGN=CENTER | LEFT | RIGHT
BACKGROUND=string
BGCOLOR=color
BORDER=integer
BORDERCOLOR=color
BORDERCOLORDARK=color
BORDERCOLORLIGHT=color
CELLPADDING=string
CELLSPACING=string
COLS=string
DATASRC=id
FRAME=ABOVE | BELOW | BORDER |
BOX | INSIDES | LHS | RHS |
VOID | VSIDES
HEIGHT=string
ID=string
RULES=ALL | COLS | GROUPS |
NONE | ROWS
STYLE=string
TITLE=string
WIDTH=string
event = script
>
```

**Netscape Navigator**

```
<TABLE
ALIGN="LEFT"|"RIGHT"
BGCOLOR="color"
BORDER="value"
CELLPADDING="value"
CELLSPACING="value"
HEIGHT="height"
HSPACE="pixHoriz"
WIDTH="pixels"|"value%"
VSPACE="pixVert"
>
```

Here's how we start the actual HTML, giving our table a border:

```
<TABLE BORDER>
      .
      .
      .
```

Next, we start the first row, using the TR (Table Row) tag. We also indicate that we want the text in this row to be aligned in the center of each cell:

```
<TABLE BORDER>
<TR ALIGN = CENTER>                                          ⇐
      .
      .
      .
```

This first row holds our table's header, and we set that header up with the TH (Table Header) tag, making the table header's text bold. We also use the COLSPAN attribute to indicate that we want the table to "span" all three columns:

```
<TABLE BORDER>
<TR ALIGN = CENTER>
<TH COLSPAN = 3>Here is a Table                              ⇐
</TH>                                                        ⇐
    .
    .
    .
```

That completes the table's header and so its first row, and we end the row with a </TR> tag:

```
<TABLE BORDER>
<TR ALIGN = CENTER>
<TH COLSPAN = 3>Here is a Table
</TH>
</TR>
    .
    .
    .
```

Now we'll work on the second row, beginning that with the TR tag:

```
<TABLE BORDER>
<TR ALIGN = CENTER>
<TH COLSPAN = 3>Here is a Table
```

```
</TH>
</TR>
<TR ALIGN = CENTER>                                            ⇐
```

In the second row, we want three cells with the text "Here," "are," and "entries":

```
       ------------------------------
       |          Here is a table         |
       |----------------------------------|
       |   Here   |  are  |  entries  |              ⇐
       |----------|-------|-----------|
       |    in    |   a   |   table   |
       ------------------------------
```

To set up each cell, we use the TD (Table Data) tag:

```
<TABLE BORDER>
<TR ALIGN = CENTER>
<TH COLSPAN = 3>Here is a Table
</TH>
</TR>
<TR ALIGN = CENTER>                                            ⇐
<TD>Here</TD>                                                  ⇐
<TD>are</TD>                                                   ⇐
<TD>entries<TD>                                                ⇐
</TR>                                                          ⇐
    .
    .
    .
```

We've created the second row of our table. Next, we add the third row of three cells with the text "in," "a," and "table":

```
       ------------------------------
       |          Here is a table         |
       |----------------------------------|
       |   Here   |  are  |  entries  |
       |----------|-------|-----------|
       |    in    |   a   |   table   |              ⇐
       ------------------------------
```

In our Web page, that looks like this:

```
<TABLE BORDER>
<TR ALIGN = CENTER>
<TH COLSPAN = 3>Here is a Table
</TH>
</TR>
<TR ALIGN = CENTER>
<TD>Here</TD>
<TD>are</TD>
<TD>entries<TD>
</TR>
<TR ALIGN = CENTER>                                              ⇐
<TD>in</TD>                                                      ⇐
<TD>a</TD>                                                       ⇐
<TD>table</TD>                                                   ⇐
</TR>                                                            ⇐
    .
    .
    .
```

Now we've set up our table; all we need to do is to finish the table's definition with the **</TABLE>** tag:

```
<TABLE BORDER>
<TR ALIGN = CENTER>
<TH COLSPAN = 3>Here is a Table
</TH>
</TR>
<TR ALIGN = CENTER>
<TD>Here</TD>
<TD>are</TD>
<TD>entries<TD>
</TR>
<TR ALIGN = CENTER>
<TD>in</TD>
<TD>a</TD>
<TD>table</TD>
</TR>
</TABLE>                                                         ⇐
```

That's it. Now the table appears in our Web page, as shown in Figure 1.5. As you can see in that figure, we do indeed have a table-spanning header, as well as two rows of three columns each. Our table is a success. Here's a tip: If you're having trouble setting up a table in HTML, try omitting the text you want in each cell—doing that makes the outline of the table much clearer as you write your HTML. You can add the text for each cell later.

There are, of course, many other objects we can use in Web pages besides tables. One of the most popular is the Web page list.

## Web Page Lists

There are several types of HTML lists: *definition lists* (a simple list), *ordered lists* (in which items are listed with numbers or letters in order), and *unordered lists* (with bullets in front of each item). We'll add an unordered list to our Web page:

```
 ----------------------------------------------------------
|<HTML>                                                    |
|                                                          |
|   ------------------------------------------------     |
|  |<HEAD>                                          |  |
|  |                                                |  |
|  |<TITLE>                                         |  |
|  |This is the title.                              |  |
|  |</TITLE>                                        |  |
|  |                                                |  |
|  |</HEAD>                                         |  |
|   ------------------------------------------------     |
|                                                          |
|   ------------------------------------------------     |
|  |<BODY>                                          |  |
|  |                                                |  |
|  |          <H1>This is our main heading</H1>     |  |
|  |                                                |  |
|  |            ---------------------               |  |
|  |           |                     |              |  |
|  |           |                     |              |  |
|  |           |                     |              |  |
|  |           |       Image         |              |  |
|  |           |                     |              |  |
|  |           |                     |              |  |
|  |            ---------------------               |  |
|  |                                                |  |
```

```
| |    -------------------------------------------  | |
| | |                                             | | |
| | |                                             | | |
| | |                    Text                     | | |
| | |                                             | | |
| |    -------------------------------------------  | |
| |                                                 | |
| |    ---------    -----------------------------    | |
| | |          |  |                             | | |
| | |          |  |                             | | |
| | | Image    |  |            Text             | | |
| | |          |  |                             | | |
| | |          |  |                             | | |
| |    ---------    -----------------------------    | |
| |                                                 | |
| |    -------------------------------------------  | |
| | | Enlarged Text                               | | |
| |    -------------------------------------------  | |
| |                                                 | |
| |                  -----------------              | |
| |                 |                 |             | |
| |                 |-----------------|             | |
| |                 |       |       |  |            | |
| |                 |-----------------|             | |
| |                 |       |       |  |            | |
| |                  -----------------              | |
| |                                                 | |
| |    *  |_____|                                   | |    ⇐
| |                                                 | |
| |    *  |_____|                                   | |
| |                                                 | |
| |    *  |_____|                                   | |
| |                                                 | |
| |</BODY>                                          | |
|    -------------------------------------------------  |
|                                                       |
|</HTML>                                                |
 -----------------------------------------------------
```

Here are the items we'll put in our list:

```
         * Here
         * is
```

```
    * a
    * list!
```

We can color our list white so it stands out, using the FONT tag:

```
<FONT COLOR = ffffff>                                          ⇐
    .
    .
    .
</FONT>                                                        ⇐
```

To set up an unordered list, we use the UL tag, which has these attributes:

**Internet Explorer**

```
<UL
ALIGN=CENTER | LEFT | RIGHT
COMPACT
ID=string
SRC=string
STYLE=string
TITLE=string
TYPE=1 | a | A | i | I
event = script
>
```

**Netscape Navigator**

```
<UL
TYPE="CIRCLE"|"DISC"|"SQUARE"
>
```

Now we're ready. Setting up our list looks like this in HTML, where we use the UL tag:

```
<FONT COLOR = ffffff>
<UL>                                                          ⇐
    .
    .
    .
</UL>                                                         ⇐
</FONT>
```

Next, all we have to do is to add the items in the list, and we do that using the <LI> (List Item) tag. <LI> is another of the very few HTML tags that don't need a closing tag:

```
<FONT COLOR = ffffff>
<UL>
<LI> Here                                                     ⇐
```

```
<LI> is                                                          ⇐
<LI> a                                                           ⇐
<LI> list!                                                       ⇐
</UL>
</FONT>
```

The result of this code appears in Figure 1.5. As you can see in that figure, our list appears with the items separated vertically, and with a bullet before each item.

We're nearing the end of our first Web page, but there's one more exciting item we can place in it: an e-mail link. When users click this link, they can send e-mail to any e-mail address you like.

## Sending E-Mail from a Web Page

Our last step will be to add an e-mail link to our Web page:

```
     -------------------------------------------------------
    |<HTML>                                                 |
    |                                                       |
    |   -------------------------------------------------   |
    |  |<HEAD>                                           |  |
    |  |                                                 |  |
    |  |<TITLE>                                          |  |
    |  |This is the title.                               |  |
    |  |</TITLE>                                         |  |
    |  |                                                 |  |
    |  |</HEAD>                                          |  |
    |   -------------------------------------------------   |
    |                                                       |
    |   -------------------------------------------------   |
    |  |<BODY>                                           |  |
    |  |                                                 |  |
    |  |          <H1>This is our main heading</H1>      |  |
    |  |                                                 |  |
    |  |             ---------------------               |  |
    |  |            |                     |              |  |
    |  |            |                     |              |  |
    |  |            |                     |              |  |
    |  |            |        Image        |              |  |
    |  |            |                     |              |  |
```

```
 | |                    |                      |                    | |
 | |               --------------------                             | |
 | |                                                                | |
 | | -------------------------------------------------              | |
 | | |                                               |              | | |
 | | |                                               |              | | |
 | | |                     Text                      |              | | |
 | | |                                               |              | | |
 | | -------------------------------------------------              | |
 | |                                                                | |
 | | ---------    -----------------------------------               | |
 | | |       |    |                                 |               | | |
 | | |       |    |                                 |               | | |
 | | | Image |    |            Text                 |               | | |
 | | |       |    |                                 |               | | |
 | | |       |    |                                 |               | | |
 | | ---------    -----------------------------------               | |
 | |                                                                | |
 | | -------------------------------------------------              | |
 | | | Enlarged Text                                                | | |
 | | -------------------------------------------------              | |
 | |                                                                | |
 | |                  ------------------                            | |
 | |                  |                |                            | |
 | |                  |----------------|                            | |
 | |                  |      |       |  |                           | |
 | |                  |----------------|                            | |
 | |                  |      |       |  |                           | |
 | |                  ------------------                            | |
 | |                                                                | |
 | |        _____                                                   | |
 | |   *   |_____|                                                  | |
 | |        _____                                                   | |
 | |   *   |_____|                                                  | |
 | |        _____                                                   | |
 | |   *   |_____|                                                  | |
 | |                                                                | |
 | | -------------------------------------------------              | |
 | | | E-mail                                        |  | |           ⇐
 | | -------------------------------------------------              | |
 | |                                                                | |
 |  -------------------------------------------------              |
 |                                                                 |
 ---------------------------------------------------
```

Adding an e-mail link to a Web page is easy—just use the keyword "MAILTO:" when specifying a hyperlink's URL. This will make the Web browser treat the URL as an e-mail address. For example, we can place the link "E-mail me at: user-name@internetprovider.com" in our Web page, where the e-mail address, user-name@internetprovider.com, is underlined. When the user clicks that e-mail address, e-mail will be sent to that e-mail address. In HTML, we set up a hyper-link to that address using the keyword "MAILTO:" this way:

```
<!-- This is a comment. You use comments to add explanatory text to
your Web pages, as we'll see in this Web page. We start the Web page
with the HTML tag, indicating this is a Web page written in HyperText
Markup Language.>
<HTML>
    .
    .
    .

<!-- Using the UL and LI tags, we can set up a bulleted list easily.>
<FONT COLOR = ffffff>
<UL>
<LI> Here
<LI> is
<LI> a
<LI> list!
</UL>
</FONT>


<!-- We can also set up an A tag to allow the user to e-mail us using
the MAILTO keyword. That looks like the following HTML.>
E-mail me at: <A HREF="MAILTO:username@internetprovider.com">
    username@internetprovider.com</A>                              ⇐
<BR>
<BR>
    .
    .
    .
```

The result appears in Figure 1.5. As you can see, the e-mail line near the bottom reads, "E-mail me at username@internetprovider.com." When users click the e-mail address, their mail program opens and they can send mail to the address you've placed in the hyperlink. It's that easy.

Let's finish our brush-up Web page now.

# Finishing Our Web Page

To finish our Web page, we might add a final message, "WELCOME TO DYNAM-IC HTML!" as an H1 heading in red. We do that like this in html.htm:

```
<!-- This is a comment. You use comments to add explanatory text to
your Web pages, as we'll see in this Web page. We start the Web page
with the HTML tag, indicating this is a Web page written in HyperText
Markup Language.>
<HTML>
    .
    .
    .

<!-- Using the UL and LI tags, we can set up a bulleted list easily.>
<FONT COLOR = ffffff>
<UL>
<LI> Here
<LI> is
<LI> a
<LI> list!
</UL>
</FONT>


<!-- We can also set up an A tag to allow the user to e-mail us using
the MAILTO keyword. That looks like the following HTML.>
E-mail me at: <A HREF="MAILTO:username@internetprovider.com">
   username@internetprovider.com</A>
<BR>
<BR>


<!-- Finally, we display a message: WELCOME TO DYMANIC HTML!>
<FONT COLOR = ff0000>                                              ⇐
<CENTER>                                                           ⇐
<H1>WELCOME TO DYNAMIC HTML!</H1>                                  ⇐
<BR>                                                               ⇐
<BR>                                                               ⇐
</CENTER>                                                          ⇐
</FONT>                                                            ⇐
    .
    .
    .
```

This heading appears at the bottom of Figure 1.5. Now we're done with the Web page on the screen, but we still have to finish off the <BODY> and <HTML> tags with </BODY> and </HTML> tags:

```
<!-- This is a comment. You use comments to add explanatory text to
your Web pages, as we'll see in this Web page. We start the Web page
with the HTML tag, indicating this is a Web page written in HyperText
Markup Language.>
<HTML>
    .
    .
    .

<!-- Using the UL and LI tags, we can set up a bulleted list easily.>
<FONT COLOR = ffffff>
<UL>
<LI> Here
<LI> is
<LI> a
<LI> list!
</UL>
</FONT>


<!-- We can also set up an A tag to allow the user to e-mail us using
the MAILTO keyword. That looks like the following HTML.>
E-mail me at: <A HREF="MAILTO:username@internetprovider.com">
    username@internetprovider.com</A>
<BR>
<BR>


<!-- Finally, we display a message: WELCOME TO DYMANIC HTML!>
<FONT COLOR = ff0000>
<CENTER>
<H1>WELCOME TO DYNAMIC HTML!</H1>
<BR>
<BR>
</CENTER>
</FONT>


<!-- The /BODY and /HTML tags finish off the Web page's body and close
the page.>
```

```
</BODY>                                                      ⇐
</HTML>                                                      ⇐
```

This finishes our entire Web page:

```
 -----------------------------------------------------------
|<HTML>                                                     |
|                                                           |
|   ------------------------------------------------------  |
|  |<HEAD>                                               | |
|  |                                                     | |
|  |<TITLE>                                              | |
|  |This is the title.                                   | |
|  |</TITLE>                                             | |
|  |                                                     | |
|  |</HEAD>                                              | |
|   ------------------------------------------------------  |
|                                                           |
|   ------------------------------------------------------  |
|  |<BODY>                                               | |
|  |                                                     | |
|  |          <H1>This is our main heading</H1>          | |
|  |                                                     | |
|  |              ---------------------                  | |
|  |             |                     |                 | |
|  |             |                     |                 | |
|  |             |                     |                 | |
|  |             |       Image         |                 | |
|  |             |                     |                 | |
|  |             |                     |                 | |
|  |              ---------------------                  | |
|  |                                                     | |
|  |   -----------------------------------------------   | |
|  |  |                                              |   | |
|  |  |                                              |   | |
|  |  |                  Text                        |   | |
|  |  |                                              |   | |
|  |   -----------------------------------------------   | |
|  |                                                     | |
|  |   ---------   --------------------------------      | |
|  |  |         | |  |                              |    | |
|  |  |         | |  |                              |    | |
```

```
  | | |  Image  | |                  Text                    | | |
  | | |         | |                                          | | |
  | | |         | |                                          | | |
  | |   --------    --------------------------------------   | |
  | |                                                        | |
  | |   ------------------------------------------------     | |
  | | | Enlarged Text                                        | | |
  | |   ------------------------------------------------     | |
  | |                                                        | |
  | |                    ------------------                  | |
  | |                  |                    |                | |
  | |                  |------------------|                  | |
  | |                  |       |        |      |             | |
  | |                  |------------------|                  | |
  | |                  |       |        |      |             | |
  | |                    ------------------                  | |
  | |         _____                                          | |
  | |   *   |_____|                                          | |
  | |         _____                                          | |
  | |   *   |_____|                                          | |
  | |         _____                                          | |
  | |   *   |_____|                                          | |
  | |                                                        | |
  | |   ------------------------------------------------     | |
  | | | E-mail                                               | | |
  | |   ------------------------------------------------     | |
  | |                                                        | |
  |  |</BODY>                                            | |    ⇐
  |    ------------------------------------------------     |
  |                                                         |
  |</HTML>                                                  |     ⇐
  ---------------------------------------------------------------
```

Our review Web page is complete, and it's a success. The complete listing for this Web page, html.htm, appears in Listing 1.1.

## Listing 1.1 html.htm

```
<!-- This is a comment. You use comments to add explanatory text to
your Web pages, as we'll see in this Web page. We start the Web page
with the HTML tag, indicating this is a Web page written in HyperText
Markup Language.>
```

**Listing 1.1  Continued**

```
<HTML>


<!-- The next section is the Web page's header. We place the title of
the Web page here. This title is displayed by Web browsers and WWW
directories. The header starts with the HEAD tag, and the title
starts with the TITLE tag.>
<HEAD>
<TITLE>Welcome to Dynamic HTML!</TITLE>
</HEAD>


<!-- Next comes the Web page's body. This is where the Web page proper
is set up, enclosed with the BODY tag.>
<BODY TEXT  = ffff00 LINK  = ff0000 ALINK = ffffff VLINK = ffff00>


<!-- Using the BACKGROUND keyword, we can tile the Web page's
background with an image of our choosing.>
<BODY BACKGROUND = "gif/back.gif">


<!-- Now we set up a visible heading for the Web page. We do that with
the H1 tag, which sets the font size to the largest heading possible.
The CENTER tag makes sure the heading appears centered in the Web
page.>
<CENTER>
<H1>Welcome to Dynamic HTML!</H1>
</CENTER>


<!-- The BR tag adds a line break, moving us down one line and
allowing us to space the elements of a Web page as we like.>
<BR>


<!-- The IMG tag indicates that we want to add a graphic image to our
Web page. In this case, we display the image file yourgif.gif.>
<CENTER>
<IMG WIDTH=236 HEIGHT=118 SRC="gif/yourgif.gif"></IMG>
```

*Continued*

**Listing 1.1  Continued**

```
</CENTER>

<!-- The P tag, which stands for paragraph, lets us format text in a
rudimentary way. All the text enclosed in the P tags will appear as
separate paragraphs on the screen.>
<P>
    Welcome to our HTML review. Understanding the basics of HTML
    is critical for the rest of our book on Dynamic HTML. If we
    don't have a good foundation, we won't be able to go very far.
    In the chapters to come, we'll build on our HTML foundation,
    adding the elements of Dynamic HTML gradually to produce some
    stellar Web pages. If that doesn't interest you, perhaps you'd
    like to take a look at <A
HREF="http://www.microsoft.com">microsoft</A>.
<BR>
<BR>
</P>


<!-- Now we'll mix text and graphics. In this case, we'll place a
sidebar image on the left of the Web page, with text on the right. We
do that with the ALIGN keyword. We'll see how to do this better using
the DIV tag later in the book.>
<IMG WIDTH=141 HEIGHT=126 SRC="gif/sidebar.gif" ALIGN=LEFT>
<FONT COLOR = "ff0000">
    This text is specially designed to appear next to a graphics image.
    In this case, we have made our text red, and it appears right next
    to the image, to the right of the image. This is a powerful
    technique, because now we can mix graphics with text. If we wanted
    the image on the right, we could simply have used the ALIGN = RIGHT
    keywords instead of ALIGN = LEFT. We will see a great deal more
    about both text handling and graphics handling in this book,
    exploiting the full power of the Internet Explorer and Dynamic
    HTML.
</FONT>
</IMG>
<BR>
<BR>


<!-- The FONT tag lets us adjust the size of the text we display. In
```

**Listing 1.1  Continued**

```
this case, we set the font size to 5 temporarily.>
<FONT SIZE = 5>
We can also use the FONT tag this way....
</FONT>
<BR>
<BR>


<!-- Tables are a big part of Web pages. In this case, we add a new
table with a spanning header row, and two rows of three columns each.
The TR tag starts a table row, the TH tag a table head, and the TD tag
specifies table data.>
<CENTER>
<TABLE BORDER>
<TR ALIGN = CENTER>
<TH COLSPAN = 3>Here is a Table
</TH>
</TR>
<TR ALIGN = CENTER>
<TD>Here</TD>
<TD>are</TD>
<TD>entries<TD>
</TR>
<TR ALIGN = CENTER>
<TD>in</TD>
<TD>a</TD>
<TD>table</TD>
</TR>
</TABLE>
</CENTER>


<!-- Using the UL and LI tags, we can set up a bulleted list easily.>
<FONT COLOR = ffffff>
<UL>
<LI> Here
<LI> is
<LI> a
<LI> list!
</UL>
```

*Continued*

**Listing 1.1  Continued**

```
</FONT>


<!-- We can also set up an A tag to allow the user to e-mail us using
the MAILTO keyword. That looks like the following HTML.>
E-mail me at: <A HREF="MAILTO:username@internetprovider.com">
   username@internetprovider.com</A>
<BR>
<BR>


<!-- Finally, we display a message: WELCOME TO DYMANIC HTML!>
<FONT COLOR = ff0000>
<CENTER>
<H1>WELCOME TO DYNAMIC HTML!</H1>
<BR>
<BR>
</CENTER>
</FONT>


<!-- The /BODY and /HTML tags finish off the Web page's body and close
the page.>
</BODY>
</HTML>
```

# What's Ahead

Now we've brought ourselves up to speed in standard HTML. If you've had some trouble with this chapter, you should probably take a look at a good standard HTML book like Ian Graham's *HTML Sourcebook* (John Wiley & Sons, 1995) before progressing. If, on the other hand, you're comfortable with all you've seen—or if it's all old hat to you—then it's time to move on to Chapter 2. In that chapter, we'll start to work with the scripting languages we'll use with Dynamic HTML: VBScript and JavaScript. We'll work through the basics of scripting and then proceed to work with Dynamic HTML itself. Let's turn to Chapter 2 now and get a good grounding in scripting our Web pages.

# CHAPTER TWO

# SCRIPTING YOUR WEB PAGE

I n this chapter, we'll start building on our HTML foundation as we make our Web pages come alive and *do* something. This will be our first step toward using Dynamic HTML. Dynamic HTML works by making more of the elements of a Web page *scriptable*, and this chapter is about writing scripts. What does this mean? With standard HTML, you can only use the mouse and keyboard with Web page *controls* like text boxes, buttons, and so on. With Dynamic HTML, much more of the Web page comes alive—you can click anywhere in a Web page and make that Web page respond. Bringing much more of your Web page to life is what Dynamic HTML is all about. In fact, as we'll see in Chapter 5, Internet Explorer makes just about every tag active, from the <TABLE> tag to the <H1> tag—and all these tags can act as only controls could before, accepting and making use of the user's actions. Netscape Navigator also supports this aspect of Dynamic HTML, but not quite as fully as Internet Explorer does.

To put Dynamic HTML to work, we'll use a scripting language. Dynamic HTML itself doesn't do more than give us the chance to respond to the user; we have to script our responses to the user ourselves. There are two popular scripting languages: JavaScript and VBScript. Netscape Navigator supports JavaScript, and Internet Explorer supports both JavaScript and VBScript. If all other things were equal, we'd use JavaScript in this book. However, Microsoft appears to strongly prefer VBScript over JavaScript for Dynamic HTML applications. The numerous examples at Microsoft's Web site are all written in VBScript, the company's online documentation for Dynamic HTML also uses VBScript, and there are things you can do with Internet Explorer in VBScript that you simply can't do with JavaScript. For those reasons, we'll see how to use *both* JavaScript and VBScript in this book, making it easier for Internet Explorer programmers to choose which one they want and to use the Microsoft resources available at the Microsoft Web site. VBScript and JavaScript are not such different languages; by working through both, we'll be better prepared to program Dynamic HTML pages. Afterward, if you want to stick to pure JavaScript, that's fine, but reading this book will also prepare you for using VBScript, which many readers say they find easier to work with, and which is what the bulk of programmers appear to use with Internet Explorer today.

In fact, the Microsoft and Netscape implementations of Dynamic HTML are so different that, even if this book used JavaScript for all examples, we wouldn't be able to run our examples in both browsers any more than if we wrote all Internet Explorer examples in VBScript and all Netscape Navigator examples in JavaScript. This difference between Dynamic HTML implementations is a real inconvenience, and to work around it, Chapter 3 presents a way to not only detect which browser your page is being loaded into, but to *rewrite* your Web page on the fly to tailor the code to the browser your page is in. This may be the only practical way of dealing with the large-scale differences between browsers.

This chapter, then, focuses on the basics of using both JavaScript and VBScript, because using scripting languages will let us make use of what Dynamic HTML has to offer. The chapter covers how to embed scripts into a Web page (this will be important to our work with Dynamic HTML); how to use scripting properties, methods, and events; and how to hook scripts up to Web page controls (Web page elements such as text boxes, buttons, radio buttons, list boxes, and so on). This chapter demonstrates how to support a simple text box that the user can type into, simple buttons that place text into text boxes when clicked, radio buttons, check boxes, list boxes, and more. We'll see how to do all that in both JavaScript and VBScript—then you can choose which one you want to use.

Chapter 3 describes how using Dynamic HTML means that many elements in a Web page, not just the controls we'll see in this chapter, can be scripted. The way we use scripts will be just the same in this chapter, however, so let's get started now as we see how to support text boxes in our Web pages.

## Getting Started with Text Boxes

The first Web page control we'll take a look at is the *text box*. Text boxes are those rectangular boxes that everyone is familiar with: You type text into text boxes, and in Windows, dialog boxes are full of them. In our case, we'll place a text box in our Web page like this:

Then the user can type text into the text box like this:

This method prepares our Web page to support text boxes. Let's see this in action now as we place a text box in our Web page. Let's create a new Web page named textbox.htm; we start with the normal <HTML> tag:

```
<HTML>
      .
      .
      .
```

Next, add a header and make the title of the Web page "Textbox Example":

```
<HTML>
<HEAD>                                              ⇐
<TITLE>Textbox Example</TITLE>                      ⇐
</HEAD>                                              ⇐
      .
```

.
.

Now we're ready to add the Web page's body:

```
<HTML>

<HEAD>
<TITLE>Textbox Example</TITLE>
</HEAD>

<BODY>                                                        ⇐
    .
    .
    .
</BODY>                                                       ⇐
</HTML>                                                       ⇐
```

We'll set up the new Web page's text box in the Web page's body. First, we make sure that our new text box will be centered by adding a <CENTER> tag:

```
<HTML>

<HEAD>
<TITLE>Textbox Example</TITLE>
</HEAD>

<BODY>

<CENTER>                                                      ⇐
    .
    .
    .
</CENTER>                                                     ⇐

</BODY>
</HTML>
```

Now we're ready to add the text box itself.

## Adding a Text Box to a Web Page

We add controls like text boxes to Web pages with the <INPUT> tag, which can take these attributes:

**Internet Explorer**

```
<INPUT
ACCESSKEY=string
ALIGN=ABSBOTTOM | ABSMIDDLE |
BASELINE | BOTTOM | LEFT | MIDDLE
| RIGHT | TEXTTOP | TOP
DATAFLD=string
DATASRC=string
DISABLED
ID=string
LANGUAGE=JAVASCRIPT | VBSCRIPT
MAXLENGTH=long
NAME=string
READONLY=string
SIZE=variant
STYLE=string
TABINDEX=integer
TITLE=string
TYPE=BUTTON | CHECKBOX | HIDDEN |
IMAGE | TEXTBOX | RADIO | RESET |
SELECT-MULTIPLE | SELECT-ONE |
SELECT-ONE | SUBMIT | TEXT |
TEXTAREA
VALUE=string
event = script
>
```

**Netscape Navigator
(not all attributes available for all TYPEs)**

```
<INPUT
ALIGN="LEFT"|"RIGHT"|"TOP"|
"ABSMIDDLE"|"ABSBOTTOM"|"TEXTTOP"|
"MIDDLE"|"BASELINE"|"BOTTOM"
NAME="name"
SRC="Location"
VALUE=string
TYPE=BUTTON | CHECKBOX | HIDDEN |
IMAGE | TEXTBOX | RADIO | RESET |
FILE | TEXT | PASSWORD
MAXLENGTH="maxChar"
SIZE="charsLength"
ONCLICK="JScode"
ONSELECT="jJScode"
ONBLUR="blurJScode"
ONCHANGE="changeJScode"
ONFOCUS="focusJScode"
>
```

In this case, we want a text box, so we use the <INPUT> tag with the TYPE attribute set to TEXT:

```
<HTML>

<HEAD>
<TITLE>Textbox Example</TITLE>
</HEAD>

<BODY>

<CENTER>
<INPUT TYPE = TEXT>
```

```
</CENTER>

</BODY>
</HTML>
```

Although this code creates a text box, it's only one character wide, which is not much use. Let's make the new text box 20 characters wide with the SIZE attribute:

```
<HTML>

<HEAD>
<TITLE>Textbox Example</TITLE>
</HEAD>

<BODY>

<CENTER>
<INPUT TYPE = TEXT SIZE = 20>
</CENTER>

</BODY>
</HTML>
```

This is all we need for Internet Explorer, but Netscape Navigator requires all controls to appear in a *form*:

| Internet Explorer | Netscape Navigator |
|---|---|
| `<FORM` | `<FORM` |
| `ACTION=string` | `ACTION="ServerURL"` |
| `ID=string` | `ENCTYPE="EncodingType"` |
| `METHOD=GET | POST` | `METHOD="GET"|"POST"` |
| `NAME=string` | `NAME="FormName"` |
| `STYLE=string` | `ONRESET="resetJScode"` |
| `TARGET=string` | `ONSUBMIT="submitJScode"` |
| `TITLE=string` | `TARGET="WindowName"` |
| `event = script` | `>` |
| `>` | |

Forms are specially designed to set off controls in groups. Forms do not appear on the screen; they are purely logical groupings in code. That's what a form is—a collection of controls that we want to keep together. Usually, those controls will appear near each other in the Web page, such as a text box and a Send button that allows the user to send feedback to a page's author. How forms work will become clear as we use them. Here's how we add our text box to a form:

```
<HTML>

<HEAD>
<TITLE>Textbox Example</TITLE>
</HEAD>

<BODY>

<FORM>                                                        ⇐
<CENTER>
<INPUT TYPE = TEXT SIZE = 20>
</CENTER>
</FORM>                                                       ⇐

</BODY>
</HTML>
```

This creates a new text box in our Web page, as we see in Figure 2.1. (You don't need to put controls into forms with Internet Explorer, but it doesn't hurt.) The text box appears centered in our Web page, as we intended. In addition, users can type text into that text box—all they have to do is to click the text box with the mouse, which makes a blinking caret appear in the text box, then type the text they want. They can even select, cut, copy, and paste text with our text box.

Our first control example, showing how to use a text box, is a success.

The listing for this text box Web page appears in Listing 2.1.

**Listing 2.1 textbox.htm**

```
<HTML>
<HEAD>
<TITLE>Textbox Example</TITLE>
</HEAD>
<BODY>

<FORM>
<CENTER>
<INPUT TYPE = TEXT SIZE = 20>
</CENTER>
</FORM>
```

*Continued*

**Listing 2.1 Continued**

```
</BODY>
</HTML>
```

Our first control example is fine as far as it goes, but that's not very far. The user is able to place text into the text box, but we cannot. Let's see about placing text in the text box ourselves with some scripts of our own. We'll do that in two ways: First, we'll see how to place text into the text box automatically when the Web page is first displayed in the Web browser. Next, we'll see how to add a push button that, when clicked, will place the specific text we want into the text box. Let's start by seeing how to initialize our text box using VBScript.

## Initializing Web Pages with VBScript

We can initialize our Web page to put the message, "Hello from VBScript" into the text box automatically when the Web page opens. We start by changing the title of the text box example to something more appropriate, "VBScript Initialization":

**Figure 2.1 Our first Web page text box.**

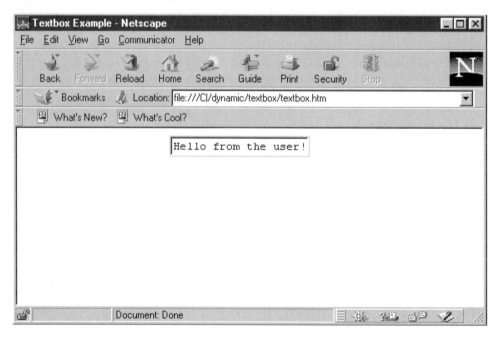

```
<HTML>
<HEAD>
<TITLE>VBScript Initialization</TITLE>                              ⇐
</HEAD>

<BODY>

<CENTER>
<INPUT TYPE = TEXT SIZE = 20>
</CENTER>

</BODY>
</HTML>
```

Next, we indicate to the Web browser that we intend to use VBScript in our Web page with the <BODY> tag's LANGUAGE attribute:

```
<HTML>
<HEAD>
<TITLE>VBScript Initializtion</TITLE>
</HEAD>

<BODY LANGUAGE = VBScript>                                          ⇐

<CENTER>
<INPUT TYPE = TEXT SIZE = 20>
</CENTER>

</BODY>
</HTML>
```

The next step is to add some VBScript code that the Web browser will run when the Web page is first loaded. To do that, we'll have to use Dynamic HTML events.

## Using Web Page Events

When the user takes some action, like clicking the mouse, typing a key, scrolling a Web page, or any other such action, the Web browser generates an *event*. For example, when the Web page is first displayed, the Web browser creates an onLoad event. This is a typical name for an event. All Internet Explorer's events appear in Table 2.1; all Netscape Navigator's events appear in Table 2.2. Notice they all start with "on."

**Table 2.1 Internet Explorer Events**

| | | |
|---|---|---|
| onabort | onafterupdate | onbeforeupdate |
| onblur | onbounce | onchange |
| onclick | ondblclick | onerror |
| onfinish | onfocus | onhelp |
| onkeydown | onkeypress | onkeyup |
| onload | onmousedown | onmousemove |
| onmouseout | onmouseover | onmouseup |
| onreadystatechange | onreset | onrowenter |
| onscroll | onselect | onstart |
| onsubmit | onunload | |

**Table 2.2 Netscape Navigator Events**

| | | |
|---|---|---|
| onAbort | onBlur | onClick |
| onChange | onDragDrop | onError |
| onFocus | onKeyDown | onKeyPress |
| onKeyUp | onLoad | onMouseDown |
| onMouseMove | onMouseOut | onMouseOver |
| onMouseUp | onMove | onReset |
| onResize | onSelect | onSubmit |
| onUnload | | |

Because we want to load our text box with the "Hello from VBScript" message, we'll use the onLoad event. In particular, we can run a VBScript *subroutine* when the onLoad event occurs. A subroutine is simply a special type of enclosed block of VBScript commands that we can refer to by name. For example, let's say that we want to run the VBScript code in a subroutine named Page_Initialize(). The parentheses after the subroutine's name indicate that we can send values to that subroutine for it to use; this is called *passing parameters to a subroutine,* and we'll see how it works soon when we turn to JavaScript. To connect a subroutine named Page_Initialize() to the onLoad event, then, we add the code "onLoad = Page_Initialize()" to the <BODY> tag:

```
<HTML>
<HEAD>
```

```
<TITLE>VBScript Initialization</TITLE>
</HEAD>

<BODY LANGUAGE = VBScript onLoad = Page_Initialize()>                    ⇐

<CENTER>
<INPUT TYPE = TEXT SIZE = 20>
</CENTER>

</BODY>
</HTML>
```

Now when the Web page is first loaded, the Web browser will search for a subroutine named Page_Initialize() to run. Our next step, then, is to create that subroutine.

## Setting Up a Script in a Web Page

Script code like the Page_Initialize() subroutine we're about to write goes into the script portion of our Web page, which is enclosed in a <SCRIPT> tag. This tag works like this:

**Internet Explorer**

```
<SCRIPT
EVENT=string
FOR=string
ID=string
IN=string
LANGUAGE=JAVASCRIPT | VBSCRIPT
LIBRARY=string
TITLE=string
>
```

**Netscape Navigator**

```
<SCRIPT
LANGUAGE="LanguageName"
SRC="Location"
>
```

The <SCRIPT> tag looks like this in our Web page:

```
<HTML>
<HEAD>
<TITLE>VBScript Initialization</TITLE>
</HEAD>

<BODY LANGUAGE = VBScript onLoad = Page_Initialize()>
```

```
<CENTER>
<INPUT TYPE = TEXT SIZE = 20>
</CENTER>

<SCRIPT>
   .
   .
   .
</SCRIPT>

</BODY>
</HTML>
```

Browsers that don't run scripts will ignore everything between the \<SCRIPT\> and \</SCRIPT\> tags, so that is where we'll place all our script code. (Some older browsers, though, might require you to enclose everything between the \<SCRIPT\> and \</SCRIPT\> tags in an HTML comment or they will display your code as text; both the Netscape and Microsoft browsers will ignore the comment tag.) As we know, there are different scripting languages, so we first indicate to the Web browser that we'll be using VBScript with the \<SCRIPT\> tag's LANGUAGE attribute:

```
<HTML>
<HEAD>
<TITLE>VBScript Initialization</TITLE>
</HEAD>

<BODY LANGUAGE = VBScript onLoad = Page_Initialize()>

<CENTER>
<INPUT TYPE = TEXT SIZE = 20>
</CENTER>

<SCRIPT LANGUAGE = VBScript>                              ⇐
   .
   .
   .
</SCRIPT>

</BODY>
</HTML>
```

Now we're ready to add some VBScript code. We start by creating our new subroutine, which we've called Page_Initialize(). We do that with the VBScript keyword SUB, giving the new subroutine the name Page_Initialize() this way:

```
<HTML>
<HEAD>
<TITLE>VBScript Initialization</TITLE>
</HEAD>

<BODY LANGUAGE = VBScript onLoad = Page_Initialize()>

<CENTER>
<INPUT TYPE = TEXT SIZE = 20>
</CENTER>

<SCRIPT LANGUAGE = VBScript>

SUB Page_Initialize()
    .
    .
    .


</SCRIPT>

</BODY>
</HTML>
```

(Unlike JavaScript, VBScript is not case-sensitive, so we could have written this keyword as "Sub" or "sub.") Next, we end the new subroutine with the VBScript instruction END SUB:

```
<HTML>
<HEAD>
<TITLE>VBScript Initialization</TITLE>
</HEAD>

<BODY LANGUAGE = VBScript onLoad = Page_Initialize()>

<CENTER>
<INPUT TYPE = TEXT SIZE = 20>
</CENTER>

<SCRIPT LANGUAGE = VBScript>
```

```
SUB Page_Initialize()
    .
    .
    .
END SUB                                                                    ⇐

</SCRIPT>

</BODY>
</HTML>
```

The VBScript code we put inside this subroutine will be executed when the Web page is first loaded. We want to place the text "Hello from VBScript" into the text box when the Web page is loaded—but how do we reach the text box from our subroutine? We do that by *naming* the text box. When we have a name for the text box, we'll be able to refer to it in our code.

Here, we'll give the text box the simple name "Textbox" by using the NAME attribute in the <INPUT> tag when we create the text box:

```
<HTML>
<HEAD>
<TITLE>VBScript Initialization</TITLE>
</HEAD>

<BODY LANGUAGE = VBScript onLoad = Page_Initialize()>

<CENTER>
<INPUT TYPE = TEXT NAME = Textbox SIZE = 20>
</CENTER>

<SCRIPT LANGUAGE = VBScript>

SUB Page_Initialize()
    .
    .
    .
END SUB

</SCRIPT>

</BODY>
</HTML>
```

Now we can refer to our text box by name, "Textbox," in our Page_Initialize() subroutine.

How do we place text into that text box? We do that by using the text box's Value property.

## Using HTML Properties

Each HTML control has built-in *properties* that we can use in our code. For example, the text in a text box is held in its value property, the color of hyperlinks is stored in the linkColor property, the size of a text box is stored in its size property, and so on. All the properties in Internet Explorer appear in Table 2.3, and all the properties for Netscape Navigator appear in Table 2.4. (Keep in mind that each of these properties applies to different controls or other page elements, and not all of them are available for any one page element.)

### Table 2.3  Internet Explorer Properties

| | | | |
|---|---|---|---|
| accessKey | action | activeElement | align |
| aLink | alinkColor | alt | altKey |
| appCodeName | appName | appVersionbackground | background-Attachment |
| backgroundColor | backgroundImage | backgroundRepeat | baseRef |
| behavior | bgColor | bgProperties | border |
| borderBottomColor | borderBottomStyle | borderBottomWidth | borderColor |
| borderColorDark | borderColorLight | borderLeftColor | borderLeftStyle |
| borderLeftWidth | borderRightColor | borderRightStyle | borderRightWidth |
| borderTopColor | borderTopStyle | borderTopWidth | bufferDepth |
| button | cancelBubble | cellPadding | cellSpacing |
| charset | checked | classid | className |
| clear | closed | code | codeBase |
| codeType | color | colorDepth | cols |
| colSpan | compact | complete | cookie |
| cookieEnabled | coords | cssText | ctrlKey |
| data | dataFld | dataFormatAs | dataSrc |
| defaultChecked | defaultSelected | defaultStatus | defaultValue |
| description | dialogArgs | direction | disabled |

*Continued*

**Table 2.3  Continued**

| | | | |
|---|---|---|---|
| display | docHeight | docLeft | docTop |
| docWidth | domain | dynsrc | enabledPlugin |
| end | event | face | fgColor |
| fileCreatedDate | fileModifiedDate | fileSize | fileUpdatedDate |
| filter | font | fontFamily | fontSize |
| fontStyle | fontVariant | fontWeight | For |
| form | frame | frameBorder | frameSpacing |
| fromElement | hash | height | host |
| hostname | href | hres | hspace |
| htmlHeight | htmlSelText | htmlText | id |
| In | indeterminate | index | isMap |
| javaEnabled | keyCode | language | lastModified |
| left | leftMargin | length | letterSpacing |
| library | lineHeight | link | linkColor |
| location | loop | lowsrc | map |
| margin | marginBottom | marginHeight | marginLeft |
| marginRight | marginTop | marginWidth | maxLength |
| method | Methods | mimeType | multiple |
| name | noHref | noResize | noShade |
| noWrap | object | opener | overflow |
| parent | parentElement | pathname | port |
| posHeight | posLeft | posTop | posWidth |
| protocol | readOnly | recordset | ref |
| referrer | rel | returnValue | retval |
| rev | rows | rowSpan | rules |
| scroll | scrollAmount | scrollDelay | scrollHeight |
| scrolling | scrollLeft | scrollTop | scrollWidth |
| search | selected | selectedIndex | self |
| shape | shiftKey | size | sourceIndex |
| span | src | srcElement | start |

**Table 2.3 Continued**

| | | | |
|---|---|---|---|
| status | strReadyState | style | suffixes |
| tabIndex | tagName | target | text |
| textAlign | textDecoration | textDecoration LineThrough | textDecoration Overline |
| textDecoration Underline | textIndent | textTransform | title |
| toElement | top | topMargin | type |
| URL | urn | useMap | userAgent |
| vAlign | value | verticalAlign | visibility |
| vLink | vlinkColor | vres | vrml |
| vspace | width | x | y |
| zIndex | | | |

**Table 2.4 Netscape Navigator Properties**

| | | | |
|---|---|---|---|
| action | alinkColor | Anchor | anchors |
| appCodeName | Applet | applets | appName |
| appVersion | Area | bgColor | Button |
| Checkbox | checked | closed | complete |
| cookie | defaultChecked | defaultSelected | defaultStatus |
| defaultValue | description | description | document |
| domain | E | elements | embeds |
| enabledPlugin | encoding | fgColor | filename |
| FileUpload | form | forms | Frame |
| frames | hash | height | Hidden |
| history | host | hostname | href |
| hspace | Image | images | index |
| lastModified | length | Link | linkColor |
| links | LN10 | LN2 | location |
| LOG10E | LOG2E | lowsrc | method |
| mimeTypes | name | opener | options |

*Continued*

**Table 2.4  Continued**

| | | | |
|---|---|---|---|
| parent | Password | pathname | PI |
| plugins | port | protocol | prototype |
| Radio | referrer | Reset | search |
| Select | selected | selectedIndex | self |
| SQRT1_2 | SQRT2 | src | status |
| Submit | suffixes | target | Text |
| text | Textarea | title | top |
| type | URL | userAgent | value |
| vlinkColor | vspace | width | window |
| window border | | | |

To place text into the text box, we'll simply place that text into the text box's Value property in our Page_Initialize() subroutine. In our Web page it looks like this:

```
<HTML>
<HEAD>
<TITLE>VBScript Initialization</TITLE>
</HEAD>

<BODY LANGUAGE = VBScript onLoad = Page_Initialize()>

<CENTER>
<INPUT TYPE = TEXT NAME = Textbox SIZE = 20>
</CENTER>

<SCRIPT LANGUAGE = VBScript>

SUB Page_Initialize()
    Textbox.Value = "Hello from VBScript"          ⇐
END SUB

</SCRIPT>

</BODY>
</HTML>
```

That completes our new Web page; when we open it up in Internet Explorer, we see that the words "Hello from VBScript" have already been loaded into the text box, as shown in Figure 2.2.

Our first VBScript Web page is a success: We've put VBScript to work, setting up a new subroutine that the Web browser calls—that is, runs—when the Web page is first loaded. The code for this Web page appears in Listing 2.2.

---

**Listing 2.2 init.htm**

```
<HTML>
<HEAD>
<TITLE>VBScript Initialization</TITLE>
</HEAD>

<BODY LANGUAGE = VBScript onLoad = Page_Initialize()>
```

*Continued*

**Figure 2.2  A text box initialized with a message in VBScript.**

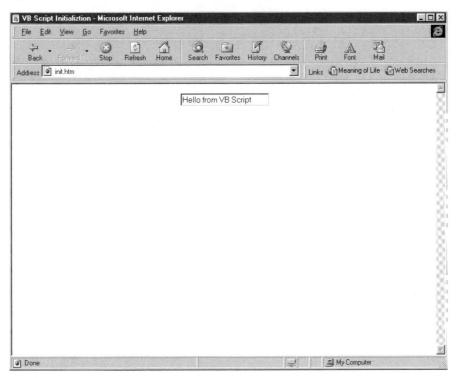

---

**Figure 2.2 Continued**

```
<CENTER>
<INPUT TYPE = TEXT NAME = Textbox SIZE = 20>
</CENTER>

<SCRIPT LANGUAGE = VBScript>

SUB Page_Initialize()
    Textbox.Value = "Hello from VBScript"
END SUB

</SCRIPT>

</BODY>
</HTML>
```

Now that we've seen how to initialize a Web page in VBScript, let's see how to do it in JavaScript.

# Initializing Web Pages with JavaScript

We begin our JavaScript example, initj.htm, by indicating that we want the onLoad event to be handled by Page_Initialize():

```
<HTML>
<HEAD>
<TITLE>JavaScript Initialization</TITLE>
</HEAD>
<BODY onLoad = "Page_Initialize()">                                    ⇐
    .
    .
    .
```

Next, we add our text box in a form, as Netscape requires. Here, we name our form Form1:

```
<HTML>
<HEAD>
<TITLE>JavaScript Initialization</TITLE>
</HEAD>
<BODY onLoad = "Page_Initialize()">

<FORM NAME = "Form1">                                                  ⇐
<CENTER>
```

```
<INPUT TYPE = TEXT NAME = Textbox SIZE = 25>                          ⇐
</CENTER>
</FORM>                                                              ⇐
```

At this point, we're ready to indicate that we are using JavaScript:

```
<HTML>
<HEAD>
<TITLE>JavaScript Initialization</TITLE>
</HEAD>
<BODY onLoad = "Page_Initialize()">

<FORM NAME = "Form1">
<CENTER>
<INPUT TYPE = TEXT NAME = Textbox SIZE = 25>
</CENTER>
</FORM>

<SCRIPT LANGUAGE = JavaScript>                                       ⇐
   .
   .
   .
```

One thing to note here is that Netscape's JavaScript has changed quite a bit over various releases (although it is backward-compatible). In particular, you might find yourself trying to use some of the new Dynamic HTML events like onMouseDown in an older Netscape Navigator version for which JavaScript can't handle such events. To avoid such situations, you can now specify the version of JavaScript you're using. The Dynamic HTML-enabled JavaScript version is JavaScript 1.2. You can specify that your script uses that version this way: <SCRIPT LANGUAGE = "JavaScript1.2">. Older versions of the browser will ignore such scripts.

In VBScript, we used subroutines; in JavaScript, we use functions. Function bodies are enclosed in curly braces, { and }. Page_Initialize() is a function:

```
<HTML>
<HEAD>
<TITLE>JavaScript Initialization</TITLE>
</HEAD>
<BODY onLoad = "Page_Initialize()">

<FORM NAME = "Form1">
```

```
<CENTER>
<INPUT TYPE = TEXT NAME = Textbox SIZE = 25>
</CENTER>
</FORM>

<SCRIPT LANGUAGE = JavaScript>

function Page_Initialize()
{

    .

    .

    .

}
```

To reach the text box and change its value property, we need to refer to its form (although Internet Explorer's JavaScript implementation does not require this). We do that with the *document object*, which we'll see more of soon. We place text in the text box by referring to the text box as document.Form1.Textbox, separating each item with a period (.). Note that JavaScript, unlike VBScript, is case-sensitive for all names:

```
<HTML>
<HEAD>
<TITLE>JavaScript Initialization</TITLE>
</HEAD>
<BODY onLoad = "Page_Initialize()">

<FORM NAME = "Form1">
<CENTER>
<INPUT TYPE = TEXT NAME = Textbox SIZE = 25>
</CENTER>
</FORM>

<SCRIPT LANGUAGE = JavaScript>

function Page_Initialize()
{
    document.Form1.Textbox.value = "Hello from JavaScript"          ⇐
}

</script>
</BODY>
</HTML>
```

That's all it takes. Our new Web page appears in Figure 2.3. Now we're programming with JavaScript!

The code for this Web page, initj.htm, appears in Listing 2.3. (Simple pages like this one work in both Netscape Navigator and Internet Explorer, but most Dynamic HTML examples will not, unfortunately.) Note that in general, when we write a Web page in both VBScript and JavaScript, we'll add a "j" at the end of the .htm file for the JavaScript version (and we'll include both .htm files in the same folder in the Web site).

So far, then, we've used scripts to place text into a text box when a page loads. However, we'll usually respond to the user's actions with our Web pages. For example, we might put a button into our Web pages and connect it to our code. Let's look into that process now.

**Figure 2.3 Page initialization with JavaScript.**

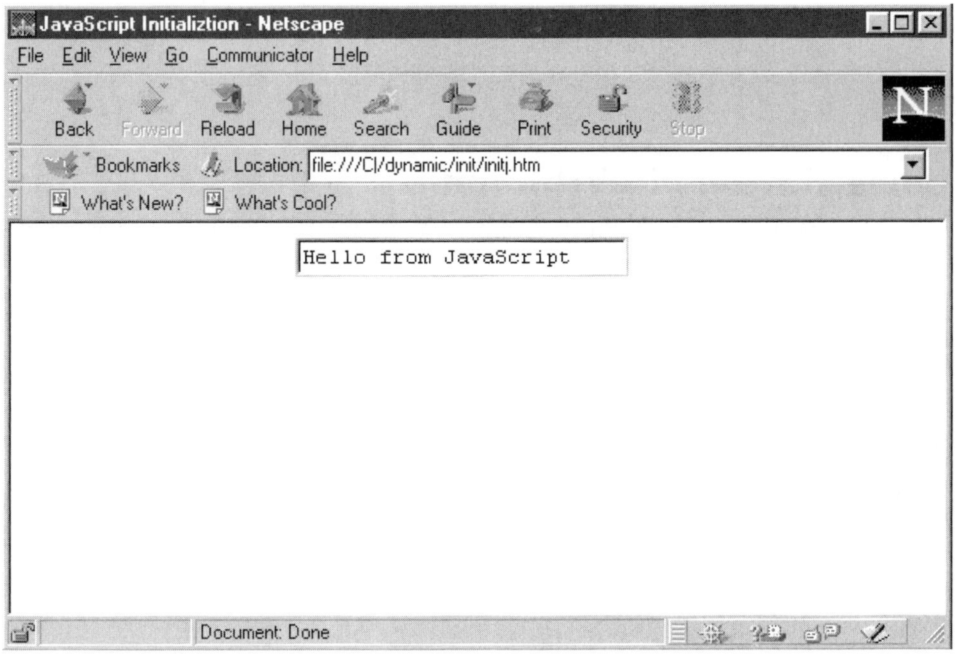

**Listing 2.3 initj.htm**

```
<HTML>
<HEAD>
<TITLE>JavaScript Initialization</TITLE>
</HEAD>
<BODY onLoad = "Page_Initialize()">

<FORM NAME = "Form1">
<CENTER>
<INPUT TYPE = TEXT NAME = Textbox SIZE = 25>
</CENTER>
</FORM>

<SCRIPT LANGUAGE = JavaScript>

function Page_Initialize()
{
    document.Form1.Textbox.value = "Hello from JavaScript"
}

</script>
</BODY>
</HTML>
```

# Using Buttons in VBScript

In this example, we'll add a button to our Web page in VBScript. In particular, we'll add a button with the caption "Show Message" and a text box to a Web page:

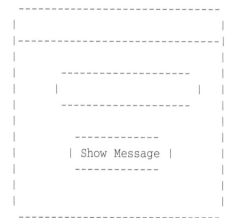

We'll place the text "Hello from VBScript" into the text box this way so that it appears when the user clicks the Show Message button:

When we install a button in our Web page, we'll be able to respond to the user's actions, which is a long way toward using true Dynamic HTML. Let's start this new example Web page, which we call buttons.htm, now.

We start with the <HTML> tag, of course, and a header with the title Buttons:

```
<HTML>

<HEAD>
<TITLE>Buttons</TITLE>
</HEAD>
        .
        .
        .
```

Next, we add a text box by using the <INPUT> tag inside the Web page's body, giving that text box the name Textbox:

```
<HTML>

<HEAD>
<TITLE>Buttons</TITLE>
</HEAD>
```

```
<BODY>

<CENTER>
<INPUT TYPE = TEXT NAME = Textbox SIZE = 20>                          ⇐
    .
    .
    .
</CENTER>

</BODY>
```

Now we're ready to add our new button. We do that with the <INPUT> tag, specifying the type of control we want as BUTTON:

```
<HTML>

<HEAD>
<TITLE>Buttons</TITLE>
</HEAD>

<BODY>

<CENTER>
<INPUT TYPE = TEXT NAME = Textbox SIZE = 20>
<BR>
<BR>
<INPUT TYPE = BUTTON >                                              ⇐
</CENTER>

</BODY>

</HTML>
```

We want our button to display the caption "Show Message." When the user clicks the button, the code will show our message. Let's give our button a caption now.

## Giving a Button a Caption

We can set the caption of a button with the button's Value property (which acts much like the Value property of a text box; a text box's Value property holds the text in the text box, just as the button's Value property holds the text in the button). In fact, we can set the button's Value property in the <INPUT> tag where we first define the button. (We can do that with other controls like text boxes as well.) Giving our button a caption looks like this in our Web page:

---

```
<HTML>

<HEAD>
<TITLE>Buttons</TITLE>
</HEAD>

<BODY>

<CENTER>
<INPUT TYPE = TEXT NAME = Textbox SIZE = 20>
<BR>
<BR>
<INPUT TYPE = BUTTON Value = "Show Message">                    ⇐
</CENTER>

</BODY>

</HTML>
```

In addition, we want to connect our button to our code. In particular, when the user clicks the button, we want to display the message in the text box. To do that, we can connect a subroutine named ShowMessage() to the button. We do that by connecting the button's onClick event to the button this way in the <INPUT> tag:

```
<HTML>

<HEAD>
<TITLE>Buttons</TITLE>
</HEAD>

<BODY>

<CENTER>
<INPUT TYPE = TEXT NAME = Textbox SIZE = 20>
<BR>
<BR>
<INPUT TYPE = BUTTON Value = "Show Message" onClick = "ShowMessage()">
</CENTER>

</BODY>

</HTML>
```

Now that we've connected the button to the ShowMessage() subroutine, we can write that new subroutine. To start, we will set up a script area in our Web page. In the last example, we set up the script area inside the body of the Web page, but it doesn't have to go there—for example, we could place it outside the body of the Web page this way:

```
<HTML>

<HEAD>
<TITLE>Buttons</TITLE>
</HEAD>

<BODY>

<CENTER>
<INPUT TYPE = TEXT NAME = Textbox SIZE = 20>
<BR>
<BR>
<INPUT TYPE = BUTTON Value = "Show Message" onClick = "ShowMessage()">
</CENTER>

</BODY>

<SCRIPT LANGUAGE = VBScript>                                    ⇐
    .
    .
    .
</SCRIPT>                                                        ⇐

</HTML>
```

We will set up the button's ShowMessage() subroutine in our script area this way:

```
<HTML>

<HEAD>
<TITLE>Buttons</TITLE>
</HEAD>

<BODY>

<CENTER>
```

```
<INPUT TYPE = TEXT NAME = Textbox SIZE = 20>
<BR>
<BR>
<INPUT TYPE = BUTTON Value = "Show Message" onClick = "ShowMessage()">
</CENTER>

</BODY>

<SCRIPT LANGUAGE = VBScript>
        Sub ShowMessage()                                              ⇐
          .
          .
          .
        End Sub                                                        ⇐
</SCRIPT>

</HTML>
```

We're ready to add the VBScript code we'll need. In this case, ShowMessage() is called when the user clicks the Show Message button. We want to place the string "Hello from VBScript" into the text box. To do that, use the text box's Value property:

```
<HTML>

<HEAD>
<TITLE>Buttons</TITLE>
</HEAD>

<BODY>

<CENTER>
<INPUT TYPE = TEXT NAME = Textbox SIZE = 20>
<BR>
<BR>
<INPUT TYPE = BUTTON Value = "Show Message" onClick = "ShowMessage()">
</CENTER>

</BODY>

<SCRIPT LANGUAGE = VBScript>
        Sub ShowMessage()
                TextBox.Value = "Hello from VBScript"                  ⇐
```

```
        End Sub
</SCRIPT>

</HTML>
```

That completes the page. Now we're ready to take a look at the page in Internet Explorer, as shown in Figure 2.4.

You can see our button with the caption "Show Message" in Figure 2.4. When the user clicks that button, the VBScript code we've placed into the page displays the "Hello from VBScript" message in the text box, as also shown in Figure 2.4. Now we're able to use button controls in our Web page; as you can see, it's only a matter of using the <INPUT> tag to set up the button, connecting a subroutine to the button with the onClick event, and adding the code you want executed when the button is clicked. The HTML code for this page appears in Listing 2.4.

**Figure 2.4 Our VBScript page supports a button and a text box.**

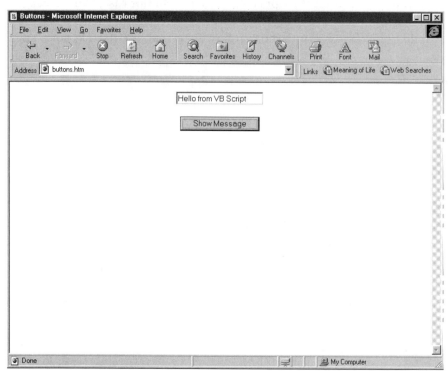

**Listing 2.4 buttons.htm**

```
<HTML>

<HEAD>
<TITLE>Buttons</TITLE>
</HEAD>

<BODY>

<CENTER>
<INPUT TYPE = TEXT NAME = Textbox SIZE = 20>
<BR>
<BR>
<INPUT TYPE = BUTTON Value = "Show Message" onClick = "ShowMessage()">
</CENTER>

</BODY>

<SCRIPT LANGUAGE = VBScript>
        Sub ShowMessage()
                TextBox.Value = "Hello from VBScript"
        End Sub
</SCRIPT>

</HTML>
```

## Another Way of Connecting Controls to Code

We've specified the name of the subroutine to call when the onClick event occurs in the above example like this:

```
<CENTER>
<INPUT TYPE = TEXT NAME = Textbox SIZE = 20>
<BR>
<BR>
<INPUT TYPE = BUTTON Value = "Show Message" onClick = "ShowMessage()">  ⇐
</CENTER>
```

However, there's another way of connecting the onClick event to a subroutine. We can simply give a name to the button via the NAME attribute, just as we did for the text box. In the button's case, we can use the name ShowButton:

```
<HTML>

<HEAD>
<TITLE>Buttons</TITLE>
</HEAD>

<BODY>

<CENTER>
<INPUT TYPE = TEXT NAME = Textbox SIZE = 20>
<BR>
<BR>
<INPUT TYPE = BUTTON Value = "Show Message" NAME = "ShowButton">      ⇐
</CENTER>

</BODY>

</HTML>
```

We can set up a subroutine with the button's name and "_OnClick" added to the end. This makes use of the VBScript default naming convention, and VBScript will know that ShowButton_OnClick() is the subroutine it should call when the user clicks the button, even though we don't tell it so:

```
<HTML>

<HEAD>
<TITLE>Buttons</TITLE>
</HEAD>

<BODY>

<CENTER>
<INPUT TYPE = TEXT NAME = Textbox SIZE = 20>
<BR>
<BR>
<INPUT TYPE = BUTTON Value = "Show Message" NAME = "ShowButton">
</CENTER>

</BODY>

<SCRIPT LANGUAGE = VBScript>
```

```
      Sub ShowButton_OnClick
              TextBox.Value = "Hello from VBScript"
      End Sub
</SCRIPT>

</HTML>
```

In general, if you want to use this way of naming your event-handling subroutines, you simply give your control a name and set up a subroutine named name_OnEvent(), where "name" is the name of the control, and "OnEvent" is the type of event you want to handle, like a click event (e.g., ShowButton_OnClick() in the above example). The new version of this Web page appears in Listing 2.5.

---

**Listing 2.5 buttons2.htm**

```
<HTML>

<HEAD>
<TITLE>Buttons</TITLE>
</HEAD>

<BODY>

<CENTER>
<INPUT TYPE = TEXT NAME = Textbox SIZE = 20>
<BR>
<BR>
<INPUT TYPE = BUTTON Value = "Show Message" NAME = "ShowButton">
</CENTER>

</BODY>

<SCRIPT LANGUAGE = VBScript>
      Sub ShowButton_OnClick
              TextBox.Value = "Hello from VBScript"
      End Sub
</SCRIPT>

</HTML>
```

Now let's take a look at how to use buttons in JavaScript. It's pretty similar to using buttons in VBScript.

# Using Buttons in JavaScript

We'll place the text "Hello from JavaScript" into the text box so that it appears when the user clicks the Show Message button:

This is just like our earlier example except it's written in JavaScript. Let's see how this works. First, we set up our form and our text box in buttonsj.htm:

```
<HTML>

<TITLE>Buttons</TITLE>

<BODY>

<CENTER>
<FORM>                                                      ⇐
<INPUT TYPE = TEXT NAME = "Textbox" SIZE = 25>              ⇐
<BR>
<BR>
      .
      .
      .
```

Next, we install our button. In the button's event handler, ShowMessage(), we'll need some way of referring to the text box to display our text. We've seen one way of doing that in this chapter already: by referring to the text box as document.form1.Textbox, where we have named our form form1.

Another way of determining which form we're working with is to pass that form itself to the event handler. In this example, we pass "this.form" to the button's event-handling function. The "this" keyword refers to the current control—the button—and the "form" keyword refers to the form property of the button:

```
<HTML>

<TITLE>Buttons</TITLE>

<BODY>

<CENTER>
<FORM>
<INPUT TYPE = TEXT NAME = "Textbox" SIZE = 25>
<BR>
<BR>
<INPUT TYPE = BUTTON Value = "Show Message" onClick =
"ShowMessage(this.form)">                                          ⇐
</FORM>
</CENTER>

</BODY>
    .
    .
    .
```

Now the form we need will be passed to the ShowMessage() function, where we name it form1. We have a way of referring to the form at this point—as form1—so we can place our message in the text box this way (note that we don't need to use the document object in this case):

```
<HTML>

<TITLE>Buttons</TITLE>

<BODY>
    .
    .
    .
</BODY>

<SCRIPT LANGUAGE = JavaScript>
    function ShowMessage(form1)                                   ⇐
    {
        form1.Textbox.value = "Hello from JavaScript"             ⇐
```

```
    }
</SCRIPT>

</HTML>
```

That's it. Our page works, as shown in Figure 2.5. Now we're able to use buttons in JavaScript!

The code for this page, buttonsj.htm, appears in Listing 2.6.

---

**Listing 2.6 buttonsj.htm**

```
<HTML>

<TITLE>Buttons</TITLE>

<BODY>

<CENTER>
```

---

**Figure 2.5 Supporting a button using JavaScript.**

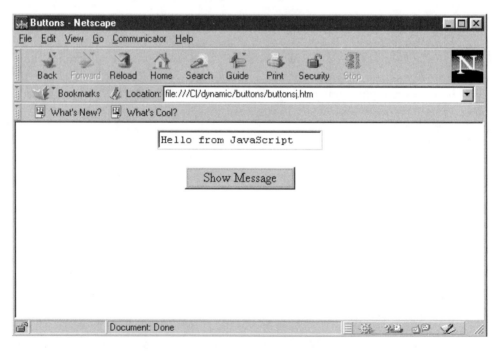

**Listing 2.6 Continued**

```
<FORM>
<INPUT TYPE = TEXT NAME = "Textbox" SIZE = 25>
<BR>
<BR>
<INPUT TYPE = BUTTON Value = "Show Message" onClick =
"ShowMessage(this.form)">
</FORM>
</CENTER>

</BODY>

<SCRIPT LANGUAGE = JavaScript>
    function ShowMessage(form1)
    {
        form1.Textbox.value = "Hello from JavaScript"
    }
</SCRIPT>

</HTML>
```

We've gotten a good look at buttons now, but buttons like the ones we've seen are only one type of control available to us. Another type of control is the check box control.

# Using Check Boxes with VBScript

If you've used Windows, you've seen *check boxes*—they're those controls that, when clicked, display a small check mark. When you click them again, the check mark disappears. Check boxes allow the user to specify a number of options at once, because when you click a check box, it stays checked until you click it again. For example, we can display five check boxes in a Web page like this:

```
      ------------------------------
     |                              |
     |-----------------------------|
     |      Click a check box...    |
     |                              |
     |      [ ] Check 1             |
     |      [ ] Check 2             |
     |      [ ] Check 3             |
     |      [ ] Check 4             |
     |      [ ] Check 5             |
```

```
   |                            |
   |      -------------------   |
   |     |                   |  |
   |      -------------------   |
   |                            |
    ----------------------------
```

Then when the user clicks a check box, we can display which one they've clicked in a text box:

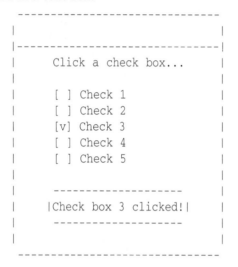

```
     ----------------------------------
    |                                  |
    |----------------------------------|
    |      Click a check box...        |
    |                                  |
    |        [ ] Check 1               |
    |        [ ] Check 2               |
    |        [v] Check 3               |
    |        [ ] Check 4               |
    |        [ ] Check 5               |
    |                                  |
    |        -------------------       |
    |       |Check box 3 clicked!|     |
    |        -------------------       |
    |                                  |
     ----------------------------------
```

They can click as many check boxes as they like (although we'll only display the most recently clicked one in our text box). Let's see how to work with check boxes in VBScript now. We start our new Web page, which we'll name checks.htm, with a header and a prompt to the user, "Click a check box...":

```
<HTML>

<HEAD>
<TITLE>Check box example</TITLE>
</HEAD>

<BODY>

<CENTER>
<H1>Click a check box...</H1>
     .
     .
     .
```

To arrange our check boxes, we'll put them in a table. To add a little splash of color, we can give that table a cyan background using the <TABLE> tag's BGCOLOR attribute:

```
<HTML>

<HEAD>
<TITLE>Check box example</TITLE>
</HEAD>

<BODY>

<CENTER>
<H1>Click a check box...</H1>

<TABLE BORDER BGCOLOR = CYAN WIDTH = 200>          ⇐
    .
    .
    .
</TABLE>                                            ⇐
    .
    .
    .
```

Setting up the check boxes is easy; we use the <INPUT> tag, setting the ATTRIBUTE tag to CHECKBOX. In addition, we connect each check box to a subroutine: Check1Clicked() for the first check box, Check2Clicked() for the second check box, and so on:

```
<HTML>

<HEAD>
<TITLE>Check box example</TITLE>
</HEAD>

<BODY>

<CENTER>
<H1>Click a check box...</H1>

<TABLE BORDER BGCOLOR = CYAN WIDTH = 200>
    <TR><TD><INPUT TYPE = CHECKBOX NAME = Check1 onClick =
Check1Clicked()>Check 1</TD></TR>                  ⇐
```

```
    <TR><TD><INPUT TYPE = CHECKBOX NAME = Check2 onClick =
Check2Clicked()>Check 2</TD></TR>                                          ⇐
    <TR><TD><INPUT TYPE = CHECKBOX NAME = Check3 onClick =
Check3Clicked()>Check 3</TD></TR>                                          ⇐
    <TR><TD><INPUT TYPE = CHECKBOX NAME = Check4 onClick =
Check4Clicked()>Check 4</TD></TR>                                          ⇐
    <TR><TD><INPUT TYPE = CHECKBOX NAME = Check5 onClick =
Check5Clicked()>Check 5</TD></TR>                                          ⇐
</TABLE>
        .
        .
        .
```

Now we've set up five check boxes, Check1 to Check5, and connected them to event-handling subroutines (which we'll write in a moment). Next, we add the text box we'll need:

```
<HTML>

<HEAD>
<TITLE>Check box example</TITLE>
</HEAD>

<BODY>

<CENTER>
<H1>Click a check box...</H1>

<TABLE BORDER BGCOLOR = CYAN WIDTH = 200>
    <TR><TD><INPUT TYPE = CHECKBOX NAME = Check1 onClick =
Check1Clicked()>Check 1</TD></TR>
    <TR><TD><INPUT TYPE = CHECKBOX NAME = Check2 onClick =
Check2Clicked()>Check 2</TD></TR>
    <TR><TD><INPUT TYPE = CHECKBOX NAME = Check3 onClick =
Check3Clicked()>Check 3</TD></TR>
    <TR><TD><INPUT TYPE = CHECKBOX NAME = Check4 onClick =
Check4Clicked()>Check 4</TD></TR>
    <TR><TD><INPUT TYPE = CHECKBOX NAME = Check5 onClick =
Check5Clicked()>Check 5</TD></TR>
</TABLE>
<BR>
<BR>
```

```
<INPUT TYPE = TEXT NAME = TextBox SIZE = 30>          ⇐
</CENTER>
```

```
</BODY>
    .
    .
    .
```

The next step is to connect the check boxes to VBScript code. Let's connect the first check box to the subroutine Check1Clicked() now. We do that by simply setting up a script area in our Web page and placing the code for the Check1Clicked() subroutine in that area. Here, we just display the message "Check box 1 clicked!" in the text box:

```
<HTML>

<HEAD>
<TITLE>Check box example</TITLE>
</HEAD>

<BODY>

<CENTER>
<H1>Click a check box...</H1>
    .
    .
    .
</BODY>

<SCRIPT LANGUAGE = VBScript>                          ⇐

    Sub Check1Clicked()                               ⇐
        TextBox.Value = "Check box 1 clicked!"        ⇐
    End Sub                                           ⇐
    .
    .
    .
</SCRIPT>                                              ⇐

</HTML>
```

Then we do the same for the other check boxes:

```
<HEAD>
<TITLE>Check box example</TITLE>
</HEAD>

<BODY>

<CENTER>
<H1>Click a check box...</H1>
    .
    .
    .
</BODY>

<SCRIPT LANGUAGE = VBScript>

    Sub Check1Clicked()
        TextBox.Value = "Check box 1 clicked!"
    End Sub

    Sub Check2Clicked()                                          <=
        TextBox.Value = "Check box 2 clicked!"                   <=
    End Sub                                                      <=

    Sub Check3Clicked()                                          <=
        TextBox.Value = "Check box 3 clicked!"                   <=
    End Sub                                                      <=

    Sub Check4Clicked()                                          <=
        TextBox.Value = "Check box 4 clicked!"                   <=
    End Sub                                                      <=

    Sub Check5Clicked()                                          <=
        TextBox.Value = "Check box 5 clicked!"                   <=
    End Sub                                                      <=

</SCRIPT>

</HTML>
```

Now we're ready to take a look at our new Web page in Internet Explorer, as shown in Figure 2.6. You can see our check boxes in the figure; when the user clicks one, the VBScript code reports which check box was clicked, as shown in Figure 2.6.

**Figure 2.6 Supporting check boxes in a VBScript page.**

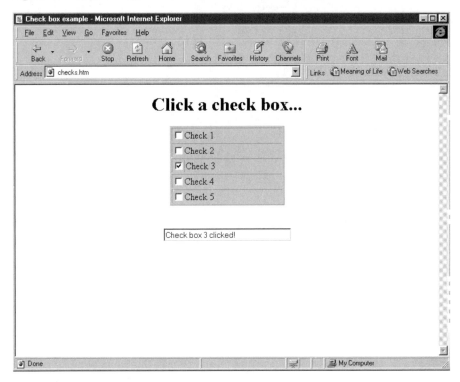

Our Web page is a success. The code for this Web page, checks.htm, appears in Listing 2.7.

**Listing 2.7 checks.htm**

```
<HTML>

<HEAD>
<TITLE>Check box example</TITLE>
</HEAD>

<BODY>

<CENTER>
<H1>Click a check box...</H1>
```

*Continued*

**Listing 2.7 Continued**

```
<TABLE BORDER BGCOLOR = CYAN WIDTH = 200>
    <TR><TD><INPUT TYPE = CHECKBOX NAME = Check1 onClick =
Check1Clicked()>Check 1</TD></TR>
    <TR><TD><INPUT TYPE = CHECKBOX NAME = Check2 onClick =
Check2Clicked()>Check 2</TD></TR>
    <TR><TD><INPUT TYPE = CHECKBOX NAME = Check3 onClick =
Check3Clicked()>Check 3</TD></TR>
    <TR><TD><INPUT TYPE = CHECKBOX NAME = Check4 onClick =
Check4Clicked()>Check 4</TD></TR>
    <TR><TD><INPUT TYPE = CHECKBOX NAME = Check5 onClick =
Check5Clicked()>Check 5</TD></TR>
</TABLE>
<BR>
<BR>
<INPUT TYPE  =  TEXT NAME  =  TextBox SIZE  =  30>
</CENTER>

</BODY>

<SCRIPT LANGUAGE = VBScript>

    Sub Check1Clicked()
        TextBox.Value = "Check box 1 clicked!"
    End Sub

    Sub Check2Clicked()
        TextBox.Value = "Check box 2 clicked!"
    End Sub

    Sub Check3Clicked()
        TextBox.Value = "Check box 3 clicked!"
    End Sub

    Sub Check4Clicked()
        TextBox.Value = "Check box 4 clicked!"
    End Sub

    Sub Check5Clicked()
        TextBox.Value = "Check box 5 clicked!"
    End Sub
```

**Listing 2.7 Continued**

```
</SCRIPT>

</HTML>
```

Now let's take a look at using check boxes in JavaScript.

# Using Check Boxes with JavaScript

Let's see how to use check boxes in a new example named checksj.htm using JavaScript. We give our form a name—form1—and add the check boxes:

```
<HTML>

<HEAD>
<TITLE>Check box example</TITLE>
</HEAD>

<BODY>

<FORM NAME = form1>
<CENTER>
<H1>Click a check box...</H1>

<TABLE BORDER BGCOLOR = CYAN WIDTH = 200>
    <TR><TD><INPUT TYPE = CHECKBOX NAME = Check1 onClick =
Check1Clicked()>Check 1</TD></TR>
    <TR><TD><INPUT TYPE = CHECKBOX NAME = Check2 onClick =
Check2Clicked()>Check 2</TD></TR>
    <TR><TD><INPUT TYPE = CHECKBOX NAME = Check3 onClick =
Check3Clicked()>Check 3</TD></TR>
    <TR><TD><INPUT TYPE = CHECKBOX NAME = Check4 onClick =
Check4Clicked()>Check 4</TD></TR>
    <TR><TD><INPUT TYPE = CHECKBOX NAME = Check5 onClick =
Check5Clicked()>Check 5</TD></TR>
</TABLE>
<BR>
<BR>
<INPUT TYPE  =  TEXT NAME  =  "TextBox" SIZE  =  30>
</CENTER>
</FORM>

</BODY>
```

Next, we add an event-handling function for each check box, written just like our JavaScript example for use with standard buttons:

```
<HTML>

<HEAD>
<TITLE>Check box example</TITLE>
</HEAD>

<BODY>
    .
    .
    .
</BODY>

<SCRIPT LANGUAGE = JavaScript>

    function Check1Clicked() {                                    ⇐
        document.form1.TextBox.value = "Check box 1 clicked!"
    }

    function Check2Clicked() {                                    ⇐
        document.form1.TextBox.value = "Check box 2 clicked!"
    }

    function Check3Clicked() {                                    ⇐
        document.form1.TextBox.value = "Check box 3 clicked!"
    }

    function Check4Clicked() {                                    ⇐
        document.form1.TextBox.value = "Check box 4 clicked!"
    }

    function Check5Clicked() {                                    ⇐
        document.form1.TextBox.value = "Check box 5 clicked!"
    }

</SCRIPT>

</HTML>
<HTML>
```

**Figure 2.7 Using check boxes with JavaScript.**

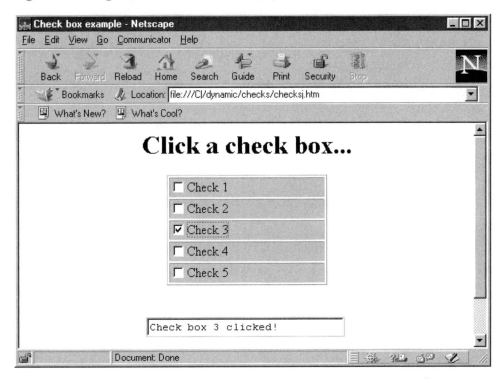

And that's all we need. Now we can use check boxes in JavaScript, as shown in Figure 2.7.

The code for this page, checksj.htm, appears in Listing 2.8.

**Listing 2.8 checksj.htm**

```
<HTML>

<HEAD>
<TITLE>Check box example</TITLE>
</HEAD>

<BODY>

<FORM NAME = form1>
<CENTER>
```

*Continued*

**Listing 2.8 Continued**

```
<H1>Click a check box...</H1>

<TABLE BORDER BGCOLOR = CYAN WIDTH = 200>
    <TR><TD><INPUT TYPE = CHECKBOX NAME = Check1 onClick =
Check1Clicked()>Check 1</TD></TR>
    <TR><TD><INPUT TYPE = CHECKBOX NAME = Check2 onClick =
Check2Clicked()>Check 2</TD></TR>
    <TR><TD><INPUT TYPE = CHECKBOX NAME = Check3 onClick =
Check3Clicked()>Check 3</TD></TR>
    <TR><TD><INPUT TYPE = CHECKBOX NAME = Check4 onClick =
Check4Clicked()>Check 4</TD></TR>
    <TR><TD><INPUT TYPE = CHECKBOX NAME = Check5 onClick =
Check5Clicked()>Check 5</TD></TR>
</TABLE>
<BR>
<BR>
<INPUT TYPE  =  TEXT NAME  =  "TextBox" SIZE  =  30>
</CENTER>
</FORM>

</BODY>

<SCRIPT LANGUAGE = JavaScript>

    function Check1Clicked() {
        document.form1.TextBox.value = "Check box 1 clicked!"
    }

    function Check2Clicked() {
        document.form1.TextBox.value = "Check box 2 clicked!"
    }

    function Check3Clicked() {
        document.form1.TextBox.value = "Check box 3 clicked!"
    }

    function Check4Clicked() {
        document.form1.TextBox.value = "Check box 4 clicked!"
    }
```

**Listing 2.8 Continued**

```
function Check5Clicked() {
        document.form1.TextBox.value = "Check box 5 clicked!"
}
```

```
</SCRIPT>
```

```
</HTML>
```

Check boxes let the user select several options at once. Another type of control—the radio button—is very similar.

## Using Radio Buttons with VBScript

*Radio buttons* are much like check boxes, except that radio buttons operate as a group: When the user selects a radio button, a black dot appears in the middle of the button; when the user clicks another radio button in the same group to select it, the first one is automatically de-selected, and the black dot in that button disappears. In this way, the user can select only one option at a time.

In our radio button example, we'll present the user with some radio buttons and a prompt, "Click a radio button..."

```
 ----------------------------
|                            |
|--------------------------- |
|      Click a radio button...  |
|                            |
|     ( ) Radio 1            |
|     ( ) Radio 2            |
|     ( ) Radio 3            |
|     ( ) Radio 4            |
|     ( ) Radio 5            |
|                            |
|     -----------------      |
|   |                 |     |
|     -----------------      |
|                            |
 ----------------------------
```

When the user clicks a radio button, a dot appears in the center of the clicked radio button, and the code reports which radio button the user clicked:

```
  ------------------------------
  |                            |
  |----------------------------|
  |    Click a radio button... |
  |                            |
  |    ( ) Radio 1             |
  |    ( ) Radio 2             |
  |    (*) Radio 3             |
  |    ( ) Radio 4             |
  |    ( ) Radio 5             |
  |                            |
  |    ----------------------  |
  |   |Radio button 3 clicked!||
  |    ----------------------  |
  |                            |
  ------------------------------
```

Then if the user clicks another radio button, the first one is automatically de-
selected, and the code reports which new radio button the user clicked:

```
  ------------------------------
  |                            |
  |----------------------------|
  |    Click a radio button... |
  |                            |
  |    ( ) Radio 1             |
  |    (*) Radio 2             |
  |    ( ) Radio 3             |
  |    ( ) Radio 4             |
  |    ( ) Radio 5             |
  |                            |
  |    ----------------------  |
  |   |Radio button 2 clicked!||
  |    ----------------------  |
  |                            |
  ------------------------------
```

Let's create this new example, radios.htm, now. This time, we set the
<INPUT> tag's TYPE attribute to RADIO so the control will be a radio control.
As with check boxes, we connect the onClick event of each button to a subroutine.
For example, we'll connect radio button 1 to the subroutine Radio1Clicked(), radio
button 2 to Radio2Clicked(), and so on.

Radio buttons are a little different from check boxes, however. We want our radio buttons to act in concert, as a group. We connect them together as a group simply by giving them all the same name—in this case, we'll use the name "RadioGroup":

```
<HTML>

<HEAD>
<TITLE>Radio button example</TITLE>
</HEAD>

<BODY>

<CENTER>
<H1>Click a radio button...</H1>

<TABLE BORDER BGCOLOR = CYAN WIDTH = 200>
    <TR><TD><INPUT TYPE = RADIO NAME = RadioGroup onClick =
Radio1Clicked()>Check 1</TD></TR>                                    ⇐
    <TR><TD><INPUT TYPE = RADIO NAME = RadioGroup onClick =
Radio2Clicked()>Check 2</TD></TR>                                    ⇐
    <TR><TD><INPUT TYPE = RADIO NAME = RadioGroup onClick =
Radio3Clicked()>Check 3</TD></TR>                                    ⇐
    <TR><TD><INPUT TYPE = RADIO NAME = RadioGroup onClick =
Radio4Clicked()>Check 4</TD></TR>                                    ⇐
    <TR><TD><INPUT TYPE = RADIO NAME = RadioGroup onClick =
Radio5Clicked()>Check 5</TD></TR>                                    ⇐
</TABLE>
<BR>
<BR>
<INPUT TYPE  =  TEXT NAME  =  TextBox SIZE  =  30>
</CENTER>

</BODY>
    .
    .
    .
```

Now that all the radio buttons have the same name, they are coordinated into a group, and only one radio button can be selected at a time.

Next, we write the click-handling subroutines Radio1Clicked() to Radio5Clicked() to report which radio button was clicked:

```
<HTML>

<HEAD>
<TITLE>Radio button example</TITLE>
</HEAD>

<BODY>
    .
    .
    .
</BODY>

<SCRIPT LANGUAGE = VBScript>

    Sub Radio1Clicked()                                        ⇐
        TextBox.Value = "Radio button 1 clicked!"              ⇐
    End Sub                                                    ⇐

    Sub Radio2Clicked()                                        ⇐
        TextBox.Value = "Radio button 2 clicked!"              ⇐
    End Sub                                                    ⇐

    Sub Radio3Clicked()                                        ⇐
        TextBox.Value = "Radio button 3 clicked!"              ⇐
    End Sub                                                    ⇐

    Sub Radio4Clicked()                                        ⇐
        TextBox.Value = "Radio button 4 clicked!"              ⇐
    End Sub                                                    ⇐

    Sub Radio5Clicked()                                        ⇐
        TextBox.Value = "Radio button 5 clicked!"              ⇐
    End Sub                                                    ⇐

</SCRIPT>

</HTML>
```

Our radios.htm Web page is ready to go, as shown in Figure 2.8. When the user clicks a radio button, that button displays a black dot, and the code reports to the user which radio button was clicked, as shown in Figure 2.8.

**Figure 2.8 Supporting radio buttons in a VBScript page.**

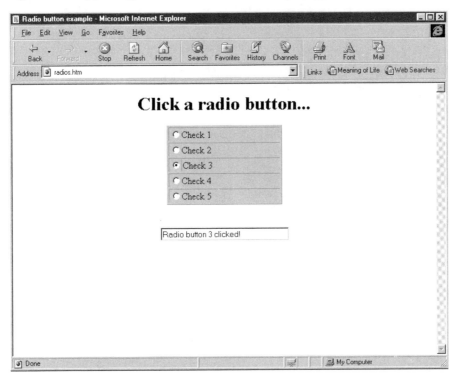

When the user clicks another radio button, the first button is automatically de-selected, and the new button is selected. Our radios.htm Web page is a success. The code for this Web page appears in Listing 2.9.

**Listing 2.9 radios.htm**

```
<HTML>

<HEAD>
<TITLE>Radio button example</TITLE>
</HEAD>

<BODY>
```

*Continued*

**Listing 2.9 Continued**

```
<CENTER>
<H1>Click a radio button...</H1>

<TABLE BORDER BGCOLOR = CYAN WIDTH = 200>
    <TR><TD><INPUT TYPE = RADIO NAME = RadioGroup onClick =
Radio1Clicked()>Check 1</TD></TR>
    <TR><TD><INPUT TYPE = RADIO NAME = RadioGroup onClick =
Radio2Clicked()>Check 2</TD></TR>
    <TR><TD><INPUT TYPE = RADIO NAME = RadioGroup onClick =
Radio3Clicked()>Check 3</TD></TR>
    <TR><TD><INPUT TYPE = RADIO NAME = RadioGroup onClick =
Radio4Clicked()>Check 4</TD></TR>
    <TR><TD><INPUT TYPE = RADIO NAME = RadioGroup onClick =
Radio5Clicked()>Check 5</TD></TR>
</TABLE>
<BR>
<BR>
<INPUT TYPE  =  TEXT NAME  =  TextBox SIZE  =  30>
</CENTER>

</BODY>

<SCRIPT LANGUAGE = VBScript>

    Sub Radio1Clicked()
        TextBox.Value = "Radio button 1 clicked!"
    End Sub

    Sub Radio2Clicked()
        TextBox.Value = "Radio button 2 clicked!"
    End Sub

    Sub Radio3Clicked()
        TextBox.Value = "Radio button 3 clicked!"
    End Sub

    Sub Radio4Clicked()
        TextBox.Value = "Radio button 4 clicked!"
    End Sub

    Sub Radio5Clicked()
        TextBox.Value = "Radio button 5 clicked!"
```

**Listing 2.9 Continued**

```
    End Sub

</SCRIPT>

</HTML>
```

Let's take a look at how to use radio buttons in JavaScript.

## Using Radio Buttons with JavaScript

We can create the same page in JavaScript just as easily:

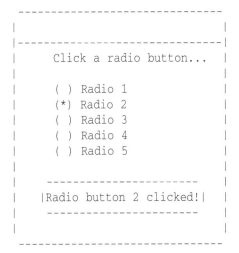

Let's create this new page, radiosj.htm, now. We start with the buttons themselves in the same group, RadioGroup, and a text box in a form named form1:

```
<HTML>

<HEAD>
<TITLE>Radio button example</TITLE>
</HEAD>

<BODY>

<FORM NAME = "form1">

<CENTER>
```

```
<H1>Click a radio button...</H1>

<TABLE BORDER BGCOLOR = CYAN WIDTH = 200>
    <TR><TD><INPUT TYPE = RADIO NAME = RadioGroup onClick =
Radio1Clicked()>Check 1</TD></TR>
    <TR><TD><INPUT TYPE = RADIO NAME = RadioGroup onClick =
Radio2Clicked()>Check 2</TD></TR>
    <TR><TD><INPUT TYPE = RADIO NAME = RadioGroup onClick =
Radio3Clicked()>Check 3</TD></TR>
    <TR><TD><INPUT TYPE = RADIO NAME = RadioGroup onClick =
Radio4Clicked()>Check 4</TD></TR>
    <TR><TD><INPUT TYPE = RADIO NAME = RadioGroup onClick =
Radio5Clicked()>Check 5</TD></TR>
</TABLE>
<BR>
<BR>
<INPUT TYPE  =  TEXT NAME  =  TextBox SIZE  =  30>
</CENTER>

</FORM>

</BODY>
```

Then, just as we've done for check boxes, we connect our radio buttons to JavaScript code:

```
<HTML>

<HEAD>
<TITLE>Radio button example</TITLE>
</HEAD>

<BODY>
    .
    .
    .
</BODY>

<SCRIPT LANGUAGE = JavaScript>

    function Radio1Clicked()                                    ⇐
    {
```

```
        document.form1.TextBox.value = "Radio button 1 clicked!"
   }

   function Radio2Clicked()                                          ⇐
   {
        document.form1.TextBox.value = "Radio button 2 clicked!"
   }

   function Radio3Clicked()                                          ⇐
   {
        document.form1.TextBox.value = "Radio button 3 clicked!"
   }

   function Radio4Clicked()                                          ⇐
   {
        document.form1.TextBox.value = "Radio button 4 clicked!"
   }

   function Radio5Clicked()                                          ⇐
   {
        document.form1.TextBox.value = "Radio button 5 clicked!"
   }

</SCRIPT>

</HTML>
```

And that's all it takes. Open the page now, as shown in Figure 2.9, and click a radio button. When you do, the page will report which button you've clicked. Our JavaScript radio button page is a success.

The code for this example, radiosj.htm, appears in Listing 2.10.

---

**Listing 2.10 radiosj.htm**

```
<HTML>

<HEAD>
<TITLE>Radio button example</TITLE>
</HEAD>

<BODY>
```

*Continued*

---

**Figure 2.9 Using radio buttons in JavaScript.**

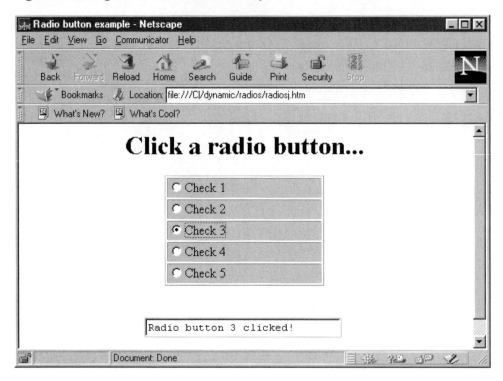

**Listing 2.10 Continued**

```
<FORM NAME = "form1">

<CENTER>
<H1>Click a radio button...</H1>

<TABLE BORDER BGCOLOR = CYAN WIDTH = 200>
    <TR><TD><INPUT TYPE = RADIO NAME = RadioGroup onClick =
Radio1Clicked()>Check 1</TD></TR>
    <TR><TD><INPUT TYPE = RADIO NAME = RadioGroup onClick =
Radio2Clicked()>Check 2</TD></TR>
    <TR><TD><INPUT TYPE = RADIO NAME = RadioGroup onClick =
Radio3Clicked()>Check 3</TD></TR>
    <TR><TD><INPUT TYPE = RADIO NAME = RadioGroup onClick =
Radio4Clicked()>Check 4</TD></TR>
```

**Listing 2.10 Continued**

```
    <TR><TD><INPUT TYPE = RADIO NAME = RadioGroup onClick =
Radio5Clicked()>Check 5</TD></TR>
</TABLE>
<BR>
<BR>
<INPUT TYPE  =  TEXT NAME  =  TextBox SIZE  =  30>
</CENTER>

</FORM>

</BODY>

<SCRIPT LANGUAGE = JavaScript>

    function Radio1Clicked()
    {
        document.form1.TextBox.value = "Radio button 1 clicked!"
    }

    function Radio2Clicked()
    {
        document.form1.TextBox.value = "Radio button 2 clicked!"
    }

    function Radio3Clicked()
    {
        document.form1.TextBox.value = "Radio button 3 clicked!"
    }

    function Radio4Clicked()
    {
        document.form1.TextBox.value = "Radio button 4 clicked!"
    }

    function Radio5Clicked()
    {
        document.form1.TextBox.value = "Radio button 5 clicked!"
    }

</SCRIPT>

</HTML>
```

We've seen how check boxes and radio buttons work, and how they are very similar. There's another control, however, that is very popular, but doesn't work like a button at all—list boxes, called select controls in HTML.

## Using List Boxes with VBScript

In our next example, we'll put together a Web page with a drop-down list box, which is called a *select control* in HTML. A select control presents the user with a list of options that opens when the user clicks the button with a downward arrow next to the select control. For example, we'll display a Web page with a prompt, "Click an item...,": a text box, and a select control within the text box:

When the user clicks the downward arrow next to the select control, the select control opens, displaying the possible options that the user can select:

```
|                         |
|        -----------      |
|       | Option 1 |V|    |
|        -----------      |
|       | Option 1 |      |
|       | Option 1 |      |
|       | Option 1 |      |
|       | Option 1 |      |
|       | Option 1 |      |
|        ----------       |
|                         |
 --------------------------
```

When the user selects an item by clicking it, the text can display which item was selected:

```
 ------------------------------
|                              |
|------------------------------|
|         Click an item...     |
|                              |
|     ----------------------   |
|    |  You chose Option 3  |  |
|     ----------------------   |
|                              |
|        -----------           |
|       | Option 3 |V|         |
|        -----------           |
|                              |
|                              |
|                              |
|                              |
|                              |
|                              |
 ------------------------------
```

Let's put together this new Web page now in VBScript, calling it select.htm. We start that file with an appropriate title, "Select Example":

<HTML>

<HEAD>
<TITLE>Select Example</TITLE>

```
</HEAD>
    .
    .
    .
```

Next, we add a prompt to the user to click an item in the select control, and add a text box so that the code can display the item the user clicked:

```
<HTML>

<HEAD>
<TITLE>Select Example</TITLE>
</HEAD>

<BODY>

<CENTER>
<H1>Click an item...</H1>                                    ⇐
<BR>                                                         ⇐
<BR>                                                         ⇐
<INPUT NAME = TextBox TYPE = Text SIZE = 20>                 ⇐
    .
    .
    .
```

Now we put in the select control itself, using the <SELECT> tag:

**Internet Explorer**

```
<SELECT
ACCESSKEY=string
ALIGN=ABSBOTTOM | ABSMIDDLE |
BASELINE | BOTTOM | LEFT | MIDDLE
| RIGHT | TEXTTOP | TOP
DATAFLD=string
DATASRC=string
DISABLED
ID=string
LANGUAGE=JAVASCRIPT | VBSCRIPT
MULTIPLE
NAME=string
READONLY=string
SIZE=variant
```

**Netscape Navigator**

```
<SELECT
NAME="selectName"
MULTIPLE
ONBLUR="blurJScode"
ONCHANGE="changeJScode"
ONCLICK="JScode"
ONFOCUS="focusJScode"
SIZE="ListLength"
>
```

```
STYLE=string
TABINDEX=integer
TITLE=string
TYPE=BUTTON | CHECKBOX | HIDDEN |
IMAGE | PASSWORD | RADIO | RESET |
SELECT-MULTIPLE | SELECT-ONE |
SELECT-ONE | SUBMIT | TEXT |
TEXTAREA
event = script
>
```

In our case, we'll name our select control Select1 and connect its onClick event to a subroutine named SelectClicked() this way:

```
<HTML>

<HEAD>
<TITLE>Select Example</TITLE>
</HEAD>

<BODY>

<CENTER>
<H1>Click an item...</H1>
<BR>
<BR>
<INPUT NAME = TextBox TYPE = Text SIZE = 20>
<BR>
<BR>
<SELECT NAME = Select1 onClick = SelectClicked()>
    .
    .
    .
```

Now that we've set up our select control, we can add the five items we want to display in that control. We do that with the <OPTION> tag.

## Adding Items to a Select Control

To add the five items we want to the select control, we use the <OPTION> tag inside the <SELECT> tag. For example, to add the items "Option 1" to "Option 5" to the select control, we use five <OPTION> tags:

```
<HTML>

<HEAD>
<TITLE>Select Example</TITLE>
</HEAD>

<BODY>

<CENTER>
<H1>Click an item...</H1>
<BR>
<BR>
<INPUT NAME = TextBox TYPE = Text SIZE = 20>
<BR>
<BR>
<SELECT NAME = Select1 onClick = SelectClicked()>
<OPTION>Option 1                                              ⇐
<OPTION>Option 2                                              ⇐
<OPTION>Option 3                                              ⇐
<OPTION>Option 4                                              ⇐
<OPTION>Option 5                                              ⇐
</SELECT>

</CENTER>

</BODY>
        .
        .
        .
```

This code adds the items we want to the select control. Now we will set up the SelectClicked() subroutine, which is called when the user clicks an item in the select control, because we need to report which item the user has selected:

```
<HTML>

<HEAD>
<TITLE>Select Example</TITLE>
</HEAD>

<BODY>
        .
```

```
      .
      .
      .
</BODY>

<SCRIPT LANGUAGE = VBSCRIPT>

Sub SelectClicked()
      .
      .
      .
End Sub

</SCRIPT>

</HTML>
```

When the Web browser calls the SelectClicked() subroutine, the code should display the item the user has clicked. We can do that with the select control's selectedIndex property. This property holds the index value of the selected item in the select control, starting with a value of 0. We've started our list of items with "Option 1," not "Option 0," however, so we simply add 1 to the value in the select control's selectedIndex property and display that value, prefixing it with the text "You chose option":

```
<HTML>

<HEAD>
<TITLE>Select Example</TITLE>
</HEAD>

<BODY>
      .
      .
      .
</BODY>

<SCRIPT LANGUAGE = VBSCRIPT>

Sub SelectClicked()
      TextBox.Value = "You chose option " & (Select1.selectedIndex + 1)
End Sub
```

```
</SCRIPT>
```

```
</HTML>
```

Note that we added the number of the item selected to the "You chose option" text with VBScript's & operator; this is how we can add text strings together—a process called *concatenation*.

Now we're ready to take a look at our Web page, as shown in Figure 2.10. As you can see in that figure, our select control appears under the text box. When the user clicks the downward arrow, the select control displays a drop-down list of options from which the user can choose. When the user selects an option, our Web page displays the option selected, as also shown in Figure 2.10.

Our VBScript select control example is a success. The HTML for this page, select.htm, appears in Listing 2.11.

**Figure 2.10 Supporting a select control in a VBScript page.**

**Listing 2.11 select.htm**

```
<HTML>

<HEAD>
<TITLE>Select Example</TITLE>
</HEAD>

<BODY>

<CENTER>
<H1>Click an item...</H1>
<BR>
<BR>
<INPUT NAME = TextBox TYPE = Text SIZE = 20>
<BR>
<BR>
<SELECT NAME = Select1 onClick = SelectClicked()>
<OPTION>Option 1
<OPTION>Option 2
<OPTION>Option 3
<OPTION>Option 4
<OPTION>Option 5
</SELECT>

</CENTER>

</BODY>

<SCRIPT LANGUAGE = VBSCRIPT>

Sub SelectClicked()
     TextBox.Value = "You chose option " & (Select1.selectedIndex +
1)
End Sub

</SCRIPT>

</HTML>
```

Let's take a look at using list boxes in JavaScript next.

# Using List Boxes with JavaScript

We'll create a JavaScript page that uses select controls, selectj.htm, now. Netscape's JavaScript for the select control does not support the onClick event, so we'll use onChange, which has the same effect when the user makes a selection in a select control:

```
<HTML>

<HEAD>
<TITLE>Select Example</TITLE>
</HEAD>

<BODY>

<FORM NAME = form1>
<CENTER>
<H1>Click an item...</H1>
<BR>
<BR>
<INPUT NAME = TextBox TYPE = Text SIZE = 20>
<BR>
<BR>
<SELECT NAME = Select1 onChange = SelectClicked()>          ⇐
<OPTION>Option 1
<OPTION>Option 2
<OPTION>Option 3
<OPTION>Option 4
<OPTION>Option 5
</SELECT>

</CENTER>
</FORM>

</BODY>
        .
        .
        .
```

In the onChange event handler, we simply use the selectedIndex property, as we did in our earlier VBScript example:

```
<HTML>

<HEAD>
<TITLE>Select Example</TITLE>
</HEAD>

<BODY>
    .
    .
    .
</BODY>

<SCRIPT LANGUAGE = JavaScript>

function SelectClicked()
{
      document.form1.TextBox.value = "You chose option " +
(document.form1.Select1.selectedIndex + 1)                        ⇐
}

</SCRIPT>

</HTML>
```

Now open the page, as shown in Figure 2.11. When you select an item in the select control, the page reports which item you've selected. Our JavaScript select example is a success.

The code for this example, selectj.htm, appears in Listing 2.12.

---

**Listing 2.12 selectj.htm**

```
<HTML>

<HEAD>
<TITLE>Select Example</TITLE>
</HEAD>

<BODY>

<FORM NAME = form1>
<CENTER>
<H1>Click an item...</H1>
```

*Continued*

---

**Figure 2.11 Supporting a select control in JavaScript.**

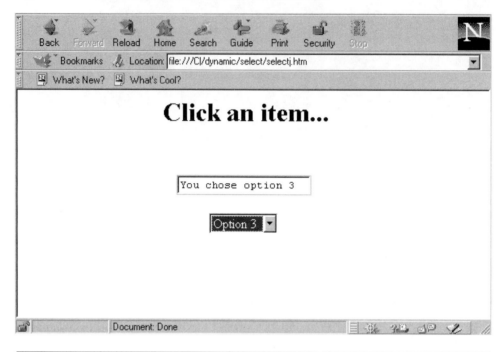

**Listing 2.12 Continued**

```
<BR>
<BR>
<INPUT NAME = TextBox TYPE = Text SIZE = 20>
<BR>
<BR>
<SELECT NAME = Select1 onChange = SelectClicked()>
<OPTION>Option 1
<OPTION>Option 2
<OPTION>Option 3
<OPTION>Option 4
<OPTION>Option 5
</SELECT>

</CENTER>
</FORM>
```

**Listing 2.12 Continued**

```
</BODY>

<SCRIPT LANGUAGE = JavaScript>

function SelectClicked()
{
      document.form1.TextBox.value = "You chose option " +
(document.form1.Select1.selectedIndex + 1)
}

</SCRIPT>

</HTML>
```

# What's Ahead

In this chapter, we learned the basics of scripting, including how to set aside an area for scripts in a Web page using the <SCRIPT> tag, how to work with HTML controls, and how to handle HTML events and properties. We've seen how to use buttons, check boxes, radio buttons, and select controls in both JavaScript and VBScript—not bad for one chapter!

So far, however, we've only been introduced to scripting and used it with the standard HTML controls. In the next chapter, we'll dig into Dynamic HTML itself, seeing how much more in a Web page is now open for us to use.

# CHAPTER THREE

# CHANGING YOUR WEB PAGE

## *on the Fly*

In this chapter, we'll go even further into scripting our Web pages as we see how to modify the actual HTML of a Web page in response to the user's actions. In other words, our HTML will become truly dynamic. We'll start by seeing how to create our entire Web page on the fly. Our first example is a Web page for a hypothetical Dynamic HTML airport, and we'll list flights out of our airport according to the time of day. Next, we'll continue with another example that lets the user specify if we should load a large graphic image or a small one (the smaller one saves downloading time)—*before* those images are loaded. After that, we'll see how to rewrite an entire Web page at the click of a button, how to select ranges of HTML to rewrite, and even how to target an HTML document in another frame so that we can rewrite that document as we like.

We'll finish by tackling a sticky problem: how to make a Web page rewrite itself to match the browser you've loaded it into, whether Internet Explorer or Netscape Navigator. You can modify that page yourself and use it to write different scripts depending on which browser your page is in. We'll start seeing the need for this ability in the next chapter when we deal with the new Dynamic HTML events like onMouseDown and onKeyDown, because the browsers handle these new events in very different ways.

There's a lot of material in this chapter, so let's start now with our first example: the Dynamic HTML airport.

# Taking Off from the Dynamic HTML Airport with VBScript

Let's say that we have our own airport, Dynamic HTML Airport, and that we want to post the flight departure schedule on the Web. Flights depart at different times of day, of course, so we can tailor our Web page to match the time of day: morning, afternoon, or evening. For example, in the morning, we might have our Web page display the morning flight times and destinations:

```
---------------------------
|       Morning Flights   |
|------------------------ |
|Pittsburgh     | 6:30 AM |
|San Francisco  | 7:00 AM |
|Boston         | 7:30 AM |
|Santa Cruz     | 8:00 AM |
|Ithaca         | 8:30 AM |
|Paris          | 9:00 AM |
|London         | 9:30 AM |
---------------------------
```

In the afternoon, we can display the afternoon flight times and destinations in a table like this:

```
---------------------------
|    Afternoon Flights    |
|------------------------ |
|Pittsburgh     | 12:00 PM|
|San Francisco  | 12:30 PM|
|Boston         | 1:30 PM |
|Santa Cruz     | 3:30 PM |
|Ithaca         | 4:00 PM |
|Paris          | 4:30 PM |
|London         | 5:00 PM |
---------------------------
```

Let's see this in action now with VBScript by creating an example page named depart.htm. We start depart.htm by identifying VBScript as our scripting language in the \<BODY> tag:

```
<HTML>

<BODY>
```

```
<SCRIPT LANGUAGE = VBScript>
   .
   .
   .
```

We'll simply place code after the <SCRIPT> tag, outside any subroutine, which means that this code will be executed immediately by the Web browser. To write our Web page's HTML, we will use the document object's write() method. This is the method you use to write directly to the Web page itself. We'll use document.write() to write HTML that the Web browser will read. Because we can use this method to write HTML directly, document.write() is one of the most powerful methods available to us.

## Writing HTML When a Page Is Loaded

To start our depart.htm page, we might display a welcoming message, "Welcome to the Dynamic HTML airport!" and display the current time of day using the VBScript Time function:

```
<HTML>

<BODY>
<SCRIPT LANGUAGE = VBScript>
document.write "<CENTER>"
document.write "<H1>"
document.write "Welcome to the Dynamic HTML airport!"
document.write "</H1>"
document.write "<H2>"
document.write Time                                              ⇐
document.write "</H2>"
document.write "</CENTER>"
   .
   .
   .
```

This code actually writes the following HTML to our Web page:

```
<CENTER>
<H1>
Welcome to the Dynamic HTML airport!
</H1>
<H2>
[Time of day]
```

```
</H2>
</CENTER>
```

Our HTML appears in the page—now we're writing Web pages on the fly!

Note that we enclose all the actual HTML we want to write to our page in quotes. If you want to write a quote to the `<A HREF = "http://www.microsoft.com">`, use double quotes like this in VBScript: `document.write("<A HREF = ""http://www.microsoft.com"">")`. If you want to write a string or numeric value, such as the value returned by the VBScript Time function, to the Web page, we don't put it in quotes, like this:

```
document.write "<H2>"
document.write Time                          ⇐
document.write "</H2>"
```

Now we can create our table showing the departing flights, based on the time of day.

## Determining the Time of Day

We can check the time of day with the VBScript Now object, which returns the current time. When we pass the time of day to the VBScript Hour function like this:

```
Hour(Now)
```

that function returns the current hour of the day.

First, our code will check if it's too early or too late, in which case we can notify the user that the airport is closed using the VBScript If statement (which must have a corresponding End If at the end of the statement):

```
<HTML>

<BODY>
<SCRIPT LANGUAGE = VBScript>
document.write "<CENTER>"
document.write "<H1>"
document.write "Welcome to the Dynamic HTML airport!"
document.write "</H1>"
document.write "<H2>"
document.write Time
document.write "</H2>"
document.write "</CENTER>"
```

```
If Hour(Now) < 6 OR Hour(Now) > 22 Then                              ⇐
        document.write "<CENTER>"                                    ⇐
        document.write "<H1>"                                        ⇐
        document.write "Airport is closed."                          ⇐
        document.write "</H1>"                                       ⇐
        document.write "</CENTER>"                                   ⇐
End If                                                               ⇐
    .
    .
    .
```

On the other hand, if the current time of day is morning (between 6:00 A.M. and noon in this example), we'll display the table of morning flights:

```
        -----------------------------
        |         Morning Flights    |
        |--------------------------- |
        |Pittsburgh        | 6:30 AM |
        |San Francisco     | 7:00 AM |
        |Boston            | 7:30 AM |
        |Santa Cruz        | 8:00 AM |
        |Ithaca            | 8:30 AM |
        |Paris             | 9:00 AM |
        |London            | 9:30 AM |

        -----------------------------
```

Here's the HTML we'll use for our table; for an added touch of color, we can give it a yellow background by inserting the BGCOLOR attribute to the <TABLE> tag:

```
<TABLE BORDER BGCOLOR = "#ffff00">
        <TR><TH COLSPAN = 2>Morning Flights</TH></TR>
        <TR><TD>Pittsburgh</TD><TD>6:30 AM</TD></TR>
        <TR><TD>San Francisco</TD><TD>7:00 AM</TD></TR>
        <TR><TD>Boston</TD><TD>7:30 AM</TD></TR>
        <TR><TD>Santa Cruz</TD><TD>8:00 AM</TD></TR>
        <TR><TD>Ithaca</TD><TD>8:30 AM</TD></TR>
        <TR><TD>Paris</TD><TD>9:00 AM</TD></TR>
        <TR><TD>London</TD><TD>9:30 AM</TD></TR>
        </TABLE>
```

Here's how we write the actual HTML code for the table into our Web page using the document.write() method, after making sure the time of day is between 6:00 A.M. and noon:

```
<HTML>

<BODY>
<SCRIPT LANGUAGE = VBScript>

        .

        .


If Hour(Now) < 6 OR Hour(Now) > 22 Then
        document.write "<CENTER>"
        document.write "<H1>"
        document.write "Airport is closed."
        document.write "</H1>"
        document.write "</CENTER>"
End If

If Hour(Now) >= 6 AND Hour(Now) < 12 Then                              ⇐
    document.write "<CENTER>"                                          ⇐
    document.write "<TABLE BORDER BGCOLOR = ""#ffff00"">"              ⇐
    document.write "<TR><TH COLSPAN = 2>Morning Flights</TH></TR>"     ⇐
    document.write "<TR><TD>Pittsburgh</TD><TD>6:30 AM</TD></TR>"      ⇐
    document.write "<TR><TD>San Francisco</TD><TD>7:00 AM</TD></TR>"   ⇐
    document.write "<TR><TD>Boston</TD><TD>7:30 AM</TD></TR>"          ⇐
    document.write "<TR><TD>Santa Cruz</TD><TD>8:00 AM</TD></TR>"      ⇐
    document.write "<TR><TD>Ithaca</TD><TD>8:30 AM</TD></TR>"          ⇐
    document.write "<TR><TD>Paris</TD><TD>9:00 AM</TD></TR>"           ⇐
    document.write "<TR><TD>London</TD><TD>9:30 AM</TD></TR>"          ⇐
    document.write "</TABLE>"                                          ⇐
    document.write "</CENTER>"                                         ⇐
End If                                                                 ⇐

        .

        .

        .
```

That takes care of the morning flights. Next, we add the script that writes the HTML for the afternoon (from noon to 5:00 P.M.) and evening (from 5:00 P.M. to 10:00 P.M.) flights. Use the If statement again:

```
<HTML>

<BODY>
<SCRIPT LANGUAGE = VBScript>

        .
```

```
                .
                .
                .
If Hour(Now) >= 12 AND Hour(Now) < 17 Then
        document.write "<CENTER>"
        document.write "<TABLE BORDER BGCOLOR = ""#ffff00"">"
        document.write "<TR><TH COLSPAN = 2>Afternoon
Flights</TH></TR>"
        document.write "<TR><TD>Pittsburgh</TD><TD>12:00 PM</TD></TR>"
        document.write "<TR><TD>San Francisco</TD><TD>12:30
PM</TD></TR>"
        document.write "<TR><TD>Boston</TD><TD>1:30 PM</TD></TR>"
        document.write "<TR><TD>Santa Cruz</TD><TD>3:30 PM</TD></TR>"
        document.write "<TR><TD>Ithaca</TD><TD>4:00 AM</TD></TR>"
        document.write "<TR><TD>Paris</TD><TD>4:30 PM</TD></TR>"
        document.write "<TR><TD>London</TD><TD>5:00 PM</TD></TR>"
        document.write "</TABLE>"
        document.write "</CENTER>"
End If

If Hour(Now) >= 17 AND Hour(Now) < 22 Then
        document.write "<CENTER>"
        document.write "<TABLE BORDER BGCOLOR = ""#ffff00"">"
        document.write "<TR><TH COLSPAN = 2>Evening Flights</TH></TR>"
        document.write "<TR><TD>Pittsburgh</TD><TD>6:30 PM</TD></TR>"
        document.write "<TR><TD>San Francisco</TD><TD>7:00
PM</TD></TR>"
        document.write "<TR><TD>Boston</TD><TD>7:30 PM</TD></TR>"
        document.write "<TR><TD>Santa Cruz</TD><TD>8:00 PM</TD></TR>"
        document.write "<TR><TD>Ithaca</TD><TD>8:30 PM</TD></TR>"
        document.write "<TR><TD>Paris</TD><TD>9:00 PM</TD></TR>"
        document.write "<TR><TD>London</TD><TD>9:30 PM</TD></TR>"
        document.write "</TABLE>"
        document.write "</CENTER>"
End If
</SCRIPT>
</HTML>
```

That completes the Web page. Open it now in Internet Explorer, as shown in Figure 3.1. As you can see, the page displays the time of day, literally writing itself in response to the current hour.

Our first on-the-fly VBScript Web page is a success!

The code for this Web page, depart.htm, appears in Listing 3.1.

## Listing 3.1 depart.htm

```
<HTML>

<BODY>
<SCRIPT LANGUAGE = VBScript>
document.write "<CENTER>"
document.write "<H1>"
document.write "Welcome to the Dynamic HTML airport!"
document.write "</H1>"
```

**Figure 3.1 The Dynamic HTML airport Web page displays the time of day.**

**Listing 3.1 Continued**

```
document.write "<H2>"
document.write Time
document.write "</H2>"
document.write "</CENTER>"

If Hour(Now) < 6 OR Hour(Now) > 22 Then
        document.write "<CENTER>"
        document.write "<H1>"
        document.write "Airport is closed."
        document.write "</H1>"
        document.write "</CENTER>"
End If

If Hour(Now) >= 6 AND Hour(Now) < 12 Then
        document.write "<CENTER>"
        document.write "<TABLE BORDER BGCOLOR = ""#ffff00"">"
        document.write "<TR><TH COLSPAN = 2>Morning Flights</TH></TR>"
        document.write "<TR><TD>Pittsburgh</TD><TD>6:30 AM</TD></TR>"
        document.write "<TR><TD>San Francisco</TD><TD>7:00
AM</TD></TR>"
        document.write "<TR><TD>Boston</TD><TD>7:30 AM</TD></TR>"
        document.write "<TR><TD>Santa Cruz</TD><TD>8:00 AM</TD></TR>"
        document.write "<TR><TD>Ithaca</TD><TD>8:30 AM</TD></TR>"
        document.write "<TR><TD>Paris</TD><TD>9:00 AM</TD></TR>"
        document.write "<TR><TD>London</TD><TD>9:30 AM</TD></TR>"
        document.write "</TABLE>"
        document.write "</CENTER>"
End If

If Hour(Now) >= 12 AND Hour(Now) < 17 Then
        document.write "<CENTER>"
        document.write "<TABLE BORDER BGCOLOR = ""#ffff00"">"
        document.write "<TR><TH COLSPAN = 2>Afternoon
Flights</TH></TR>"
        document.write "<TR><TD>Pittsburgh</TD><TD>12:00 PM</TD></TR>"
        document.write "<TR><TD>San Francisco</TD><TD>12:30
PM</TD></TR>"
        document.write "<TR><TD>Boston</TD><TD>1:30 PM</TD></TR>"
        document.write "<TR><TD>Santa Cruz</TD><TD>3:30 PM</TD></TR>"
        document.write "<TR><TD>Ithaca</TD><TD>4:00 AM</TD></TR>"
```

*Continued*

**Listing 3.1 Continued**

```
        document.write "<TR><TD>Paris</TD><TD>4:30 PM</TD></TR>"
        document.write "<TR><TD>London</TD><TD>5:00 PM</TD></TR>"
        document.write "</TABLE>"
        document.write "</CENTER>"
End If

If Hour(Now) >= 17 AND Hour(Now) < 22 Then
        document.write "<CENTER>"
        document.write "<TABLE BORDER BGCOLOR = ""#ffff00"">"
        document.write "<TR><TH COLSPAN = 2>Evening Flights</TH></TR>"
        document.write "<TR><TD>Pittsburgh</TD><TD>6:30 PM</TD></TR>"
        document.write "<TR><TD>San Francisco</TD><TD>7:00
PM</TD></TR>"
        document.write "<TR><TD>Boston</TD><TD>7:30 PM</TD></TR>"
        document.write "<TR><TD>Santa Cruz</TD><TD>8:00 PM</TD></TR>"
        document.write "<TR><TD>Ithaca</TD><TD>8:30 PM</TD></TR>"
        document.write "<TR><TD>Paris</TD><TD>9:00 PM</TD></TR>"
        document.write "<TR><TD>London</TD><TD>9:30 PM</TD></TR>"
        document.write "</TABLE>"
        document.write "</CENTER>"
End If
</SCRIPT>

</HTML>
```

Now let's take a look at the JavaScript version.

# Taking Off from the Dynamic HTML Airport with JavaScript

We start our JavaScript version of the Dynamic HTML airport Web page, departj.htm, by getting the time of day. In particular, we create a new JavaScript *Date* object and store it in our program. Unlike other programming languages, VBScript and JavaScript don't have variable types like char and int; instead, you use *var* in JavaScript and *Dim* in VBScript. In this case, we create a Date object and store it as dateNow:

```
<HTML>

<BODY>
<SCRIPT LANGUAGE = JavaScript>
var dateNow = new Date()                                    ⇐
```

.
.
.

This new object holds the current date and time. To get the current hour, we use its getHours() method this way, storing the current hour of the day in a new variable named timeNow:

```
<HTML>

<BODY>
<SCRIPT LANGUAGE = JavaScript>
var dateNow = new Date()
var timeNow = dateNow.getHours()                                    ⇐
   .
   .
   .


<HTML>
```

Besides getting the current hour, we can use the toLocaleString() method to display the current time of day when we display our greeting to the user. Note that now we need to enclose the argument we pass to the document.write() method in parentheses in JavaScript:

```
<BODY>
<SCRIPT LANGUAGE = JavaScript>
var dateNow = new Date()
var timeNow = dateNow.getHours()
document.write( "<CENTER>")
document.write( "<H1>")
document.write( "Welcome to the Dynamic HTML airport!")
document.write( "</H1>")
document.write( "<H2>")
document.write( dateNow.toLocaleString() )                          ⇐
document.write( "</H2>")
document.write( "</CENTER>")
   .
   .
   .
```

Next, we check to make sure the airport is open, just as we did in our VBScript example, but note that we have to enclose the conditional part of the if statement in parentheses and use the JavaScript || operator instead of the VBScript OR operator:

```
<HTML>

<BODY>
<SCRIPT LANGUAGE = JavaScript>
var dateNow = new Date()
var timeNow = dateNow.getHours()
document.write( "<CENTER>")
document.write( "<H1>")
document.write( "Welcome to the Dynamic HTML airport!")
document.write( "</H1>")
document.write( "<H2>")
document.write( dateNow.toLocaleString() )
document.write( "</H2>")
document.write( "</CENTER>")

if (timeNow < 6 || timeNow > 22){                    ⇐
        document.write( "<CENTER>")
        document.write( "<H1>")
        document.write( "Airport is closed." )
        document.write( "</H1>")
        document.write( "</CENTER>")
}
        .
        .
        .
```

At this point, we're ready to place the correct time-of-day table on the screen. We check the hour of the day using the JavaScript && operator instead of the VBScript AND operator:

```
<HTML>

<BODY>
<SCRIPT LANGUAGE = JavaScript>
var dateNow = new Date()
var timeNow = dateNow.getHours()
document.write( "<CENTER>")
document.write( "<H1>")
document.write( "Welcome to the Dynamic HTML airport!")
document.write( "</H1>")
```

```
document.write( "<H2>")
document.write( dateNow.toLocaleString() )
document.write( "</H2>")
document.write( "</CENTER>")

if (timeNow < 6 || timeNow > 22){
        document.write( "<CENTER>")
        document.write( "<H1>")
        document.write( "Airport is closed." )
        document.write( "</H1>")
        document.write( "</CENTER>")
}

if (timeNow > 6 && timeNow < 12 ) {                                    ⇐
        document.write( "<CENTER>")
        document.write( "<TABLE BORDER BGCOLOR = '#ffff00'>")
        document.write( "<TR><TH COLSPAN = 2>Morning
Flights</TH></TR>")
        document.write( "<TR><TD>Pittsburgh</TD><TD>6:30
AM</TD></TR>")
        document.write( "<TR><TD>San Francisco</TD><TD>7:00
AM</TD></TR>")
        document.write( "<TR><TD>Boston</TD><TD>7:30 AM</TD></TR>")
        document.write( "<TR><TD>Santa Cruz</TD><TD>8:00
AM</TD></TR>")
        document.write( "<TR><TD>Ithaca</TD><TD>8:30 AM</TD></TR>")
        document.write( "<TR><TD>Paris</TD><TD>9:00 AM</TD></TR>")
        document.write( "<TR><TD>London</TD><TD>9:30 AM</TD></TR>")
        document.write( "</TABLE>")
        document.write( "</CENTER>")
}
    .
    .
    .
```

This is very like our **VBScript** version, but one last thing to note is that when you want to use quotation marks in a line you're writing with write(), you should use single quotes instead of the double quotes we used in VBScript:

```
document.write( "<TABLE BORDER BGCOLOR = '#ffff00'>")
```

That's it. This JavaScript version creates the same display as our earlier VBScript version, shown in Figure 3.1. The listing for this page, departj.htm, appears in Listing 3.2.

## Listing 3.2 departj.htm

```
<HTML>

<BODY>
<SCRIPT LANGUAGE = JavaScript>
var dateNow = new Date()
var timeNow = dateNow.getHours()
document.write( "<CENTER>")
document.write( "<H1>")
document.write( "Welcome to the Dynamic HTML airport!")
document.write( "</H1>")
document.write( "<H2>")
document.write( dateNow.toLocaleString() )
document.write( "</H2>")
document.write( "</CENTER>")

if (timeNow < 6 || timeNow > 22){
        document.write( "<CENTER>")
        document.write( "<H1>")
        document.write( "Airport is closed." )
        document.write( "</H1>")
        document.write( "</CENTER>")
}

if (timeNow > 6 && timeNow < 12 ) {
        document.write( "<CENTER>")
        document.write( "<TABLE BORDER BGCOLOR = '#ffff00'>")
        document.write( "<TR><TH COLSPAN = 2>Morning
Flights</TH></TR>")
        document.write( "<TR><TD>Pittsburgh</TD><TD>6:30
AM</TD></TR>")
        document.write( "<TR><TD>San Francisco</TD><TD>7:00
AM</TD></TR>")
        document.write( "<TR><TD>Boston</TD><TD>7:30 AM</TD></TR>")
        document.write( "<TR><TD>Santa Cruz</TD><TD>8:00
AM</TD></TR>")
        document.write( "<TR><TD>Ithaca</TD><TD>8:30 AM</TD></TR>")
```

**Listing 3.2 Continued**

```
        document.write( "<TR><TD>Paris</TD><TD>9:00 AM</TD></TR>")
        document.write( "<TR><TD>London</TD><TD>9:30 AM</TD></TR>")
        document.write( "</TABLE>")
        document.write( "</CENTER>")
}

if ( timeNow >= 12 && timeNow < 17 ) {
        document.write( "<CENTER>")
        document.write( "<TABLE BORDER BGCOLOR = '#ffff00'>")
        document.write( "<TR><TH COLSPAN = 2>Afternoon
Flights</TH></TR>")
        document.write( "<TR><TD>Pittsburgh</TD><TD>12:00
PM</TD></TR>")
        document.write( "<TR><TD>San Francisco</TD><TD>12:30
PM</TD></TR>")
        document.write( "<TR><TD>Boston</TD><TD>1:30 PM</TD></TR>")
        document.write( "<TR><TD>Santa Cruz</TD><TD>3:30
PM</TD></TR>")
        document.write( "<TR><TD>Ithaca</TD><TD>4:00 PM</TD></TR>")
        document.write( "<TR><TD>Paris</TD><TD>4:30 PM</TD></TR>")
        document.write( "<TR><TD>London</TD><TD>5:00 PM</TD></TR>")
        document.write( "</TABLE>")
        document.write( "</CENTER>")
}

if ( timeNow >= 17 && timeNow < 22 ) {
        document.write( "<CENTER>")
        document.write( "<TABLE BORDER BGCOLOR = '#ffff00'>")
        document.write( "<TR><TH COLSPAN = 2>Evening
Flights</TH></TR>")
        document.write( "<TR><TD>Pittsburgh</TD><TD>6:30
PM</TD></TR>")
        document.write( "<TR><TD>San Francisco</TD><TD>7:00
PM</TD></TR>")
        document.write( "<TR><TD>Boston</TD><TD>7:30 PM</TD></TR>")
        document.write( "<TR><TD>Santa Cruz</TD><TD>8:00
PM</TD></TR>")
        document.write( "<TR><TD>Ithaca</TD><TD>8:30 PM</TD></TR>")
        document.write( "<TR><TD>Paris</TD><TD>9:00 PM</TD></TR>")
        document.write( "<TR><TD>London</TD><TD>9:30 PM</TD></TR>")
        document.write( "</TABLE>")
        document.write( "</CENTER>")
```

*Continued*

**Listing 3.2 Continued**

```
}
</SCRIPT>

</HTML>
```

We've made a good start in seeing how to write Web pages dynamically with the depart.htm example. We'll continue now with another example that asks the user whether or not to load a big graphics file before actually loading it, to save download time if the user wishes to do so.

# Loading Graphics on the Fly with VBScript

In this next example, we'll rewrite a Web page according to user input. We'll let the user decide to load a large graphics file into the Web page or a smaller one to save download time. When the page first loads, we present the user with a dialog box asking if we should load the big graphics file:

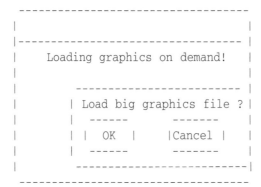

If the user clicks OK, we load and display the large graphics image:

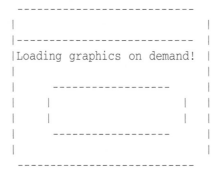

On the other hand, if the user does not want to load the big image, we can load a smaller one:

```
 ---------------------------
|                           |
|-------------------------  |
|Loading graphics on demand! |
|                           |
|                           |
|            ------          |
|           |      |         |
|            ------          |
|                           |
|                           |
 ---------------------------
```

Let's put this to work now in VBScript with a new page named loader.htm. The two images we'll use, image1.gif and image2.gif, appear in Figure 3.2.

We start our VBScript example, loader.htm, with a visible header that says, "Loading graphics on demand!":

```
<HTML>

<HEAD>
```

**Figure 3.2 The two images our loader page will use.**

```
<TITLE>Load big or little graphics example</TITLE>
</HEAD>

<BODY>

<CENTER>

<H1>Loading graphics on demand!</H1>
        .
        .
        .
```

Next, we use the VBScript confirm() function to place a dialog box on the screen asking the question "Load big graphics file?":

```
<HTML>

<HEAD>
<TITLE>Load big or little graphics example</TITLE>
</HEAD>

<BODY>

<CENTER>

<H1>Loading graphics on demand!</H1>

<SCRIPT LANGUAGE = VBScript>
        If (confirm("Load big graphics file?")) Then          ⇐
          .
          .
          .
```

(We'll see more about the confirm() function and other dialog boxes later.) If the user clicks the OK button, the confirm() function returns a value of true, and we want the browser to load the big graphics file, image1.gif:

```
<HTML>

<HEAD>
<TITLE>Load big or little graphics example</TITLE>
</HEAD>

<BODY>
```

```
<CENTER>

<H1>Loading graphics on demand!</H1>

<SCRIPT LANGUAGE = VBScript>
        If (confirm("Load big graphics file?")) Then
                document.write "<BR><BR><IMG WIDTH=236 HEIGHT=118
SRC=""gif/image1.gif""></IMG>"                                           ⇐
    .
    .
    .
```

If the user did not click the OK button, on the other hand, we want the browser to load the smaller image, image2.gif, so we write this HTML:

```
<HTML>

<HEAD>
<TITLE>Load big or little graphics example</TITLE>
</HEAD>

<BODY>

<CENTER>

<H1>Loading graphics on demand!</H1>
<SCRIPT LANGUAGE = VBScript>
        If (confirm("Load big graphics file?")) Then
                document.write "<BR><BR><IMG WIDTH=236 HEIGHT=118
SRC=""gif/image1.gif""></IMG>"
        Else
                document.write "<BR><BR><IMG WIDTH=150 HEIGHT=75
SRC=""gif/image2.gif""></IMG>"                                           ⇐
        End If                                                          ⇐
</SCRIPT>

</CENTER>

</BODY>

</HTML>
```

That's all we need. Now open the Web page in Internet Explorer, displaying the confirm box, as shown in Figure 3.3.

If the user clicks the confirm box's OK button, the script writes the HTML to load the big image, and the user's screen will look as shown in Figure 3.4.

If, on the other hand, the user does not want to load in the big image and clicks the Cancel button, the script writes the HTML to load in the smaller image, and the user's screen will look as shown in Figure 3.5.

Our example is a success. Now we're writing Web pages in response to user input; in fact, they *write themselves* in response to user input.

The code for this page, loader.htm, appears in Listing 3.3.

**Figure 3.3 Our Web page asks if it should load graphics.**

## Listing 3.3 loader.htm

```
<HTML>

<HEAD>
<TITLE>Load big or little graphics example</TITLE>
</HEAD>

<BODY>

<CENTER>

<H1>Loading graphics on demand!</H1>

<SCRIPT LANGUAGE = VBScript>
```

*Continued*

## Figure 3.4 Loading the big graphics image.

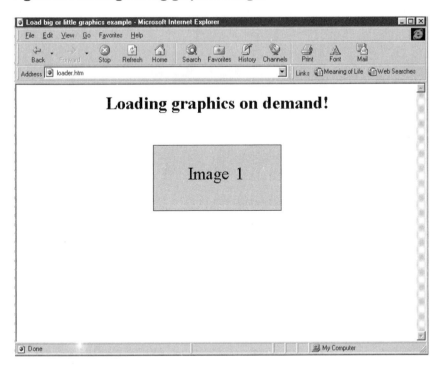

**Figure 3.5 Loading the smaller graphics image.**

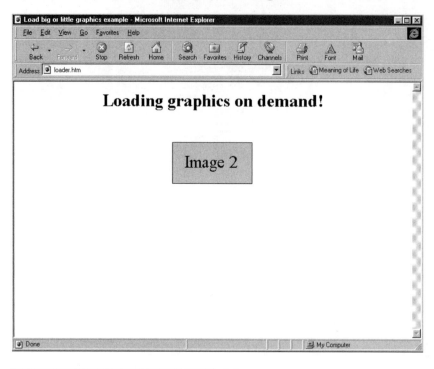

**Listing 3.3 Continued**

```
      If (confirm("Load big graphics file?")) Then
            document.write "<BR><BR><IMG WIDTH=236 HEIGHT=118
SRC=""gif/image1.gif""></IMG>"
      Else
            document.write "<BR><BR><IMG WIDTH=150 HEIGHT=75
SRC=""gif/image2.gif""></IMG>"
      End If
</SCRIPT>

</CENTER>

</BODY>

</HTML>
```

It's as easy to write this example in JavaScript. Let's take a look at that process now.

# Loading Graphics on the Fly with JavaScript

Let's put together the JavaScript version of our loader example, loaderj.htm. Like VBScript, JavaScript has a confirm() function we can use to check if the user wants to load the larger graphic image:

```
<SCRIPT LANGUAGE = JavaScript>
        if(confirm("Load big graphics file?"))
                document.write("<BR><BR><IMG WIDTH=236 HEIGHT=118
SRC='gif/image1.gif'></IMG>")
        else
    .
    .
    .
```

If the user does not want to load the image, the browser can load the smaller image, just as it did in the VBScript version:

```
</SCRIPT>
<SCRIPT LANGUAGE = JavaScript>
        if(confirm("Load big graphics file?"))
                document.write("<BR><BR><IMG WIDTH=236 HEIGHT=118
SRC='gif/image1.gif'></IMG>")
        else                                                        ⇐
                document.write("<BR><BR><IMG WIDTH=150 HEIGHT=75
SRC='gif/image2.gif'></IMG>")                                       ⇐
</SCRIPT>
```

And that's all we need. Now our JavaScript version functions just as the VBScript version did. The code for this example, loaderj.htm, appears in Listing 3.4.

---

**Listing 3.4 loaderj.htm**

```
<HTML>

<HEAD>
<TITLE>Load big or little graphics example</TITLE>
</HEAD>
```

*Continued*

---

**Listing 3.4 Continued**

```
<BODY>

<CENTER>

<H1>Loading graphics on demand!</H1>

<SCRIPT LANGUAGE = JavaScript>
        if(confirm("Load big graphics file?"))
                document.write("<BR><BR><IMG WIDTH=236 HEIGHT=118
SRC='gif/image1.gif'></IMG>")
        else
                document.write("<BR><BR><IMG WIDTH=150 HEIGHT=75
SRC='gif/image2.gif'></IMG>")
</SCRIPT>

</CENTER>

</BODY>

</HTML>
```

So far, we've written HTML to a Web page only when the page is first loaded, but in fact we can write HTML at any time. To see how this works, we'll write a new example, writer.htm, which rewrites itself completely when the user clicks a button.

## Rewriting HTML at Any Time with VBScript

Our new Web page will start by displaying a button with the caption "Rewrite the page's HTML":

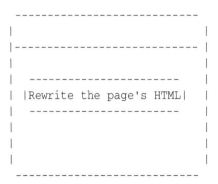

When the user clicks that button, the entire Web page will be rewritten, presenting the user with a visible heading that reads "This page was rewritten!":

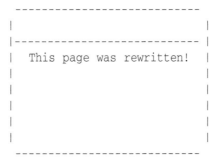

Let's put together writer.htm now in VBScript. We start with the button we'll need to let the user rewrite the page, and we connect that button to a subroutine named rewrite():

```
<HTML>

<TITLE>Rewrite the Web page example</TITLE>

<BODY>

<CENTER>
<INPUT TYPE=BUTTON Value="Rewrite the page's HTML" onClick = rewrite()>  ⇐
</CENTER>

</BODY>
        .
        .
        .
```

Next, we add the rewrite() subroutine:

```
<HTML>

<TITLE>Rewrite the Web page example</TITLE>

<BODY>

<CENTER>
<INPUT TYPE = BUTTON Value = "Rewrite the page's HTML" onClick =
rewrite()>
```

```
</CENTER>

</BODY>

<SCRIPT LANGUAGE = VBScript>                                    ⇐
        Sub rewrite()                                           ⇐
          .
          .
          .
        End Sub                                                 ⇐
</SCRIPT>                                                        ⇐
   .
   .
   .
```

When the user clicks the button, we can rewrite the page's HTML to this code:

```
<HTML>

<HEAD>
<TITLE>This page was rewritten!</TITLE>
</HEAD>

<CENTER>
<H1>This page was rewritten!</H1>
This page was rewritten using Dynamic HTML.
<BR>
We used the document.write() method to
rewrite this page's HTML on the fly.
<CENTER>

</HTML>
```

We create this code using the document.write() method, which looks like this:

```
<HTML>

<TITLE>Rewrite the Web page example</TITLE>

<BODY>

<CENTER>
```

```
<INPUT TYPE = BUTTON Value = "Rewrite the page's HTML" onClick =
rewrite()>
</CENTER>

</BODY>

<SCRIPT LANGUAGE = VBScript>
    Sub rewrite()
        document.write("<HTML>")                                      ⇐
        document.write("<HEAD>")                                      ⇐
        document.write("<TITLE>This page was rewritten!</TITLE>")     ⇐
        document.write("</HEAD>")                                     ⇐
        document.write("<CENTER>")                                    ⇐
        document.write("<H1>This page was rewritten!</H1>")           ⇐
        document.write("This page was rewritten using Dynamic HTML.") ⇐
        document.write("<BR>")                                        ⇐
        document.write("We used the document.write() method to ")     ⇐
        document.write("rewrite this page's HTML on the fly.")
        document.write("<CENTER>")                                    ⇐
        document.write("</HTML>")                                     ⇐
    End Sub
</SCRIPT>

</HTML>
```

Open this page now, as shown in Figure 3.6.

When the user clicks the button, the script rewrites the Web page entirely, as shown in Figure 3.7.

In this way, we're able to rewrite entire VBScript Web pages on the fly, at any time. This capability is an improvement of Dynamic HTML over earlier HTML, because although earlier versions let you rewrite a Web page, you could do so only as that page was loaded. Using Dynamic HTML, we can now rewrite the HTML of a Web page at any time. (Note that rewriting a page like this affects only the page as stored in the browser, not the original Web page at its original URL.)

The code for this VBScript Web page, writer.htm, appears in Listing 3.5.

---

**Listing 3.5 writer.htm**

```
<HTML>

<TITLE>Rewrite the Web page example</TITLE>
```

*Continued*

---

**Figure 3.6 Web page before rewriting.**

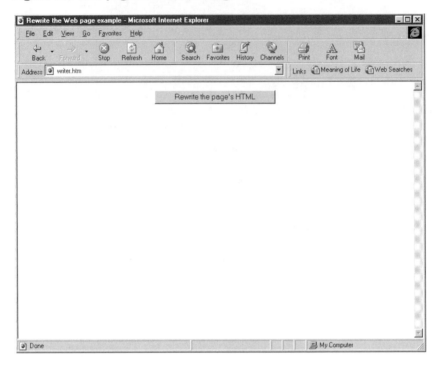

---

**Listing 3.5 Continued**

```
<BODY>

<CENTER>
<INPUT TYPE = BUTTON Value = "Rewrite the page's HTML" onClick =
rewrite()>
</CENTER>

</BODY>

<SCRIPT LANGUAGE = VBScript>
        Sub rewrite()
                document.write("<HTML>")
                document.write("<HEAD>")
                document.write("<TITLE>This page was
rewritten!</TITLE>")
```

**Listing 3.5 Continued**

```
                document.write("</HEAD>")
                document.write("<CENTER>")
                document.write("<H1>This page was rewritten!</H1>")
                document.write("This page was rewritten using Dynamic
HTML.")
                document.write("<BR>")
                document.write("We used the document.write() method
to ")
                document.write("rewrite this page's HTML on the
fly.")
                document.write("<CENTER>")
                document.write("</HTML>")
        End Sub
</SCRIPT>

</HTML>
```

**Figure 3.7 Rewritten Web page in response to a button click.**

It's also possible to rewrite a page on the fly in JavaScript. We'll look at that next.

## Rewriting HTML at Any Time with JavaScript

Creating our writer example in JavaScript, writerj.htm, is very simple. We just set up the button the user will click to rewrite the page, connecting it to a click event handler named rewrite():

```
<HTML>

<TITLE>Rewrite the Web page example</TITLE>

<BODY>

<CENTER>
<FORM>
<INPUT TYPE = BUTTON Value = "Rewrite the page's HTML" onClick =
rewrite()>
</FORM>
</CENTER>

</BODY>
          .
          .
          .
```

Then we simply create the code that will rewrite the page when the button is clicked in the rewrite() function:

```
<HTML>

<TITLE>Rewrite the Web page example</TITLE>

<BODY>
          .
          .
          .
</BODY>

<SCRIPT LANGUAGE = "JavaScript">
        function rewrite()                                        ⇐
```

```
            {
                    document.write("<HTML>")
                    document.write("<HEAD>")
                    document.write("<TITLE>This page was
rewritten!</TITLE>")
                    document.write("</HEAD>")
                    document.write("<CENTER>")
                    document.write("<H1>This page was rewritten!</H1>")
                    document.write("This page was rewritten using Dynamic
HTML.")
                    document.write("<BR>")
                    document.write("We used the document.write() method
to ")
                    document.write("rewrite this page's HTML on the
fly.")
                    document.write("<CENTER>")
                    document.write("</HTML>")
            }
</SCRIPT>

</HTML>
```

This new example, writerj.htm, runs in Netscape Navigator just as writer.htm runs in Internet Explorer. Our writer page is a success! The code for this example, writerj.htm, appears in Listing 3.6.

---

### Listing 3.6 writerj.htm

```
<HTML>

<TITLE>Rewrite the Web page example</TITLE>

<BODY>

<CENTER>
<FORM>
<INPUT TYPE = BUTTON Value = "Rewrite the page's HTML" onClick =
rewrite()>
</FORM>
</CENTER>

</BODY>
```

*Continued*

---

**Listing 3.6 Continued**

```
<SCRIPT LANGUAGE = "JavaScript">
        function rewrite()
        {
                document.write("<HTML>")
                document.write("<HEAD>")
                document.write("<TITLE>This page was
rewritten!</TITLE>")
                document.write("</HEAD>")
                document.write("<CENTER>")
                document.write("<H1>This page was rewritten!</H1>")
                document.write("This page was rewritten using Dynamic
HTML.")
                document.write("<BR>")
                document.write("We used the document.write() method
to ")
                document.write("rewrite this page's HTML on the
fly.")
                document.write("<CENTER>")
                document.write("</HTML>")
        }
</SCRIPT>

</HTML>
```

So far, we've seen how to completely rewrite a Web page. What if we only want to change *part* of a Web page? We can do that in Internet Explorer (but not in Netscape Navigator yet) by setting up a *range* to paste our HTML to. We'll see how to do this next.

## Pasting HTML by Elements

Let's say that we have an Internet Explorer Web page displaying a visible <H1> header with the text "Dynamic HTML" as well as a text prompt to the user to click that header:

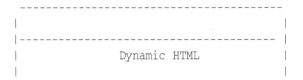

```
|Click the above header to change it... |
|                                        |
|                                        |
|                                        |
 ----------------------------------------
```

When the user clicks the header reading "Dynamic HTML," we can cause that header (and nothing else) to be rewritten, turning it into a scrolling Internet Explorer marquee using Explorer's <MARQUEE> tag:

```
 ----------------------------------------
|                                        |
|----------------------------------------|
|This marquee was written on the fly!    |
|                                        |
|Click the above header to change it... |
|                                        |
|                                        |
|                                        |
 ----------------------------------------
```

The text in the marquee, "This marquee was written on the fly!" will scroll from right to left across the page. Let's see this at work now by first taking a look at how Internet Explorer marquees work.

## Using Internet Explorer Marquees

You can set up all kinds of effects with marquees in Internet Explorer. For example, if you set the browser's **BEHAVIOR** attribute to **ALTERNATE**, the text in the marquee will bounce back and forth. (You can watch as that happens with the marquee's onBounce event.) In general, this is how you use the <MARQUEE> tag:

**Internet Explorer**

```
<MARQUEE
ALIGN=ABSBOTTOM | ABSMIDDLE | BASELINE | BOTTOM | LEFT | MIDDLE |
RIGHT | TEXTTOP | TOP
BEHAVIOR=ALTERNATE | SCROLL | SLIDE
BGCOLOR=color
DATAFLD=string
DATAFORMATAS=string
DATASRC=string
DIRECTION=DOWN | LEFT | RIGHT | UP
HEIGHT=string
```

```
HSPACE=variant
ID=string
LOOP=string
SCROLLAMOUNT=long
SCROLLDELAY=long
STYLE=string
TITLE=string
VSPACE=string
WIDTH=long
event = script
>
```

Let's start our new example Internet Explorer Web page that shows how to use Dynamic HTML to rewrite just a part of the Web page. We will call this new example dynam.htm and start by displaying the static <H1> header that we'll change, as well as a prompt to the user to click that header. We'll connect the <H1> tag's onClick event to a subroutine named changeHeader(). (Note that the Netscape Navigator <H1> tag doesn't support onClick events yet.) We also give the tag the ID "Header":

```
<HTML>

<HEAD>
<TITLE>Changing HTML on the fly</TITLE>
</HEAD>

<BODY>

<CENTER>
<H1 ID = Header onClick = "changeHeader()">Dynamic HTML</H1>          ⇐

Click the above header to change it....                               ⇐
</CENTER>

</BODY>
        .
        .
        .
```

Next, we'll add the changeHeader() subroutine:

```
<HTML>
```

```
<HEAD>
<TITLE>Changing HTML on the fly</TITLE>
</HEAD>

<BODY>

<CENTER>
<H1 ID = Header onClick = "changeHeader()">Dynamic HTML</H1>

Click the above header to change it....
</CENTER>

</BODY>


<SCRIPT LANGUAGE = VBScript>                                    ⇐

Sub changeHeader()                                             ⇐
    .
    .
    .
End Sub                                                        ⇐

</SCRIPT>                                                       ⇐
    .
    .
    .
```

The next step is to make sure we change just the <H1> header when it's clicked, not the whole Web page.

## Replacing HTML and Text

In Internet Explorer, each HTML element has the following properties: innerText, outerText, innerHTML, and outerHTML. We can use those properties to rewrite the contents of those elements.

In particular, the innerText property lets you change the text between the start and end tags of the element you're working with (including the text of any elements the element itself contains). The outerText property lets you change all the element's text—including the start and end tags.

The innerHTML property lets you change the HTML between the start and end tags of an element. Finally, the outerHTML property lets you change all the HTML of the element, including the start and end tags.

In our example, we'll add our marquee using the <H1> tag's innerHTML property this way:

```
<HTML>

<HEAD>
<TITLE>Changing HTML on the fly</TITLE>
</HEAD>

<BODY ID = body1>

<CENTER>
<H1 ID = Header onClick = "changeHeader()">Dynamic HTML</H1>

Click the above header to change it....
</CENTER>

</BODY>


<SCRIPT LANGUAGE = VBScript>

Sub changeHeader()
        Header.innerHTML ="<MARQUEE>This marquee was written on the
fly!</MARQUEE>"                                                        ⇐
End Sub

</SCRIPT>

</HTML>
```

Now when the user clicks the <H1> tag, it will change into a marquee. (If you wanted to respond to double clicks on the <H1> tag, you can use its onDblClick event instead.)

Open the Web page now in Internet Explorer, as shown in Figure 3.8.

**Figure 3.8 Our Web page will rewrite its header when that header is clicked.**

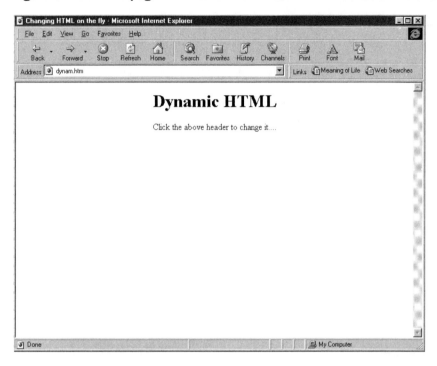

When you click the header, it changes into a scrolling marquee, as shown in Figure 3.9. Our new dynamic HTML example is a success. Now we're able to change just a single element of an Internet Explorer Web page as we like.

The code for this Web page, dynam.htm, appears in Listing 3.7.

**Listing 3.7 dynam.htm**

```
<HTML>

<HEAD>
<TITLE>Changing HTML on the fly</TITLE>
</HEAD>

<BODY ID = body1>
```

*Continued*

**Figure 3.9 Our Web page has changed its header to a marquee.**

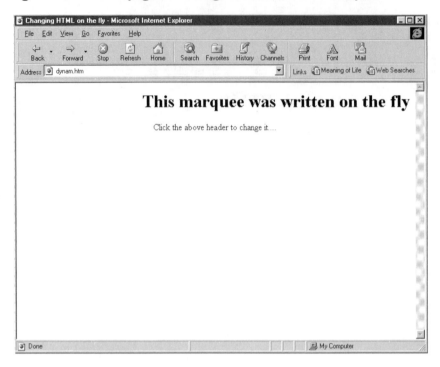

**Listing 3.7 Continued**

```
<CENTER>
<H1 ID = Header onClick = "changeHeader()">Dynamic HTML</H1>

Click the above header to change it....
</CENTER>

</BODY>


<SCRIPT LANGUAGE = VBScript>

Sub changeHeader()
        Header.innerHTML ="<MARQUEE>This marquee was written on the
fly!</MARQUEE>"
```

**Listing 3.7 Continued**

```
End Sub

</SCRIPT>

</HTML>
```

We've seen how to work with an individual HTML element now—in particular, we used an <H1> tag and rewrote it as a marquee. However, it's possible to simply select some arbitrary text in an Internet Explorer page and rewite *only* that text. Let's see how that works with an example now.

# Pasting HTML with Specific Text Ranges

Let's say that we wanted some of the text in an Internet Explorer page to change when the user clicks a button. This is useful if you want to tailor your page to the user's interests, without having to read in additional pages from the Web. In our example, we'll present the user with a button that displays the caption, "Change the text" as well as text reading simply, "Here is the text.":

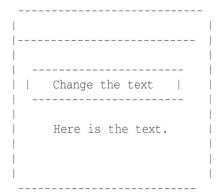

When the user clicks the button, our Web page will rewrite the text (and only the text) to read "Here is the new text!":

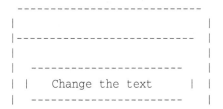

```
|                              |
|      Here is the new text!   |
|                              |
|                              |
|                              |
  ----------------------------
```

To select and change the text we want to work with, we'll use a text *range*. An
Internet Explorer text range specifies a section of the text in your page, and you can
use the range object's member functions—like pasteHTML()—to work with and
change the text in such a range.

Let's see this in action in a new Internet Explorer example named ranger.htm.
We start by placing the text we'll display in our Web page, as well as a button with
the caption "Change the text." We connect the button's onClick event to a subroutine named ChangeText():

```
<HTML>

<HEAD>
<TITLE>Text Range example</TITLE>
</HEAD>

<BODY>

<CENTER>
<INPUT TYPE = BUTTON Value = "Change the text" onClick = ChangeText()>  ⇐
<BR>
<BR>
Here is the text.                                                      ⇐
</CENTER>

</BODY>
    .
    .
    .
```

Next, we add the subroutine ChangeText():

```
<HTML>

<HEAD>
<TITLE>Text Range example</TITLE>
</HEAD>

<BODY>
```

```
<CENTER>
<INPUT TYPE = BUTTON Value = "Change the text" onClick = ChangeText()>
<BR>
<BR>
Here is the text.
</CENTER>

</BODY>

<SCRIPT LANGUAGE = VBScript>
        Sub ChangeText()                                            ⇐
          .
          .
          .
        End Sub                                                     ⇐
</SCRIPT>

</BODY>

</HTML>
```

In ChangeText(), create a new VB Script object named r, which will be our new text range:

```
<HTML>

<HEAD>
<TITLE>Text Range example</TITLE>
</HEAD>

<BODY ID = body1>

<CENTER>
<INPUT TYPE = BUTTON Value = "Change the text" onClick = ChangeText()>
<BR>
<BR>
Here is the text.
</CENTER>

</BODY>

<SCRIPT LANGUAGE = VBScript>
        Sub ChangeText()
                Dim r                                               ⇐
```

```
                        .
                        .
                        .
            End Sub
</SCRIPT>

</BODY>

</HTML>
```

Now we create this new object using the **VBScript** set keyword, creating a new text range corresponding to the document's body:

```
<HTML>

<HEAD>
<TITLE>Text Range example</TITLE>
</HEAD>

<BODY ID = body1>

<CENTER>
<INPUT TYPE = BUTTON Value = "Change the text" onClick = ChangeText()>
<BR>
<BR>
Here is the text.
</CENTER>

</BODY>

<SCRIPT LANGUAGE = VBScript>
        Sub ChangeText()
            Dim r
            set r = document.body.createTextRange()              ⇐
                .
                .
                .
        End Sub
</SCRIPT>

</BODY>

</HTML>
```

Now we have a text range to work with. We set that text range to encompass the text we're looking for with the range's findText() method this way:

```
<HTML>

<HEAD>
<TITLE>Text Range example</TITLE>
</HEAD>

<BODY ID = body1>

<CENTER>
<INPUT TYPE = BUTTON Value = "Change the text" onClick = ChangeText()>
<BR>
<BR>
Here is the text.
</CENTER>

</BODY>

<SCRIPT LANGUAGE = VBScript>
        Sub ChangeText()
            Dim r
            set r = document.body.createTextRange()
            r.findText("Here is the text.")                    ⇐
                .
                .
                .

        End Sub
</SCRIPT>

</BODY>

</HTML>
```

Finally, we paste the new text in place with the range's pasteHTML() method this way:

```
<HTML>

<HEAD>
<TITLE>Text Range example</TITLE>
</HEAD>
```

```
<BODY ID = body1>

<CENTER>
<INPUT TYPE = BUTTON Value = "Change the text" onClick = ChangeText()>
<BR>
<BR>
Here is the text.
</CENTER>

</BODY>

<SCRIPT LANGUAGE = VBScript>
        Sub ChangeText()
            Dim r
            set r = document.body.createTextRange()
            r.findText("Here is the text.")
            r.pasteHTML("Here is the new text!")                    ⇐
        End Sub
</SCRIPT>

</BODY>

</HTML>
```

That's all there is to it; that completes the page—open it now in Internet Explorer, as shown in Figure 3.10.

Now click the button—when you do, the script we've written rewrites the text in the page to "Here is the new text!", as shown in Figure 3.11. Our dynam.htm example is a success. Now we can reach and change any section of text we like in an Internet Explorer Web page.

The code for this example, ranger.htm, appears in Listing 3.8.

## Listing 3.8 ranger.htm

```
<HTML>

<HEAD>
<TITLE>Text Range example</TITLE>
</HEAD>

<BODY ID = body1>

<CENTER>
```

**Figure 3.10 We will change (only) the text in this page by rewriting it.**

**Listing 3.8 Continued**

```
<INPUT TYPE = BUTTON Value = "Change the text" onClick = ChangeText()>
<BR>
<BR>
Here is the text.
</CENTER>

</BODY>

<SCRIPT LANGUAGE = VBScript>
        Sub ChangeText()
            Dim r
            set r = document.body.createTextRange()
            r.findText("Here is the text.")
            r.pasteHTML("Here is the new text!")
        End Sub
```

*Continued*

**Figure 3.11 We have changed the text in our Web page.**

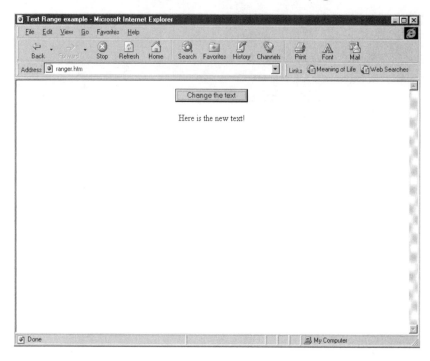

**Listing 3.8 Continued**

```
</SCRIPT>

</BODY>

</HTML>
```

So far, then, we've seen how to make the HTML in our Web pages dynamic, but we've only worked with simple Web pages. What if we wanted to modify a document appearing in another frame? We'll see how to do that next, using both the Internet Explorer and the Netscape Navigator.

# Targeted Frames in VBScript

In our next example, we'll write HTML to a page in another frame to see how to gain more control over our Web pages. For example, we might modify the airport departures example from the beginning of the chapter to use frames like this:

```
 --------------------------------------------------------
|                                                        |
|------------------------------------------------------- |
|                    |                                   |
|  1. Airport Hours  |        Welcome to the             |
|                    |        Dynamic HTML               |
|  2. Morning Flights|          Airport!                 |
|                    |                                   |
|  3. Afternoon Flights |                                |
|                    |                                   |
|                    |                                   |
|  4. Evening Flights|                                   |
|                    |                                   |
 --------------------------------------------------------
```

When the user clicks the Airport Hours hyperlink in the frame on the left, the page can show the airport's hours in the right frame:

```
 --------------------------------------------------------
|                                                        |
|------------------------------------------------------- |
|                    |                                   |
|  1. Airport Hours  |       The Dynamic HTML            |
|                    |          Airport Hours            |
|  2. Morning Flights|                                   |
|                    |   The Dynamic HTML Airport is     |
|  3. Afternoon Flights |    open from 6AM to 10PM        |
|                    |          EST daily.               |
|  4. Evening Flights|                                   |
|                    |                                   |
|                    |                                   |
|                    |                                   |
 --------------------------------------------------------
```

When the user clicks the Morning Flights entry in the left frame, we can *rewrite* the HTML in the second frame (as opposed to loading a new Web page into that frame) to show a table holding the departure times for the morning flights:

```
 --------------------------------------------------------
|                                                        |
|------------------------------------------------------- |
|                    |   -------------------------       |
```

```
|   1. Airport Hours      |    |      Morning Flights       |  |
|                         |    |----------------------------|  |
|   2. Morning Flights    |    |Pittsburgh     | 6:30 AM    |  |
|                         |    |San Francisco  | 7:00 AM    |  |
|   3. Afternoon Flights  |    |Boston         | 7:30 AM    |  |
|                         |    |Santa Cruz     | 8:00 AM    |  |
|   4. Evening Flights    |    |Ithaca         | 8:30 AM    |  |
|                         |    |Paris          | 9:00 AM    |  |
|                         |    |London         | 9:30 AM    |  |
|                         |    |---------------------------    |
|                         |                                      |
----------------------------------------------------------------
```

When the user clicks the Afternoon Flights entry, we can rewrite the HTML in the right frame to display the afternoon flights schedule table:

```
    ----------------------------------------------------------
   |                                                          |
   |----------------------------------------------------------|
   |                         |     ----------------------------|
   |   1. Airport Hours      |    | Afternoon Flights       |  |
   |                         |    |-----------------------     |  |
   |   2. Morning Flights    |    |Pittsburgh     | 12:00 PM  |  |
   |                         |    |San Francisco  | 12:30 PM  |  |
   |   3. Afternoon Flights  |    |Boston         | 1:30 PM   |  |
   |                         |    |Santa Cruz     | 3:30 PM   |  |
   |   4. Evening Flights    |    |Ithaca         | 4:00 PM   |  |
   |                         |    |Paris          | 4:30 PM   |  |
   |                         |    |London         | 5:00 PM   |  |
   |                         |    |---------------------------    |
   |                         |                                    |
    ----------------------------------------------------------
```

Let's put this example together now. We'll start the airport.htm file by creating two column frames, taking up 40 percent and 60 percent of the page, respectively. We do that using the <FRAMESET> tag, which lets us specify the relative widths of the columns we want to create this way:

```
<HTML>

<HEAD>
<TITLE>Targeted frames</TITLE>
</HEAD>
```

```
<FRAMESET COLS = "40%, 60%">                                    ⇐
    .
    .
    .
```

Next, we display a new page, menu.htm, in the first frame, and another new page, welcome.htm, in the second frame. We also name the second frame "display" because we need some way of targeting that frame, as we'll see:

```
<HTML>

<HEAD>
<TITLE>Targeted frames</TITLE>
</HEAD>

<FRAMESET COLS = "40%, 60%">
<FRAME SRC = menu.htm >                                         ⇐
<FRAME SRC = welcome.htm NAME = "display">                      ⇐
</FRAMESET>
</HTML>
```

The welcome.htm page simply holds a message of welcome to the user:

```
<HTML>

<HEAD>
<TITLE>Welcome to the Dynamic HTML Airport</TITLE>
</HEAD>

<BODY>

<CENTER>
<H1>Welcome to the Dynamic HTML Airport!</H1>
</CENTER>

</BODY>

</HTML>
```

So far, our display in the Web browser looks like this:

```
 --------------------------------------------------------
|                                                      |  |
|-------------------------------------------------|    |  |
|                           |                          |  |
|                           |         Welcome to the   |  |
|                           |         Dynamic HTML      |  |
|                           |            Airport!       |  |
|                           |                          |  |
|                           |                          |  |
|                           |                          |  |
|                           |                          |  |
|                           |                          |  |
|                           |                          |  |
 --------------------------------------------------------
```

Now we're ready to write menu.htm, which will go into the left-hand frame. (This file, menu.htm, is where the action is in this example.)

## Writing a File to Target a Frame

The menu.htm page will appear in the left frame of the Web browser, and we'll support a number of entries the user can click to cause new data to appear in the right frame:

```
     --------------------------------------------------------
    |                                                      |  |
    |-------------------------------------------------|    |  |
    |                           |                          |  |
    |   1. Airport Hours        |         Welcome to the   |  |
    |                           |         Dynamic HTML      |  |
    |   2. Morning Flights      |            Airport!       |  |
    |                           |                          |  |
    |   3. Afternoon Flights    |                          |  |
    |                           |                          |  |
    |   4. Evening Flights      |                          |  |
    |                           |                          |  |
    |                           |                          |  |
     --------------------------------------------------------
            menu.htm                    welcome.htm
```

We'll place our entries—Airport Hours, Morning Flights, Afternoon Flights, and so on—in an ordered list (i.e., these items will be numbered automatically when displayed) using the <OL> tag:

**Internet Explorer**

```
<OL
ALIGN=CENTER | LEFT | RIGHT
COMPACT
ID=string
START=string
STYLE=string
STRING=string
TITLE=string
TYPE=string
event = scrpit
>
```

**Netscape Navigator**

```
<OL
START="value"
TYPE="value"
>
```

For the first entry in menu.htm, we use a hyperlink with the text "Airport Hours" and with its TARGET attribute set to the right-hand frame, which we've named display. This link is to a new page named hours.htm, which is loaded into the right-hand frame when the user clicks this hyperlink:

```
<HTML>

<BODY LINK = 0000>

<OL>

<LI><A HREF = "hours.htm" TARGET = "display">        ⇐
    Airport Hours                                    ⇐
</A>                                                 ⇐
</LI>                                                ⇐
    .
    .
    .
```

The hours.htm file simply indicates to the user the hours for our airport:

```
<HTML>

<HEAD>
<TITLE>Airport Hours</TITLE>
</HEAD>

<BODY>
```

```
<CENTER>
<H1>The Dynamic HTML Airport Hours</H1>
<BR>
<BR>
The Dynamic HTML airport is open from 6 AM to 10 PM EST daily.
</CENTER>

</BODY>

</HTML>
```

Now we will make active the other entries in menu.htm: "Morning Flights," "Afternoon Flights," and "Evening Flights."

## Writing to Targeted Frames

When the user clicks the flight schedule entries in menu.htm, we won't load in a new Web page; instead, we'll write HTML directly to the page in the right-hand frame. To do that, we start by connecting those entries to the VBScript subroutines Morning(), Afternoon(), and Evening(). We'll display these entries with the <A> tag, just like the Airport Hours hyperlink we've already made active, and even underline (using the <U> tag) the entries to make them look like hyperlinks. They aren't hyperlinks, though; instead, we'll connect them to VBScript subroutines with the <A> tag's onClick event and rewrite the document in the right-hand frame in code. Here's how we connect the schedule entries to the correct VBScript subroutines:

```
<HTML>

<BODY LINK = 0000>

<OL>

<LI><A HREF = "hours.htm" TARGET = "display">
    Airport Hours
</A>
</LI>

<LI><A onClick = "Morning()">                                    ⇐
    <U>Morning Flights</U>                                       ⇐
</A>                                                             ⇐

<LI><A onClick = "Afternoon()">                                 ⇐
```

```
    <U>Afternoon Flights</U>                                        ⇐
</A>                                                                ⇐

<LI><A onClick = "Evening()">                                       ⇐
    <U>Evening Flights</U>                                          ⇐
</A>                                                                ⇐

</OL>

</BODY>
    .
    .
    .
```

When the user clicks one of those entries, the Web browser will call the associated subroutine. For example, when the user clicks the Morning Flights entry, the code in the Morning() subroutine will be executed:

```
<HTML>

<BODY LINK = 0000>
    .
    .
    .
</BODY>

<SCRIPT LANGUAGE = VBScript>
        Sub Morning()                                               ⇐
        .
        .
        .
        End Sub                                                     ⇐
</SCRIPT>
```

In this subroutine, we want to write new HTML to the right-hand frame. However, our code is in the left-hand frame. How do we reach the other frame? We do that with the frames collection.

## Using the Frames Collection

The *frames collection* holds all the frames in our window. The left-hand frame was added first, so it's frames(0) in the frames collection, and the right-hand frame is frames(1).

We want to use the write() method of the document in the right-hand frame, so we address that document as frames(1).document and its write() method as frames(1).document.write()—but that's not enough. The frames collection belongs to the window object; however, the code we're executing is in a frame and does not represent the whole window. To get the main window object, we use the *parent* object. In other words, to write to the document in the right-hand frame with code in the left-hand frame, we must call parent.frames(1).document.write(). That's how we'll rewrite the HTML in the target frame.

It seems as though we're all set, but there is one more thing to consider.

## Opening a Document to Reset It

All the examples in this chapter so far were designed to rewrite a page only once, but in our current example, the user might click the "Morning Hours" entry in the left-hand frame to write HTML to the right-hand frame, and then click the "Afternoon Hours" entry, writing more HTML to the right-hand frame.

When you simply call write(), however, you just write more HTML starting at the last location you've written to in the document. But we want to start the whole document over from scratch so we can change from the morning schedule of flights to the afternoon schedule, for example. To do that, we *open* the document using the open() method; this places us at the beginning of the document:

```
<HTML>

<BODY LINK = 0000>
        .
        .
        .
</BODY>

<SCRIPT LANGUAGE = VBScript>
        Sub Morning()
        parent.frames(1).document.open()                          ⇐
            .
            .
            .

        End Sub
</SCRIPT>
```

Now we're ready to write the HTML to the right-hand frame to display our morning schedule. Note that we close the document after writing it, with the close() method:

```
<HTML>

<BODY LINK = 0000>
     .
     .
     .
</BODY>

<SCRIPT LANGUAGE = VBScript>
    Sub Morning()
        parent.frames(1).document.open()
        parent.frames(1).document.write "<CENTER>"
        parent.frames(1).document.write "<TABLE BORDER BGCOLOR =
""#ffff00"">"
        parent.frames(1).document.write "<TR><TH COLSPAN = 2>Morning
Flights</TH></TR>"
        parent.frames(1).document.write
"<TR><TD>Pittsburgh</TD><TD>6:30 AM</TD></TR>"
        parent.frames(1).document.write "<TR><TD>San
Francisco</TD><TD>7:00 AM</TD></TR>"
        parent.frames(1).document.write "<TR><TD>Boston</TD><TD>7:30
AM</TD></TR>"
        parent.frames(1).document.write "<TR><TD>Santa
Cruz</TD><TD>8:00 AM</TD></TR>"
        parent.frames(1).document.write "<TR><TD>Ithaca</TD><TD>8:30
AM</TD></TR>"
        parent.frames(1).document.write "<TR><TD>Paris</TD><TD>9:00
AM</TD></TR>"
        parent.frames(1).document.write "<TR><TD>London</TD><TD>9:30
AM</TD></TR>"
        parent.frames(1).document.write "</TABLE>"
        parent.frames(1).document.write "</CENTER>"
        parent.frames(1).document.close()
    End Sub
        .
        .
        .
```

In the same way, we can write the other two schedules:

```
<HTML>

<BODY LINK = 0000>
     .
     .
```

```
        .
</BODY>

<SCRIPT LANGUAGE = VBScript>
        Sub Morning()

        .

        .

        .

    Sub Afternoon()
        parent.frames(1).document.open()
        parent.frames(1).document.write "<CENTER>"
        parent.frames(1).document.write "<TABLE BORDER BGCOLOR =
""#ffff00"">"
        parent.frames(1).document.write "<TR><TH COLSPAN = 2>Afternoon
Flights</TH></TR>"
        parent.frames(1).document.write
"<TR><TD>Pittsburgh</TD><TD>12:00 PM</TD></TR>"
        parent.frames(1).document.write "<TR><TD>San
Francisco</TD><TD>12:30 PM</TD></TR>"
        parent.frames(1).document.write "<TR><TD>Boston</TD><TD>1:30
PM</TD></TR>"
        parent.frames(1).document.write "<TR><TD>Santa
Cruz</TD><TD>3:30 PM</TD></TR>"
        parent.frames(1).document.write "<TR><TD>Ithaca</TD><TD>4:00
AM</TD></TR>"
        parent.frames(1).document.write "<TR><TD>Paris</TD><TD>4:30
PM</TD></TR>"
        parent.frames(1).document.write "<TR><TD>London</TD><TD>5:00
PM</TD></TR>"
        parent.frames(1).document.write "</TABLE>"
        parent.frames(1).document.write "</CENTER>"
        parent.frames(1).document.close()
    End Sub
    Sub Evening()
        parent.frames(1).document.open()
        parent.frames(1).document.write "<CENTER>"
        parent.frames(1).document.write "<TABLE BORDER BGCOLOR =
""#ffff00"">"
        parent.frames(1).document.write "<TR><TH COLSPAN = 2>Evening
Flights</TH></TR>"
        parent.frames(1).document.write
"<TR><TD>Pittsburgh</TD><TD>6:30 PM</TD></TR>"
```

```
        parent.frames(1).document.write "<TR><TD>San
Francisco</TD><TD>7:00 PM</TD></TR>"
        parent.frames(1).document.write "<TR><TD>Boston</TD><TD>7:30
PM</TD></TR>"
        parent.frames(1).document.write "<TR><TD>Santa
Cruz</TD><TD>8:00 PM</TD></TR>"
        parent.frames(1).document.write "<TR><TD>Ithaca</TD><TD>8:30
PM</TD></TR>"
        parent.frames(1).document.write "<TR><TD>Paris</TD><TD>9:00
PM</TD></TR>"
        parent.frames(1).document.write "<TR><TD>London</TD><TD>9:30
PM</TD></TR>"
        parent.frames(1).document.write "</TABLE>"
        parent.frames(1).document.write "</CENTER>"
        parent.frames(1).document.close()
    End Sub
</SCRIPT>
</HTML>
```

That's it. Our VBScript frames example is complete.

Now open airport.htm in Internet Explorer. When the user clicks the Morning Flights entry, the browser displays the morning schedule of flights, as shown in Figure 3.12.

When the user clicks the Afternoon Flights entry, the page displays the afternoon flights table, as shown in Figure 3.13. Our example is a success. Now we're able to write HTML to documents in other frames.

The code for this page appears in several listings: airport.htm in Listing 3.9, menu.htm in Listing 3.10, welcome.htm in Listing 3.11, and hours.htm in Listing 3.12.

**Listing 3.9 airport.htm**

```
<HTML>

<HEAD>
<TITLE>Targeted frames</TITLE>
</HEAD>

<FRAMESET COLS = "40%, 60%">
<FRAME SRC = menu.htm >
<FRAME SRC = welcome.htm NAME = "display">
```

*Continued*

**Figure 3.12 The morning schedule of flights rewritten to a new frame using VBScript.**

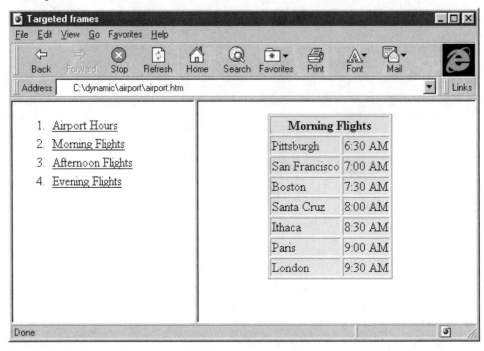

---

**Listing 3.9 Continued**

```
</FRAMESET>
</HTML>
```

---

**Listing 3.10 menu.htm**

```
<HTML>
<BODY LINK = 0000>

<OL>

<LI><A HREF = "hours.htm" TARGET = "display">
    Airport Hours
</A>
```

**Listing 3.10 Continued**

```
</LI>

<LI><A onClick = "Morning()">
    <U>Morning Flights</U>
</A>

<LI><A onClick = "Afternoon()">
    <U>Afternoon Flights</U>
</A>

<LI><A onClick = "Evening()">
    <U>Evening Flights</U>
</A>

</OL>
```

*Continued*

**Figure 3.13 The afternoon schedule of flights rewritten to a new frame.**

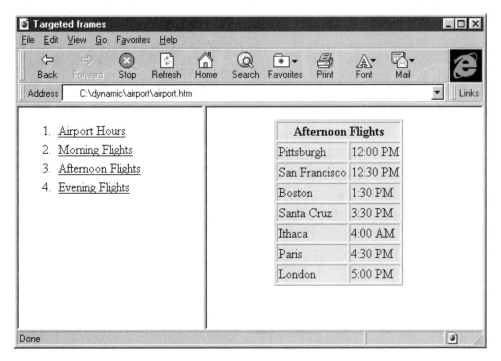

**Listing 3.10 Continued**

```
</BODY>

<SCRIPT LANGUAGE = VBScript>
        Sub Morning()
        parent.frames(1).document.open()
        parent.frames(1).document.write "<CENTER>"
        parent.frames(1).document.write "<TABLE BORDER BGCOLOR =
""#ffff00"">"
        parent.frames(1).document.write "<TR><TH COLSPAN = 2>Morning
Flights</TH></TR>"
        parent.frames(1).document.write
"<TR><TD>Pittsburgh</TD><TD>6:30 AM</TD></TR>"
        parent.frames(1).document.write "<TR><TD>San
Francisco</TD><TD>7:00 AM</TD></TR>"
        parent.frames(1).document.write "<TR><TD>Boston</TD><TD>7:30
AM</TD></TR>"
        parent.frames(1).document.write "<TR><TD>Santa
Cruz</TD><TD>8:00 AM</TD></TR>"
        parent.frames(1).document.write "<TR><TD>Ithaca</TD><TD>8:30
AM</TD></TR>"
        parent.frames(1).document.write "<TR><TD>Paris</TD><TD>9:00
AM</TD></TR>"
        parent.frames(1).document.write "<TR><TD>London</TD><TD>9:30
AM</TD></TR>"
        parent.frames(1).document.write "</TABLE>"
        parent.frames(1).document.write "</CENTER>"
        parent.frames(1).document.close()
        End Sub
        Sub Afternoon()
        parent.frames(1).document.open()
        parent.frames(1).document.write "<CENTER>"
        parent.frames(1).document.write "<TABLE BORDER BGCOLOR =
""#ffff00"">"
        parent.frames(1).document.write "<TR><TH COLSPAN = 2>Afternoon
Flights</TH></TR>"
        parent.frames(1).document.write
"<TR><TD>Pittsburgh</TD><TD>12:00 PM</TD></TR>"
        parent.frames(1).document.write "<TR><TD>San
Francisco</TD><TD>12:30 PM</TD></TR>"
```

**Listing 3.10 Continued**

```
        parent.frames(1).document.write "<TR><TD>Boston</TD><TD>1:30
PM</TD></TR>"
        parent.frames(1).document.write "<TR><TD>Santa
Cruz</TD><TD>3:30 PM</TD></TR>"
        parent.frames(1).document.write "<TR><TD>Ithaca</TD><TD>4:00
AM</TD></TR>"
        parent.frames(1).document.write "<TR><TD>Paris</TD><TD>4:30
PM</TD></TR>"
        parent.frames(1).document.write "<TR><TD>London</TD><TD>5:00
PM</TD></TR>"
        parent.frames(1).document.write "</TABLE>"
        parent.frames(1).document.write "</CENTER>"
        parent.frames(1).document.close()
        End Sub
        Sub Evening()
        parent.frames(1).document.open()
        parent.frames(1).document.write "<CENTER>"
        parent.frames(1).document.write "<TABLE BORDER BGCOLOR =
""#ffff00"">"
        parent.frames(1).document.write "<TR><TH COLSPAN = 2>Evening
Flights</TH></TR>"
        parent.frames(1).document.write
"<TR><TD>Pittsburgh</TD><TD>6:30 PM</TD></TR>"
        parent.frames(1).document.write "<TR><TD>San
Francisco</TD><TD>7:00 PM</TD></TR>"
        parent.frames(1).document.write "<TR><TD>Boston</TD><TD>7:30
PM</TD></TR>"
        parent.frames(1).document.write "<TR><TD>Santa
Cruz</TD><TD>8:00 PM</TD></TR>"
        parent.frames(1).document.write "<TR><TD>Ithaca</TD><TD>8:30
PM</TD></TR>"
        parent.frames(1).document.write "<TR><TD>Paris</TD><TD>9:00
PM</TD></TR>"
        parent.frames(1).document.write "<TR><TD>London</TD><TD>9:30
PM</TD></TR>"
        parent.frames(1).document.write "</TABLE>"
        parent.frames(1).document.write "</CENTER>"
        parent.frames(1).document.close()
        End Sub
</SCRIPT>
</HTML>
```

## Listing 3.11 welcome.htm

```
<HTML>

<HEAD>
<TITLE>Welcome to the Dynamic HTML Airport</TITLE>
</HEAD>

<BODY>

<CENTER>
<H1>Welcome to the Dynamic HTML Airport!</H1>
</CENTER>

</BODY>

</HTML>
```

## Listing 3.12 hours.htm

```
<HTML>

<HEAD>
<TITLE>Airport Hours</TITLE>
</HEAD>

<BODY>

<CENTER>
<H1>The Dynamic HTML Airport Hours</H1>
<BR>
<BR>
The Dynamic HTML airport is open from 6 AM to 10 PM EST daily.
</CENTER>

</BODY>

</HTML>
```

Now that we've seen how to do this in VBScript, let's take a look at the same process in JavaScript.

# Writing HTML to Targeted Frames with JavaScript

It turns out that writing this example in JavaScript is just about as easy as writing it in VBScript. We just use functions instead of subroutines, enclose the arguments to document.write() in parentheses, and instead of two double quotes, use single quotes, and that's almost all there is to it. We'll call this new JavaScript Web page airportj.htm; note that it loads in the JavaScript version of the menu.htm page, menuj.htm:

```
<HTML>

<HEAD>
<TITLE>Targeted frames</TITLE>
</HEAD>

<FRAMESET COLS = "40%, 60%">
<FRAME SRC = menuj.htm >                                    ⇐
<FRAME SRC = welcome.htm NAME = "display">
</FRAMESET>
</HTML>
```

Now we can write the menuj.htm page. This page lists the entries from which the user can select and rewrites the target page. We start menuj.htm with the entries the user may select. There is one point to notice here: The onClick events in hyperlinks are inactive in Netscape unless we include the HREF attribute, so we just give that attribute the menu page itself, menuj.htm:

```
<HTML>

<BODY LINK = 0000>

<FORM>
<OL>

<LI><A HREF = "hours.htm" TARGET = "display">
    Airport Hours
</A>
</LI>

<LI><A HREF = "menuj.htm" onClick = "Morning()">        ⇐
    <U>Morning Flights</U>
</A>
```

```
<LI><A HREF = "menuj.htm" onClick = "Afternoon()">                    ⇐
    <U>Afternoon Flights</U>
</A>

<LI><A HREF = "menuj.htm" onClick = "Evening()">                      ⇐
    <U>Evening Flights</U>
</A>

</OL>
</FORM>

</BODY>
    .
    .
    .
```

Now we'll write the functions Morning(), Afternoon(), and Evening(), which look very much like their VBScript counterparts. The major difference is that JavaScript uses brackets, [ and ], to refer to members of an array instead of VBScript's ( and ):

```
<HTML>

<BODY LINK = 0000>
    .
    .
    .
</BODY>

<SCRIPT LANGUAGE = JavaScript>
        function Morning()
        {
        parent.frames[1].document.open()
        parent.frames[1].document.write( "<CENTER>")
        parent.frames[1].document.write( "<TABLE BORDER BGCOLOR =
'#ffff00'>")
        parent.frames[1].document.write( "<TR><TH COLSPAN = 2>Morning
Flights</TH></TR>")
        parent.frames[1].document.write(
"<TR><TD>Pittsburgh</TD><TD>6:30 AM</TD></TR>")
```

```
        parent.frames[1].document.write( "<TR><TD>San
Francisco</TD><TD>7:00 AM</TD></TR>")
        parent.frames[1].document.write( "<TR><TD>Boston</TD><TD>7:30
AM</TD></TR>")
        parent.frames[1].document.write( "<TR><TD>Santa
Cruz</TD><TD>8:00 AM</TD></TR>")
        parent.frames[1].document.write( "<TR><TD>Ithaca</TD><TD>8:30
AM</TD></TR>")
        parent.frames[1].document.write( "<TR><TD>Paris</TD><TD>9:00
AM</TD></TR>")
        parent.frames[1].document.write( "<TR><TD>London</TD><TD>9:30
AM</TD></TR>")
        parent.frames[1].document.write( "</TABLE>")
        parent.frames[1].document.write( "</CENTER>")
        parent.frames[1].document.close()
        }
        function Afternoon()
        {
        parent.frames[1].document.open()
        parent.frames[1].document.write( "<CENTER>")
        parent.frames[1].document.write( "<TABLE BORDER BGCOLOR =
'#ffff00'>")
        parent.frames[1].document.write( "<TR><TH COLSPAN =
2>Afternoon Flights</TH></TR>")
        parent.frames[1].document.write(
"<TR><TD>Pittsburgh</TD><TD>12:00 PM</TD></TR>")
        parent.frames[1].document.write( "<TR><TD>San
Francisco</TD><TD>12:30 PM</TD></TR>")
        parent.frames[1].document.write( "<TR><TD>Boston</TD><TD>1:30
PM</TD></TR>")
        parent.frames[1].document.write( "<TR><TD>Santa
Cruz</TD><TD>3:30 PM</TD></TR>")
        parent.frames[1].document.write( "<TR><TD>Ithaca</TD><TD>4:00
AM</TD></TR>")
        parent.frames[1].document.write( "<TR><TD>Paris</TD><TD>4:30
PM</TD></TR>")
        parent.frames[1].document.write( "<TR><TD>London</TD><TD>5:00
PM</TD></TR>")
        parent.frames[1].document.write( "</TABLE>")
        parent.frames[1].document.write( "</CENTER>")
        parent.frames[1].document.close()
        }
```

```
        function Evening()
        {
        parent.frames[1].document.open()
        parent.frames[1].document.write( "<CENTER>")
        parent.frames[1].document.write( "<TABLE BORDER BGCOLOR =
'#ffff00'>")
        parent.frames[1].document.write( "<TR><TH COLSPAN = 2>Evening
Flights</TH></TR>")
        parent.frames[1].document.write(
"<TR><TD>Pittsburgh</TD><TD>6:30 PM</TD></TR>")
        parent.frames[1].document.write( "<TR><TD>San
Francisco</TD><TD>7:00 PM</TD></TR>")
        parent.frames[1].document.write( "<TR><TD>Boston</TD><TD>7:30
PM</TD></TR>")
        parent.frames[1].document.write( "<TR><TD>Santa
Cruz</TD><TD>8:00 PM</TD></TR>")
        parent.frames[1].document.write( "<TR><TD>Ithaca</TD><TD>8:30
PM</TD></TR>")
        parent.frames[1].document.write( "<TR><TD>Paris</TD><TD>9:00
PM</TD></TR>")
        parent.frames[1].document.write( "<TR><TD>London</TD><TD>9:30
PM</TD></TR>")
        parent.frames[1].document.write( "</TABLE>")
        parent.frames[1].document.write( "</CENTER>")
        parent.frames[1].document.close()
        }
</SCRIPT>
</HTML>
```

And that's all it takes. Open this new page in Netscape Navigator and click an entry. The browser will rewrite the page, as shown in Figure 3.14. Now we're rewriting targeted frames with JavaScript!

The code for this example, airportj.htm and menuj.htm, appears in Listings 3.13 and 3.14, respectively.

---

**Listing 3.13 airportj.htm**

```
<HTML>

<HEAD>
<TITLE>Targeted frames</TITLE>
</HEAD>
```

---

**Figure 3.14 HTML written to another frame using JavaScript.**

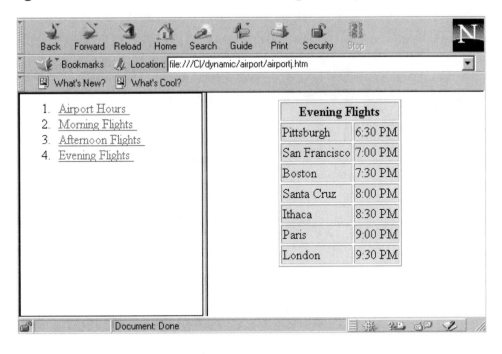

---

**Listing 3.13 Continued**

```
<FRAMESET COLS = "40%, 60%">
<FRAME SRC = menuj.htm >
<FRAME SRC = welcome.htm NAME = "display">
</FRAMESET>
</HTML>
```

**Listing 3.14 menuj.htm**

```
<HTML>

<BODY LINK = 0000>

<FORM>
<OL>
```

*Continued*

**Listing 3.14 Continued**

```
<LI><A HREF = "hours.htm" TARGET = "display">
    Airport Hours
</A>
</LI>

<LI><A HREF = "menuj.htm" onClick = "Morning()">
    <U>Morning Flights</U>
</A>

<LI><A HREF = "menuj.htm" onClick = "Afternoon()">
    <U>Afternoon Flights</U>
</A>

<LI><A HREF = "menuj.htm" onClick = "Evening()">
    <U>Evening Flights</U>
</A>

</OL>
</FORM>

</BODY>

<SCRIPT LANGUAGE = JavaScript>
        function Morning()
        {
        parent.frames[1].document.open()
        parent.frames[1].document.write( "<CENTER>")
        parent.frames[1].document.write( "<TABLE BORDER BGCOLOR =
'#ffff00'>")
        parent.frames[1].document.write( "<TR><TH COLSPAN = 2>Morning
Flights</TH></TR>")
        parent.frames[1].document.write(
"<TR><TD>Pittsburgh</TD><TD>6:30 AM</TD></TR>")
        parent.frames[1].document.write( "<TR><TD>San
Francisco</TD><TD>7:00 AM</TD></TR>")
        parent.frames[1].document.write( "<TR><TD>Boston</TD><TD>7:30
AM</TD></TR>")
        parent.frames[1].document.write( "<TR><TD>Santa
Cruz</TD><TD>8:00 AM</TD></TR>")
        parent.frames[1].document.write( "<TR><TD>Ithaca</TD><TD>8:30
AM</TD></TR>")
```

**Listing 3.14 Continued**

```
        parent.frames[1].document.write( "<TR><TD>Paris</TD><TD>9:00
AM</TD></TR>")
        parent.frames[1].document.write( "<TR><TD>London</TD><TD>9:30
AM</TD></TR>")
        parent.frames[1].document.write( "</TABLE>")
        parent.frames[1].document.write( "</CENTER>")
        parent.frames[1].document.close()
        }
        function Afternoon()
        {
        parent.frames[1].document.open()
        parent.frames[1].document.write( "<CENTER>")
        parent.frames[1].document.write( "<TABLE BORDER BGCOLOR =
'#ffff00'>")
        parent.frames[1].document.write( "<TR><TH COLSPAN =
2>Afternoon Flights</TH></TR>")
        parent.frames[1].document.write(
"<TR><TD>Pittsburgh</TD><TD>12:00 PM</TD></TR>")
        parent.frames[1].document.write( "<TR><TD>San
Francisco</TD><TD>12:30 PM</TD></TR>")
        parent.frames[1].document.write( "<TR><TD>Boston</TD><TD>1:30
PM</TD></TR>")
        parent.frames[1].document.write( "<TR><TD>Santa
Cruz</TD><TD>3:30 PM</TD></TR>")
        parent.frames[1].document.write( "<TR><TD>Ithaca</TD><TD>4:00
AM</TD></TR>")
        parent.frames[1].document.write( "<TR><TD>Paris</TD><TD>4:30
PM</TD></TR>")
        parent.frames[1].document.write( "<TR><TD>London</TD><TD>5:00
PM</TD></TR>")
        parent.frames[1].document.write( "</TABLE>")
        parent.frames[1].document.write( "</CENTER>")
        parent.frames[1].document.close()
        }
        function Evening()
        {
        parent.frames[1].document.open()
        parent.frames[1].document.write( "<CENTER>")
        parent.frames[1].document.write( "<TABLE BORDER BGCOLOR =
'#ffff00'>")
```

*Continued*

**Listing 3.14 Continued**

```
        parent.frames[1].document.write( "<TR><TH COLSPAN = 2>Evening
Flights</TH></TR>")
        parent.frames[1].document.write(
"<TR><TD>Pittsburgh</TD><TD>6:30 PM</TD></TR>")
        parent.frames[1].document.write( "<TR><TD>San
Francisco</TD><TD>7:00 PM</TD></TR>")
        parent.frames[1].document.write( "<TR><TD>Boston</TD><TD>7:30
PM</TD></TR>")
        parent.frames[1].document.write( "<TR><TD>Santa
Cruz</TD><TD>8:00 PM</TD></TR>")
        parent.frames[1].document.write( "<TR><TD>Ithaca</TD><TD>8:30
PM</TD></TR>")
        parent.frames[1].document.write( "<TR><TD>Paris</TD><TD>9:00
PM</TD></TR>")
        parent.frames[1].document.write( "<TR><TD>London</TD><TD>9:30
PM</TD></TR>")
        parent.frames[1].document.write( "</TABLE>")
        parent.frames[1].document.write( "</CENTER>")
        parent.frames[1].document.close()
        }
</SCRIPT>
</HTML>
```

The major difference between the two browsers we're working with so far has been the language we're using: VBScript or JavaScript. However, in the next chapter, the differences will become major, especially when we deal with the new Dynamic HTML events. For that reason, the last example we'll look at in this chapter is a Web page that rewrites itself based on the Web browser you're loading it into. You can modify this page if you like to write entire pages on the fly, using Netscape or Microsoft code as appropriate.

# Rewriting a Web Page
# Depending on the Browser

In our last example for this chapter, we'll cause a Web page to rewrite itself depending on which browser it's being loaded into. For example, if a user loads a page into Netscape Navigator, the user will see this message written in HTML:

---

```
|            What's your browser?             |
|                                             |
|      You're running Netscape Navigator 4.0  |
|                                             |
|                                             |
|                                             |
 ---------------------------------------------
```

If a user loads the page into Internet Explorer, the user will see this message written in HTML:

```
 ---------------------------------------------
|                                             |
|---------------------------------------------|
|            What's your browser?             |
|                                             |
| You're running Microsoft Internet Explorer 4.0 |
|                                             |
|                                             |
|                                             |
 ---------------------------------------------
```

This example is actually easier to write than you might think. All we have to do is to use JavaScript to check the appName and appVersion properties of the navigator object, which is an object common to both browsers. If we're running in Internet Explorer, appName will be a string reading, "Microsoft Internet Explorer," so we can display that fact in HTML with document.write() and the appVersion property:

```
<HTML>

<HEAD>
<TITLE>What's your browser?</TITLE>
</HEAD>

<BODY>
<CENTER>
<H1>What's your browser?</H1>
</CENTER>

<SCRIPT LANGUAGE = JavaScript>

    if (navigator.appName == "Microsoft Internet Explorer") {
        document.write("<H3><CENTER>")
```

```
        document.write("You're running Microsoft Internet Explorer " +
navigator.appVersion)
        document.write("</H3></CENTER>")
    }
    .
    .
    .
```

On the other hand, if the user is loading the page in Netscape Navigator, appName will be "Netscape," so we display that fact in HTML, along with the Netscape version this way:

```
<HTML>

<HEAD>
<TITLE>What's your browser?</TITLE>
</HEAD>

<BODY>
<CENTER>
<H1>What's your browser?</H1>
</CENTER>

<SCRIPT LANGUAGE = JavaScript>

    if (navigator.appName == "Microsoft Internet Explorer") {          ⇐
        document.write("<H3><CENTER>")                                 ⇐
        document.write("You're running Microsoft Internet Explorer " +
navigator.appVersion)                                                  ⇐
        document.write("</H3></CENTER>")                               ⇐
    }

    if(navigator.appName == "Netscape") {
        document.write("<H3><CENTER>")
        document.write("You're running Netscape Navigator " + naviga-
tor.appVersion)
        document.write("</H3></CENTER>")
    }

</SCRIPT>

</BODY>

</HTML>
```

If you open this page in Netscape 4.0, you'll see the result shown in Figure 3.15, where the page reports it is running in that browser.

On the other hand, if you open the page in Internet Explorer, you'll see a result more like that in Figure 3.16, where the page reports it is running in Explorer. Our browser.htm example is a success. Now we can determine the type and version of the browser and write our Web page accordingly.

The code for Figure 3.15, browser.htm, appears in Listing 3.15.

**Listing 3.15 browser.htm**

```
<HTML>

<HEAD>
<TITLE>What's your browser?</TITLE>
</HEAD>
```

*Continued*

**Figure 3.15 Message stating the page is loaded in Netscape Navigator.**

**Figure 3.16 Message stating the page is loaded in Internet Explorer.**

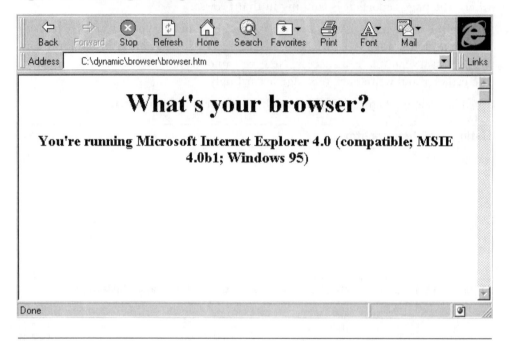

**Listing 3.15 Continued**

```
<BODY>
<CENTER>
<H1>What's your browser?</H1>
</CENTER>

<SCRIPT LANGUAGE = JavaScript>

    if (navigator.appName == "Microsoft Internet Explorer") {
        document.write("<H3><CENTER>")
        document.write("You're running Microsoft Internet Explorer " +
navigator.appVersion)
        document.write("</H3></CENTER>")
    }

    if(navigator.appName == "Netscape") {
```

```
      document.write("<H3><CENTER>")
      document.write("You're running Netscape Navigator " + naviga-
tor.appVersion)
      document.write("</H3></CENTER>")
   }

</SCRIPT>

</BODY>

</HTML>
```

## What's Ahead

That completes this chapter. We've come far, seeing how to write a Web page on the fly according to the time of day, directions from the user, and button clicks. We've seen how to rewrite an element in our Web page in response to a mouse click, how to change text using text ranges, and how to write HTML to documents in other frames. And we've even seen how to determine what browser our page is being loaded in and how to write our page accordingly. Our HTML has truly become dynamic.

In the next chapter, we'll start exploring more of what Dynamic HTML has to offer us: mouse and text effects. These effects are a big part of Dynamic HTML.

# CHAPTER FOUR

# POWERFUL MOUSE

## *and Text Effects*

**T**his chapter examines what Dynamic HTML can do when it comes to using the mouse and handling text. This is an important part of making Web pages "come alive," because as the user moves the mouse over your Web page, you can cause hyperlinks to be highlighted when the mouse is near them, make text "grow" or shrink, change images, and more.

We'll start by seeing how handling the mouse works in Dynamic HTML with an example named mouser.htm. This Web page will report to us on the location of mouse events, such as when a mouse button was pressed, where the mouse is when the user moves it, and so on.

This is also a chapter on text handling. For example, we'll let the user *select* (that is, highlight) everything in a Web page with the click of a button. In addition, we'll also read the text that the user has selected with the mouse and display it in a text box.

We'll even read characters from the keyboard. In the example in this chapter, we'll read keys *directly* from the keyboard as the user types them, and we'll handle them in our page.

Finally, we'll work with *styles* in this chapter. We'll create style classes and apply those classes to text. We'll also redefine the style of standard HTML elements. For example, we'll redefine the size of the text in <H1> headers to be 52 point (which is a great deal larger than the default size). Finally, we'll get an introduction to *cascading style sheets* (CSS) when we see how styles can be *inherited*.

Regrettably, Internet Explorer and Netscape Navigator diverge for all topics in this chapter: mouse handling, keyboard handling, and style sheets. This means that although the topics we'll cover will be the same for both browsers, the details will be different. There's a lot coming up in this chapter, though, so let's start at once with the mouse.

## Using the Mouse in Internet Explorer

Our first Web page example in this chapter will show us how to work with the mouse in Internet Explorer. In particular, our page will display the header "Mouse demo" and a text box:

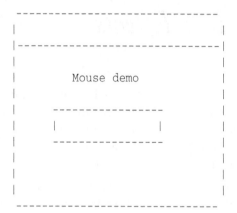

We'll be able to report on the user's mouse actions in the text box. For example, if the user clicks the mouse at a certain location in our page, we'll report that location's coordinates. The first coordinate is the $x$ coordinate, which indicates the mouse's horizontal position in pixels; the second coordinate is the $y$ coordinate, which indicates the mouse's vertical position in pixels (positive $y$ is downward in Web pages):

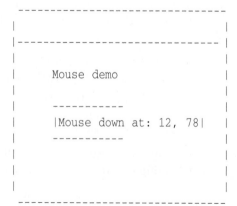

When the user moves the mouse, we can report its new position:

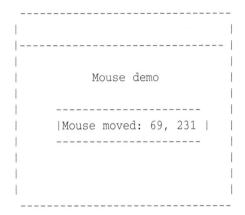

We'll also note when the mouse is over our Internet Explorer page and when it's been moved away from our page. Let's start this example, mouser.htm, now. We begin with the header "Mouse demo" and the text box we'll use to report the user's actions:

```
<HTML>

<HEAD>
<TITLE>Mouser</TITLE>
</HEAD>

<BODY>

<CENTER>
<H1>Mouse demo</H1>                              ⇐
<BR>
<BR>
<INPUT ID = Textbox TYPE = TEXT SIZE = 20>
</CENTER>

</BODY>
        .
        .
        .
```

Now we'll start handling the mouse. (In this example, we'll examine the mouse's actions on the document, but keep in mind that most visible HTML elements in Internet Explorer can now handle the same mouse events as the ones we'll take a look at, so you could use the same events in headers, images, tables, and so on!) We'll start with a simple mouse event: onMouseOver.

## The onMouseOver Event

The document's onMouseOver event occurs when the user moves the mouse over the document. We'll simply report to the user that the mouse is over the document this way:

```
<HTML>

<HEAD>
<TITLE>Mouser</TITLE>
</HEAD>

<BODY>
    .
    .
    .
</BODY>

<SCRIPT LANGUAGE= "VBSCRIPT">

    SUB document_onMouseOver                              ⇐
        Textbox.Value = "Mouse Over"                      ⇐
    END SUB                                               ⇐
    .
    .
    .
```

When we open this page in Internet Explorer and move the mouse over the document, the Web page reports that action, as shown in Figure 4.1.

We'll use onMouseOver extensively in this chapter. Now let's take a look at the onMouseOut event.

## The onMouseOut Event

The document's onMouseOut event occurs when the mouse leaves the document. We can report that this way in our Web page's HTML:

**Figure 4.1 Using the onMouseOver event.**

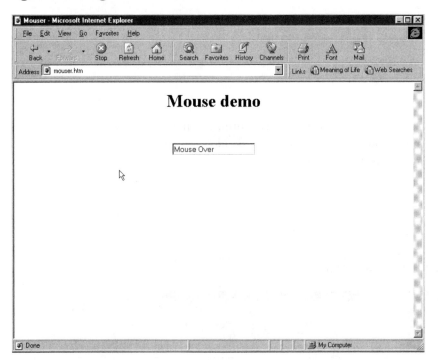

```
<HTML>

<HEAD>
<TITLE>Mouser</TITLE>
</HEAD>

<BODY>
    .
    .
    .
</BODY>

<SCRIPT LANGUAGE= "VBSCRIPT">

    SUB document_onMouseOver
```

```
        Textbox.Value = "Mouse Over"
END SUB
SUB document_onMouseOut                                              ⇐
        Textbox.Value = "Mouse Out"                                  ⇐
END SUB                                                              ⇐
    .
    .
    .
```

Open the page now in Internet Explorer, as shown in Figure 4.2. When you move the mouse out of the document's window, the Web page reports that the mouse is out. So far, the mouser Web page is a success.

Next, we'll take a look at the onMouseDown event.

**Figure 4.2 Using the onMouseOut event.**

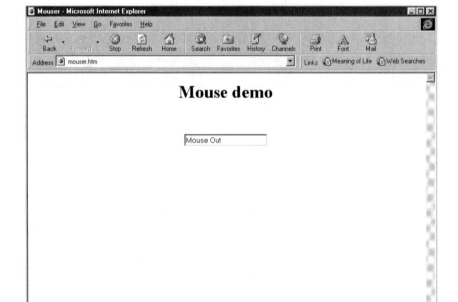

## The onMouseDown Event

The onMouseDown event handler looks like this in general:

```
Private Sub object_onMouseDown()
```

Note that we are passed no parameters here—how do we know where the mouse went down? It turns out that we can use the *event* object, which is a member of the window object. To find the x position of the mouse, then, we'd use the value window.event.x (this value is a long integer; long integers have twice as much storage space allocated to them—usually 4 bytes—as standard integer variables), and the window.event.y value holds the y location of the mouse.

The window.event.button parameter is 1 if the left mouse button is down, 2 if the right mouse button is down, and 4 if the middle mouse button is down (note that these values add: if both the left and right mouse buttons are down, the button parameter will hold 3, for example).

The window.event.shiftKey parameter is 1 if the Shift key was pressed when the mouse button was pressed, 2 if the Ctrl key was pressed, and 4 if the Alt key was pressed.

We can report the x and y position at which the user pressed the mouse button this way in OnMouseDown():

```
<HTML>

<HEAD>
<TITLE>Mouser</TITLE>
</HEAD>

<BODY>
    .
    .
    .
</BODY>

<SCRIPT LANGUAGE= "VBSCRIPT">

    SUB document_onMouseOver()
        Textbox.Value = "Mouse Over"
    END SUB

    SUB document_onMouseOut()
        Textbox.Value = "Mouse Out"
    END SUB
```

```
SUB document_onMouseDown()                                              ⇐
     Textbox.Value = "Mouse down at: " & window.event.x & "," &
window.event.y                                                          ⇐
   END SUB                                                              ⇐
   .
   .
   .
```

That's all there is to it—open the Web page in Internet Explorer and click the mouse somewhere in the document. When you do, the Web page reports the location of the mouse, as also shown in Figure 4.3. Now we're able to locate the mouse!

The last mouse event is the onMouseMove event.

## The onMouseMove Event

Here's how you use the onMouseMove event:

```
Private Sub object_onMouseMove()
```

**Figure 4.3 Using the onMouseDown event.**

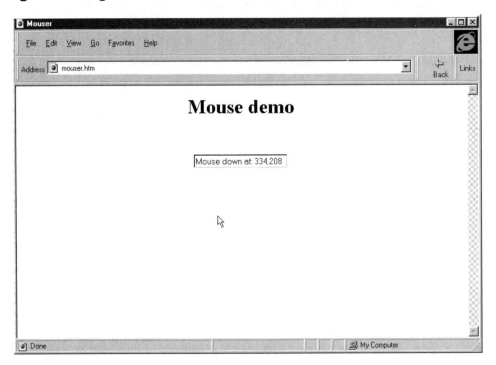

You get the mouse location and button state as you do in the onMouseDown() event with the event object. In our example, we can report the location to which the user has moved the mouse—note that when we add the document_onMouseMove() subroutine to our Web page that the page will no longer report when the mouse is over the document, because the mouse move event handler is called after the mouse over event handler (which means the mouse move message will overwrite the mouse over message). Here's the code for the mouse move event:

```
<HTML>

<HEAD>
<TITLE>Mouser</TITLE>
</HEAD>

<BODY>
    .
    .
    .
</BODY>

<SCRIPT LANGUAGE= "VBSCRIPT">

    SUB document_onMouseOver()
        Textbox.Value = "Mouse Over"
    END SUB

    SUB document_onMouseOut()
        Textbox.Value = "Mouse Out"
    END SUB

    SUB document_onMouseDown()
        Textbox.Value = "Mouse down at: " & window.event.x & "," &
window.event.y
    END SUB

    SUB document_onMouseMove()                                       ⇐
        Textbox.Value = "Mouse moved: " & window.event.x & "," &
window.event.y                                                       ⇐
    END SUB                                                          ⇐
```

```
</SCRIPT>

</BODY>
</HTML>
```

Open the Web page in Internet Explorer now, as shown in Figure 4.4, and move the mouse in the document; when you do, the Web page displays the new location of the mouse.

We've seen how to work with the mouse now, and that's a crucial part of Dynamic HTML, as we'll see in this chapter. The code for this Internet Explorer page, mouser.htm, appears in Listing 4.1.

**Figure 4.4 Using the onMouseMove event.**

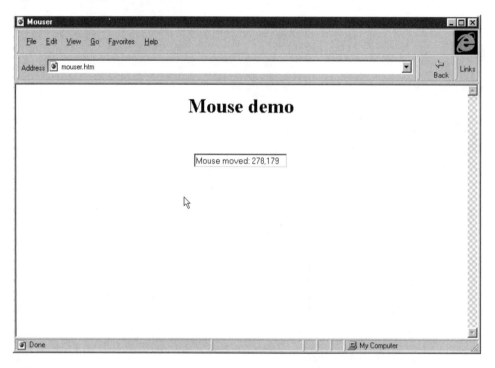

**Listing 4.1 mouser.htm**

```
<HTML>

<HEAD>
```

**Listing 4.1 Continued**

```
<TITLE>Mouser</TITLE>
</HEAD>

<BODY>

<CENTER>
<H1>Mouse demo</H1>
<BR>
<BR>
<INPUT ID = Textbox TYPE = TEXT SIZE = 20>
</CENTER>

</BODY>

<SCRIPT LANGUAGE= "VBSCRIPT">
    SUB document_onMouseOver()
        Textbox.Value = "Mouse Over"
    END SUB

    SUB document_onMouseOut()
        Textbox.Value = "Mouse Out"
    END SUB

    SUB document_onMouseDown()
        Textbox.Value = "Mouse down at: " & window.event.x & "," &
window.event.y
    END SUB

    SUB document_onMouseMove()
        Textbox.Value = "Mouse moved: " & window.event.x & "," &
window.event.y
    END SUB

</SCRIPT>

</BODY>
</HTML>
```

Now we've seen how to use the mouse in the Internet Explorer. Let's take a look at using the mouse in Netscape Navigator next—where things are almost completely different.

## Table 4.1 Netscape Navigator Event Object Properties

| Event Property | Means This |
| --- | --- |
| type | Event type |
| layerX | The cursor's horizontal position relative to the layer in which the event occurred |
| layerY | The cursor's vertical position in pixels, relative to the layer in which the event occurred |
| pageX | The cursor's horizontal position in pixels, relative to the page |
| pageY | The cursor's vertical position in pixels, relative to the page |
| screenX | The cursor's horizontal position in pixels, relative to the screen |
| screenY | The cursor's vertical position in pixels, relative to the screen |
| which | The mouse button that was pressed or the ASCII value of a pressed key |
| modifiers | The modifier keys associated with a mouse or key event; possible values are ALT_MASK, CONTROL_MASK, SHIFT_MASK, and META_MASK |
| data | An array of strings containing the URLs of the dropped objects (use with the dragdrop event) |

# Using the Mouse in Netscape Navigator

When you use the mouse in Netscape Navigator, you still use the onMouseDown, onMouseUp, onMouseOver, and onMouseOut events, but the way you handle those events is different from Internet Explorer. In Netscape Navigator, your event-handling function is passed to an event object. The Netscape event object has several properties that tell you the mouse's location and more, as shown in Table 4.1.

Let's put together the mouser example for Netscape Navigator, mouserj.htm, now. We start with the text box we'll use to report mouse events:

```
<HTML>

<HEAD>
<TITLE>Mouser</TITLE>
</HEAD>


<BODY>
```

```
<CENTER>
<FORM name = "form1">

<H1>Mouse demo</H1>
<BR>
<BR>
<INPUT TYPE = "text" name = "Textbox" SIZE = 30>                    ⇐
</FORM>
     .
     .
     .
```

Next, we connect the mouseDown event to our code. We can't just use the VBScript shorthand technique of connecting the document's onMouseDown event to a subroutine named document_onMouseDown() here; instead, we must explicitly connect the document object's onMouseDown event to the function mouseDownhandler(). We do the same for the onMouseUp event, connecting that to the mouseUpHandler() function:

```
<HTML>

<HEAD>
<TITLE>Mouser</TITLE>
</HEAD>

<BODY>
     .
     .
     .
</BODY>

<SCRIPT LANGUAGE= "JavaScript">

    document.onMouseDown = mouseDownHandler              ⇐
    document.onMouseUp = mouseUpHandler                  ⇐
     .
     .
     .
```

We note in passing here that although Netscape is usually very strongly case-sensitive, one exception is event naming—an event like onMouseDown is the same as onmousedown, ONMOUSEDOWN, and so on.

Next, we write those two mouse-handling functions, naming the event object passed and getting the *x* and *y* screen coordinates of the mouse from the e.screenX and e.screenY:

```
<HTML>

<HEAD>
<TITLE>Mouser</TITLE>
</HEAD>


<BODY>
    .
    .
    .
</BODY>

<SCRIPT LANGUAGE= "JavaScript">

    document.onMouseDown = mouseDownHandler
    document.onMouseUp = mouseUpHandler

    function mouseDownHandler(e)
    {
        document.form1.Textbox.value = "Mouse down at: " + e.screenX +
", " + e.screenY                                                    ⇐
    }

    function mouseUpHandler(e)
    {
        document.form1.Textbox.value = "Mouse up at: " + e.screenX +
", " + e.screenY                                                    ⇐
    }
    .
    .
    .
```

That completes the onMouseDown and onMouseUp event handlers.

Next, let's add handlers for the onMouseOver and onMouseOut events. The document object does not support these events in Netscape Navigator, but hyperlinks do, so we add a hyperlink and connect its onMouseOver and onMouseOut events to the matching event handlers:

```
<HTML>
<HEAD>
<TITLE>Mouser</TITLE>
</HEAD>

<BODY>

<CENTER>
<FORM name = "form1">

<H1>Mouse demo</H1>
<BR>
<BR>
<INPUT TYPE = "text" name = "Textbox" SIZE = 30>
<BR>
<BR>
<A HREF = "mouserj.htm" onMouseOver = "mouseOverHandler()"
    onMouseOut = "mouseOutHandler()">                          ⇐
    Move the mouse over this hyperlink!</A>
</FORM>

</CENTER>

</BODY>
```

Then we just write those event handlers:

```
<HTML>

<HEAD>
<TITLE>Mouser</TITLE>
</HEAD>

<BODY>
    .
    .
    .
```

```
</BODY>

<SCRIPT LANGUAGE= "JavaScript">

    document.onMouseDown = mouseDownHandler
    document.onMouseUp = mouseUpHandler
    function mouseDownHandler(e)
    {
        document.form1.Textbox.value = "Mouse down at: " + e.screenX +
", " + e.screenY
    }

    function mouseUpHandler(e)
    {
        document.form1.Textbox.value = "Mouse up at: " + e.screenX +
", " + e.screenY
    }

    function mouseOverHandler(e)                                    ⇐
    {
        document.form1.Textbox.value = "Mouse is over the hyperlink"
    }

    function mouseOutHandler(e)                                     ⇐
    {
        document.form1.Textbox.value = "Mouse has left the hyperlink"
    }

</SCRIPT>

</HTML>
```

That's all we need. Open the Web page in Netscape Navigator, as shown in Figure 4.5. When you click the mouse in the page, you'll see mouse down and mouse up events displayed, and when you move the mouse over or out of the hyperlink, you'll see those events displayed. Now we're using the mouse in Netscape Navigator.

The code for this example, mouserj.htm, appears in Listing 4.2.

**Figure 4.5 Using the mouse directly in Netscape Navigator.**

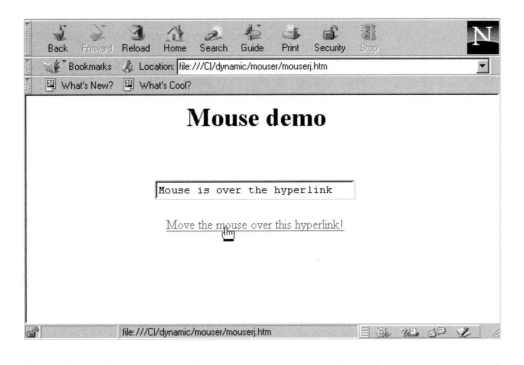

**Listing 4.2 mouserj.htm**

```
<HTML>

<HEAD>
<TITLE>Mouser</TITLE>
</HEAD>


<BODY>

<CENTER>
<FORM name = "form1">
```

*Continued*

**Listing 4.2 Continued**

```
<H1>Mouse demo</H1>
<BR>
<BR>
<INPUT TYPE = "text" name = "Textbox" SIZE = 30>
<BR>
<BR>
<A HREF = "mouserj.htm" onMouseOver = "mouseOverHandler()"
    onMouseOut = "mouseOutHandler()">
    Move the mouse over this hyperlink!</A>
</FORM>

</CENTER>

</BODY>


<SCRIPT LANGUAGE= "JavaScript">

    document.onMouseDown = mouseDownHandler
    document.onMouseUp = mouseUpHandler

    function mouseDownHandler(e)
    {
        document.form1.Textbox.value = "Mouse down at: " + e.screenX +
", " + e.screenY
    }

    function mouseUpHandler(e)
    {
        document.form1.Textbox.value = "Mouse up at: " + e.screenX +
", " + e.screenY
    }

    function mouseOverHandler(e)
    {
        document.form1.Textbox.value = "Mouse is over the hyperlink"
    }

    function mouseOutHandler(e)
    {
        document.form1.Textbox.value = "Mouse has left the hyperlink"
```

**Listing 4.2 Continued**

```
    }
</SCRIPT>
</HTML>
```

Now that we've worked with the mouse, let's turn to working with text for a moment—then we'll combine the two, handling both the mouse and text together.

# Selecting Text from Code in Internet Explorer

We've seen Internet Explorer text ranges in the last chapter. Now we'll take a more detailed look at Internet Explorer text ranges.

The user can select text in a Web page simply by dragging the mouse over the text. In this new example and the next one, we'll see how to work with selected text. In our first example, the user will select everything in an Internet Explorer Web page with the click of a mouse. Let's call this new example selectit.htm.

We start by placing some items into our Web page—some text, a button with the caption "Click me to select everything," and a text box. We also connect the button to a subroutine named SelectAll():

```
<HTML>

<HEAD>
<TITLE>Select everything example</TITLE>
</HEAD>


<BODY ID = BODY1>

<CENTER>
<BR>
Here is some text.                                          ⇐
<BR>
<BR>
<INPUT TYPE = BUTTON VALUE = "Click me to select everything" onClick =
SelectAll()></INPUT>                                        ⇐
<BR>
<BR>
<INPUT TYPE = TEXT SIZE = 20></INPUT>                       ⇐

</CENTER>
```

```
</BODY>
   .
   .
   .
```

To select everything in the page, the user clicks the button, calling the SelectAll() subroutine. In that subroutine, we'll start by creating a text range named textrange. We set aside storage space for the textrange object with the VBScript Dim keyword and create a text range for our page's entire body with the CreateTextRange() method:

```
<HTML>

<HEAD>
<TITLE>Select everything example</TITLE>
</HEAD>


<BODY ID = BODY1>
   .
   .
   .
</BODY>

<SCRIPT LANGUAGE = VBSCRIPT>

SUB SelectAll()
        Dim textrange                                      ⇐
        set textrange = BODY1.CreateTextRange()            ⇐
         .
         .
         .

END SUB
   .
   .
   .
```

Note the VBScript keyword set; you must use this keyword when assigning an object such as a text range to a variable like textrange. (You don't use the set keyword for normal assignments like integer15 = 5, only for objects.) We'll see a great deal more about objects later in this book.

Now that we have our text range, we can select everything in the document with the text range's select() method. That method highlights everything in the text range on the screen, and because our text range includes the whole body, that's everything in the page:

```
<HTML>

<HEAD>
<TITLE>Select everything example</TITLE>
</HEAD>
<BODY ID = BODY1>
     .
     .
     .
</BODY>

<SCRIPT LANGUAGE = VBSCRIPT>

SUB SelectAll()
        Dim textrange
        set textrange = BODY1.CreateTextRange()
        textrange.select()                                      ⇐
END SUB

</SCRIPT>

</HTML>
```

That's all we need. Now open the Web page in Internet Explorer, as shown in Figure 4.6, and click the button. When you do, everything in the page is selected, as shown in Figure 4.6. The user can then copy the selected text to the clipboard. In fact, you can even support cut-and-paste operations in your page by modifying the HTML to match the user's wishes.

We've selected everything in our Web page, but note that you can place only part of the page into a text range, and when you execute the select() method, just that part of the page will be selected.

The code for this page, selectit.htm, appears in Listing 4.3.

**Listing 4.3 selectit.htm**

```
<HTML>

<HEAD>
```

*Continued*

**Figure 4.6 Selecting everything in a Web page with the select() method.**

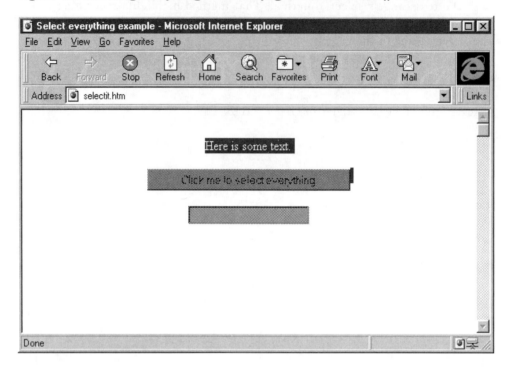

**Listing 4.3 Continued**

```
<TITLE>Select everything example</TITLE>
</HEAD>


<BODY ID = BODY1>

<CENTER>
<BR>
Here is some text.
<BR>
<BR>
<INPUT TYPE = BUTTON VALUE = "Click me to select everything" onClick =
SelectAll()></INPUT>
<BR>
```

**Listing 4.3 Continued**

```
<BR>
<INPUT TYPE = TEXT SIZE = 20></INPUT>

</CENTER>

</BODY>

<SCRIPT LANGUAGE = VBSCRIPT>

SUB SelectAll()
        Dim textrange
        set textrange = BODY1.CreateTextRange()
        textrange.select()
END SUB

</SCRIPT>

</HTML>
```

That's one example showing how to work with selected text. In this example, we did the selecting ourselves. But what if the user, not our script, selects the text? Let's look into this now.

## User's Text Selections in Internet Explorer

Let's see how to work with text that the user selects with the mouse in Internet Explorer. For example, we might have a Web page with the prompt: "Select some of this text with the mouse..." and a text box:

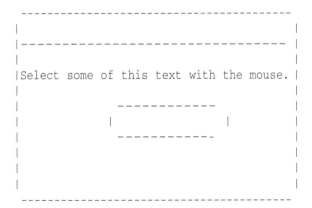

When the user selects some of the text using the mouse, the page will automatically display the selected text in the text box:

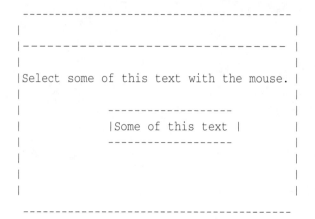

In this way, our page will be able to handle text that the user has selected as soon as it is selected.

Let's put together this Internet Explorer example, selects.htm, now. We start with the prompt to the user and the text box we'll need:

```
<HTML>

<BODY ID = BODY1>

<CENTER>
Select some of this text with the mouse...                    ⇐
<BR>
<BR>

<INPUT TYPE = TEXT NAME = textbox SIZE = 40>                   ⇐
</CENTER>

</BODY>
        .
        .
        .
```

Now that our text appears on the screen, the user can select all or part of that text with the mouse. When the user does so, the document's onClick event occurs, and we can get a text range for the text the user has selected with the selection object.

## Using the Internet Explorer Selection Object

The *selection object* is part of the document object, and we can use the selection object's CreateRange() method to get a text range for the selection the user has made. Once we have that text range, we can display the text in it using that range's text property, which holds the text in the range:

```
<HTML>

<BODY ID = BODY1>
    .
    .
    .
</BODY>

<SCRIPT LANGUAGE = VBSCRIPT>

SUB document_onClick()⇐
        Dim textrange                                          ⇐
        set textrange = document.selection.CreateRange()       ⇐
        textbox.Value = "You selected this text: """ & textrange.text
& """"                                                         ⇐
END SUB                                                        ⇐

</SCRIPT>

</HTML>
```

Open the page now in Internet Explorer and select some of the text there with the mouse—as soon as you do, the selection you've made appears in the text box, as shown in Figure 4.7. Our example works as intended; now we can determine what text the user has selected as soon as it is selected (and without the need to click any other controls).

The code for this page, selects.htm, appears in Listing 4.4.

**Figure 4.7 Reporting the text the user has selected in a Web page.**

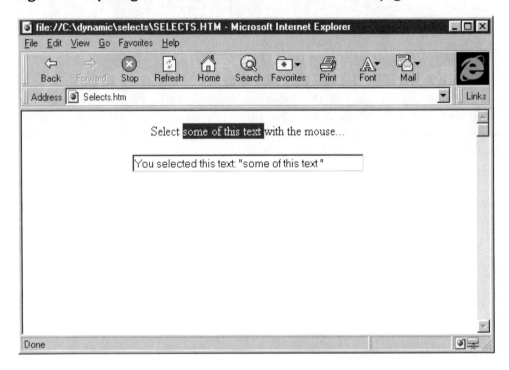

**Listing 4.4 selects.htm**

```
<HTML>

<BODY ID = BODY1>
<CENTER>
Select some of this text with the mouse...
<BR>
<BR>

<INPUT TYPE = TEXT NAME = textbox SIZE = 40>
</CENTER>

</BODY>

<SCRIPT LANGUAGE = VBSCRIPT>
```

**Listing 4.4 Continued**

```
SUB document_onClick()
        Dim textrange
        set textrange = document.selection.CreateRange()
        textbox.Value = "You selected this text: """ & textrange.text
& """"
END SUB

</SCRIPT>

</HTML>
```

Now that we've worked with text and worked with the mouse, let's put the two together as we see how to highlight and enlarge text as the user brings the mouse near that text. We do this using dynamic *styles*. Styles are something new in both browsers, and we'll see how to use them later in this chapter. Using styles, you can change the presentation of your text's color, size, indentation, and more. We'll take a look at Internet Explorer's styles first, because you can change them on the fly, which means we can enlarge or color text when the mouse moves near that text, producing some striking effects.

# Highlighting and Enlarging
# Text in Internet Explorer

Our next example will be targeted to Internet Explorer, and we'll see how to use text and the mouse together. We'll display four hyperlinks in our page:

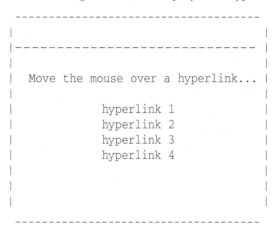

When the user moves the mouse near a hyperlink, we can "grow"—that is, enlarge—that hyperlink's text on the screen and color it. Let's put this to work now in an Internet Explorer example named hilight.htm. We start this example with the text prompt and four hyperlinks:

```
<HTML>
<HEAD>
<TITLE>Highlighting text with the mouse</TITLE>
</HEAD>

<BODY LINK = 0000>

<CENTER>
<H1>Move the mouse over a hyperlink...</H1>
<A HREF="http://www.microsoft.com" name= link1>hyperlink 1</A>
<br>
<A HREF="http://www.microsoft.com" name= link2>hyperlink 2</A>
<br>
<A HREF="http://www.microsoft.com" name= link3>hyperlink 3</A>
<br>
<A HREF="http://www.microsoft.com" name= link4>hyperlink 4</A>
</CENTER>

</BODY>
     .
     .
     .
```

Next, we can use each link's onMouseOver event to watch mouse movements. When the mouse moves over a hyperlink, we can enlarge that hyperlink and color it. For example, when the mouse is over link1, link1_onMouseOver() will be called, and we can grow and color the hyperlink's text in that subroutine. We'll choose magenta for our color and 24 points for our font size.

To change the first hyperlink text's font size to 24, we simply execute this code in Internet Explorer: link1.style.fontSize = 24. This changes the fontSize property of the link's STYLE attribute. (Styles are a topic we'll dig further into later in this chapter.) To change the link's color to magenta, we'll execute this code: link1.style.color = "magenta". In link1_onMouseOver(), that looks like the code here, where we use the name we've given the first link, link1:

```
<HTML>
```

```
<HEAD>
<TITLE>Highlighting text with the mouse</TITLE>
</HEAD>

<BODY LINK = 0000>
    .
    .
    .
</BODY>

<SCRIPT LANGUAGE= "VBSCRIPT">
    sub link1_onMouseOver                         ⇐
        link1.style.color="magenta"               ⇐
        link1.style.fontSize=24                   ⇐
    End Sub                                        ⇐
    .
    .
    .
```

We might note here that we could also use the document's anchors collection to reach the first link, because collections are also indexed by element name—that is, link1.style.color = "magenta" is the same as document.anchors ("link1").style.color = "magenta".

In future versions of Netscape Navigator, the browser will let you change the style of particular Web page elements using the STYLE attribute as we have done here with Internet Explorer (the styles you set with a tag's STYLE attribute are called *in-line* styles), but at this writing, you can't use an individual HTML tag's STYLE attribute in Navigator yet. The following code is how Netscape will implement the STYLE attribute (you can also use an HTML tag's CLASS attribute to do the same thing, as we'll see later, and that attribute does work now):

```
<HTML>
<BODY>
<P STYLE="color = 'fuchsia'">This text is fuchsia.</P>
<P>This text is in the normal color.</P>
</BODY>
</HTML>
```

When the user moves the mouse away from the hyperlink in Internet Explorer, the hyperlink's onMouseOut event occurs, and we can reset the styles of the hyperlink back to normal:

```
<HTML>
<HEAD>
<TITLE>Highlighting text with the mouse</TITLE>
</HEAD>
<BODY LINK = 0000>
    .
    .
    .
</BODY>

<SCRIPT LANGUAGE= "VBSCRIPT">
    sub link1_onMouseOver
        link1.style.color="magenta"
        link1.style.fontSize=24
    End Sub
    sub link1_onMouseOut                                    ⇐
        link1.style.color="black"                           ⇐
        link1.style.fontSize=16                             ⇐
    End Sub                                                 ⇐
    .
    .
    .
```

We add the same subroutines for the other hyperlinks:

```
<HTML>
<HEAD>
<TITLE>Highlighting text with the mouse</TITLE>
</HEAD>

<BODY LINK = 0000>
    .
    .
    .
</BODY>

<SCRIPT LANGUAGE= "VBSCRIPT">
    sub link1_onMouseOver
        link1.style.color="magenta"
        link1.style.fontSize=24
    End Sub

    sub link1_onMouseOut
```

```
            link1.style.color="black"
            link1.style.fontSize=16
    End Sub

    sub link2_onMouseOver                                    ⇐
            link2.style.color="magenta"                      ⇐
            link2.style.fontSize=24                          ⇐
    End Sub                                                  ⇐

    sub link2_onMouseOut                                     ⇐
            link2.style.color="black"                        ⇐
            link2.style.fontSize=16                          ⇐
    End Sub                                                  ⇐

    sub link3_onMouseOver                                    ⇐
            link3.style.color="magenta"                      ⇐
            link3.style.fontSize=24                          ⇐
    End Sub                                                  ⇐

    sub link3_onMouseOut                                     ⇐
            link3.style.color="black"                        ⇐
            link3.style.fontSize=16                          ⇐
    End Sub                                                  ⇐

    sub link4_onMouseOver                                    ⇐
            link4.style.color="magenta"                      ⇐
            link4.style.fontSize=24                          ⇐
    End Sub                                                  ⇐

    sub link4_onMouseOut                                     ⇐
                link4.style.color="black"                    ⇐
            link4.style.fontSize=16                          ⇐
    End Sub                                                  ⇐

</SCRIPT>

</HTML>
```

Now we open the Web page in Internet Explorer, as shown in Figure 4.8. When the user moves the mouse near a hyperlink, that hyperlink's text grows and its color changes to magenta. Now we're merging our use of the mouse with text effects.

**Figure 4.8 An enlarged and colored hyperlink in response to mouse movements.**

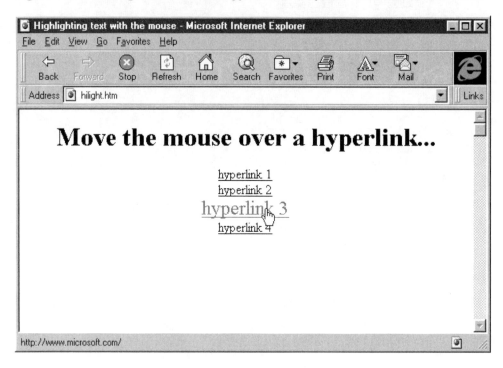

The code for this Web page, hilight.htm, appears in Listing 4.5.

**Listing 4.5 hilight.htm**

```
<HTML>
<HEAD>
<TITLE>Highlighting text with the mouse</TITLE>
</HEAD>

<BODY LINK = 0000>

<CENTER>
<H1>Move the mouse over a hyperlink...</H1>
<A HREF="http://www.microsoft.com" name= link1>hyperlink 1</A>
<br>
<A HREF="http://www.microsoft.com" name= link2>hyperlink 2</A>
```

**Listing 4.5 Continued**

```
<br>
<A HREF="http://www.microsoft.com" name= link3>hyperlink 3</A>
<br>
<A HREF="http://www.microsoft.com" name= link4>hyperlink 4</A>
</CENTER>

</BODY>

<SCRIPT LANGUAGE= "VBSCRIPT">
    sub link1_onMouseOver
        link1.style.color="magenta"
        link1.style.fontSize=24
    End Sub

    sub link1_onMouseOut
        link1.style.color="black"
        link1.style.fontSize=16
    End Sub

    sub link2_onMouseOver
        link2.style.color="magenta"
        link2.style.fontSize=24
    End Sub

    sub link2_onMouseOut
        link2.style.color="black"
        link2.style.fontSize=16
    End Sub

    sub link3_onMouseOver
        link3.style.color="magenta"
        link3.style.fontSize=24
    End Sub

    sub link3_onMouseOut
        link3.style.color="black"
        link3.style.fontSize=16
    End Sub

    sub link4_onMouseOver
        link4.style.color="magenta"
        link4.style.fontSize=24
```

*Continued*

**Listing 4.5 Continued**

```
    End Sub

    sub link4_onMouseOut
        link4.style.color="black"
        link4.style.fontSize=16
    End Sub

</SCRIPT>

</HTML>
```

In this mouse-and-text example, we only placed hyperlinks in our Web page. Now let's take a look at mixing hyperlinks and text in Internet Explorer.

# Highlighting Hyperlinks Only in Internet Explorer

In our next example, we will still highlight hyperlinks in Internet Explorer, but we will embed those hyperlinks in text—and both hyperlinks and text will be enclosed in a <DIV> tag. When the user moves the mouse over the hyperlinks, they will be highlighted, but they won't be highlighted when the user moves the mouse over the text. Let's see how this new example, hilinks.htm, works.

We start with text and a hyperlink placed in a section of the Web page (we create this section with the <DIV> tag):

```
<HTML>

<HEAD>
<TITLE>Highlighting hyperlinks</TITLE>
</HEAD>

<BODY LINK = 0000 VLINK = 0000>

<CENTER>
<H1>Highlighting hyperlinks only...</H1>
<BR>
</CENTER>

<DIV ID = DIV1>
```

```
Dynamic HTML is a product of
<A HREF = "http://www.microsoft.com">microsoft</A>
and you can jump to their site by clicking the hyperlink.
</DIV>

</BODY>
     .
     .
     .
```

When the user moves the mouse over the <DIV> section, we can determine if the mouse is over the a hyperlink by checking the onMouseMove event's source element. If that element is an <A> tag, we know that the mouse is over a hyperlink, and we will highlight it by turning its background color blue and its text white.

We will find out the source element that the mouse is over by checking Internet Explorer's event object—in particular, the srcelement property of that object. The Internet Explorer event object is a member of the window object, so that looks like this:

```
<HTML>

<HEAD>
<TITLE>Highlighting hyperlinks</TITLE>
</HEAD>

<BODY LINK = 0000 VLINK = 0000>
     .
     .
     .
</BODY>

<SCRIPT LANGUAGE = VBSCRIPT>

SUB DIV1_onMouseMove()
    DIM source                                           ⇐
    SET source = window.event.srcelement                 ⇐
     .
     .
     .
```

Note that the Internet Explorer's event object is *not* the same as the Netscape Navigator event object. The Internet Explorer event object has the following properties: id, keyCode, fromElement, toElement, srcelement, button, cancelBubble, x, y, shiftKey, ctrlKey, altKey, and returnValue.

If the type of the source element is an <A> tag, which we will check with the element's tagName property (all tags in Dynamic HTML have this property), then we set its text white and its background blue, like this:

```
<HTML>

<HEAD>
<TITLE>Highlighting hyperlinks</TITLE>
</HEAD>

<BODY LINK = 0000 VLINK = 0000>
    .
    .
    .
</BODY>

<SCRIPT LANGUAGE = VBSCRIPT>

SUB DIV1_onMouseMove()
    DIM source
    SET source = window.event.srcelement
    IF source.tagName="A" THEN                              ⇐
        source.style.color = "white"                        ⇐
        source.style.background = "blue"                    ⇐
    END IF                                                  ⇐
END SUB
    .
    .
    .
```

Similarly, when the mouse leaves the hyperlink, we set that hyperlink's colors back to normal in DIV_onMouseOut():

```
<HTML>

<HEAD>
<TITLE>Highlighting hyperlinks</TITLE>
</HEAD>

<BODY LINK = 0000 VLINK = 0000>
```

```
          .
          .
          .
</BODY>

<SCRIPT LANGUAGE = VBSCRIPT>

SUB DIV1_onMouseMove(button, shift, x, y)
    DIM source
    SET source = window.event.srcelement
    IF source.tagName="A" THEN
        source.style.color = "white"
        source.style.background = "blue"
    END IF
END SUB

SUB DIV1_onMouseOut()⇐
    DIM source                                              ⇐
    set source=window.event.srcelement                     ⇐
    IF source.tagName="A" THEN                              ⇐
        source.style.color="black"                         ⇐
        source.style.background = "white"                  ⇐
    END IF                                                  ⇐
END SUB
</SCRIPT>

</HTML>
```

Open the Web page in Internet Explorer now. When you move the mouse near the hyperlink, it is automatically highlighted, as shown in Figure 4.9—our hilinks.htm examples is a success. In this way, we can make Internet Explorer Web pages come alive as the user simply moves the mouse.

The code for this page, hilink.htm, appears in Listing 4.6.

### Listing 4.6 hilink.htm

```
<HTML>

<HEAD>
<TITLE>Highlighting hyperlinks</TITLE>
</HEAD>
```

*Continued*

**Figure 4.9 Highlighting hyperlinks with the mouse.**

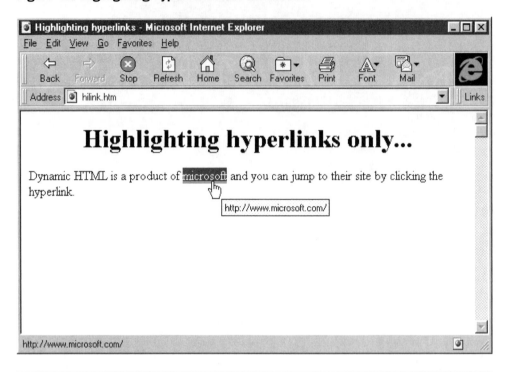

**Listing 4.6 Continued**

```
<BODY LINK = 0000 VLINK = 0000>

<CENTER>
<H1>Highlighting hyperlinks only...</H1>
<BR>
</CENTER>

<DIV ID = DIV1>
Dynamic HTML is a product of
<A HREF = "http://www.microsoft.com">microsoft</A>
and you can jump to their site by clicking the hyperlink.
</DIV>

</BODY>

<SCRIPT LANGUAGE = VBSCRIPT>
```

**Listing 4.6 Continued**

```
SUB DIV1_onMouseMove()
    DIM source
    SET source = window.event.srcelement
    IF source.tagName="A" THEN
        source.style.color = "white"
        source.style.background = "blue"
    END IF
END SUB

SUB DIV1_onMouseOut()
    DIM source
    set source=window.event.srcelement
    IF source.tagName="A" THEN
        source.style.color="black"
        source.style.background = "white"
    END IF
END SUB
</SCRIPT>

</HTML>
```

Now that we've seen that we can work with text dynamically in Internet Explorer, let's cover another text topic: reading text directly from the keyboard in both Internet Explorer and Netscape Navigator.

# Reading Keys from the Keyboard in Internet Explorer

We've worked with text in this chapter already, but not as directly as we're going to work with it now. Our next example will show us how to read straight from the keyboard in Internet Explorer. We'll just place a prompt to the user to type some characters this way, and add a text box for displaying what is typed:

```
        |           ----------------------          |
        |                                            |
        |                                            |
        |                                            |
        ------------------------------------
```

When the user does type some text, our VBScript code (and not the text box) will read that text and display it in the text box:

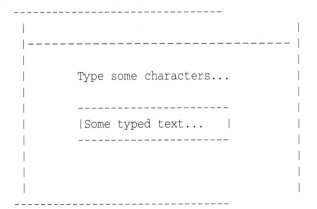

```
        ------------------------------------
        |                                            |
        |------------------------------------|
        |                                            |
        |         Type some characters...            |
        |                                            |
        |         ----------------------             |
        |         |Some typed text...  |             |
        |         ----------------------             |
        |                                            |
        |                                            |
        |                                            |
        ------------------------------------
```

Let's put together this example, keys.htm, now. We start with the prompt to the user and the text box we'll use to display what the user has typed:

```
<HTML>

<HEAD>
<TITLE>Key reading example</TITLE>
</HEAD>

<BODY ID = BODY1>

<CENTER>
<H1>Type some characters...</H1>
<BR>
<BR>
<INPUT NAME = Textbox TYPE = TEXT SIZE = 20>
</CENTER>

</BODY>
```

.

.

Next, we can read the keys the user types with the onKeyPress event. We declare the body's onKeyPress event this way, setting up a string named inString to store the characters the user types:

```
<HTML>

<HEAD>
<TITLE>Key reading example</TITLE>
</HEAD>

<BODY ID = BODY1>
   .

   .

   .

</BODY>

<SCRIPT LANGUAGE = VBSCRIPT>

Dim inString                                        ⇐

private function BODY1_onKeypress()                  ⇐
   .

   .

   .

END function                                        ⇐
   .

   .

   .
```

Now we get the typed key's numeric key code by checking the event object's keyCode property, and we add that key to the string inString, displaying that string in the text box:

```
<HTML>

<HEAD>
<TITLE>Key reading example</TITLE>
</HEAD>

<BODY ID = BODY1>
```

```
          .
          .
          .
</BODY>

<SCRIPT LANGUAGE = VBSCRIPT>

Dim inString

private function BODY1_onKeypress()

        inString = inString & chr(window.event.keyCode)        ⇐
        Textbox.Value = inString                               ⇐

END function
</SCRIPT>

</HTML>
```

---

**Listing 4.7 keys.htm**

```
<HTML>

<HEAD>
<TITLE>Key reading example</TITLE>
</HEAD>

<BODY ID = BODY1>

<CENTER>
<H1>Type some characters...</H1>
<BR>
<BR>
<INPUT NAME = Textbox TYPE = TEXT SIZE = 20>
</CENTER>

</BODY>


<SCRIPT LANGUAGE = VBSCRIPT>

Dim inString
```

---

Now open the Web page in Internet Explorer and type some characters (making sure the text box does not have the focus, or you'd simply be typing text directly into the text box). The text you type appears in the text box, as shown in Fig 4.10 ref. Now we're reading keys from the keyboard. In fact, with a little modification and the pasteHTML() method, you can type directly into Web page elements like headers and tables.

The code for this page, keys.htm, appears in Listing 4.7.

**Figure 4.10 Reading keys directly from the keyboard.**

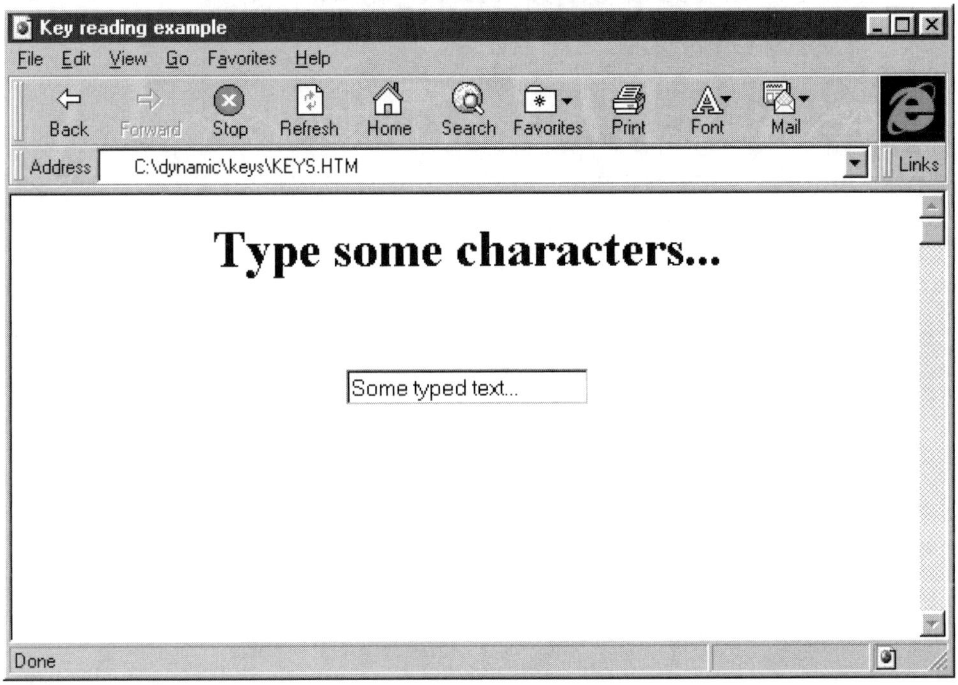

**Listing 4.7 Continued**

```
private function BODY1_onKeypress()

        inString = inString & chr(window.event.keycode)
        Textbox.Value = inString
```
*Continued*

**Listing 4.7 Continued**
```
END function
</SCRIPT>

</HTML>
```
Now that we've seen how to read text directly in Internet Explorer, let's do the same in Netscape Navigator.

# Reading Keys from the Keyboard in Netscape Navigator

We might set up a new example in Netscape Navigator in which we ask the user a difficult question:

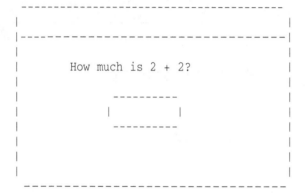

```
 --------------------------------------
|                                      |
|------------------------------------- |
|                                      |
|          How much is 2 + 2?          |
|                                      |
|            ----------                |
|           |          |               |
|            ----------                |
|                                      |
|                                      |
|                                      |
 --------------------------------------
```

If the user answers correctly by pressing "4," we display a congratulatory message:

```
 -----------------------------------
|                                   |
|---------------------------------- |
|                                   |
|          How much is 2 + 2?       |
|                                   |
|          -----------------        |
|         |Correct! 2 + 2 = 4|      |
|          -----------------        |
|                                   |
|                                   |
|                                   |
 -----------------------------------
```

Let's put together this example, keysj.htm, now. We start with our prompt and a text box in which we'll display the results of the user's text entry:

```
<HTML>

<HEAD>
<TITLE>Key reading example</TITLE>
</HEAD>

<BODY>

<CENTER>

<FORM NAME = "form1">
<BR>
<H1>How much is 2 + 2?</H1>
<BR>
<INPUT NAME = Textbox TYPE = TEXT SIZE = 20>
</FORM>
</CENTER>

</BODY>
        .
        .
        .
```

Now we indicate that Navigator should send keystrokes to the function KeyPressHandler() this way:

```
<HTML>

<HEAD>
<TITLE>Key reading example</TITLE>
</HEAD>

<BODY>
        .
        .
        .
</BODY>

<SCRIPT LANGUAGE = JavaScript>
```

```
document.onKeyPress = KeyPressHandler                                    ⇐
    .
    .
    .
```

Now we write that function, KeyPressHandler(), which is passed an event object when the user types a key. We can get the ASCII code of the key the user typed by looking at the event object's which property. If that ASCII code is the ASCII code for 4, which is 52, we should congratulate the user on being right:

```
<HTML>

<HEAD>
<TITLE>Key reading example</TITLE>
</HEAD>

<BODY>
    .
    .
    .
</BODY>
<SCRIPT LANGUAGE = JavaScript>

document.onKeyPress = KeyPressHandler

function KeyPressHandler(e)
{
    if(e.which == 52)    // ASC(52) = "4"                                ⇐
document.form1.Textbox.value = "Correct! 2 + 2 = 4"<HTML>                ⇐
        .
        .
        .
```

On the other hand, if the user types anything else, we put an error message in the text box:

```
<HEAD>
<TITLE>Key reading example</TITLE>
</HEAD>

<BODY>
    .
    .
    .
```

```
</BODY>

<SCRIPT LANGUAGE = JavaScript>

document.onKeyPress = KeyPressHandler

function KeyPressHandler(e)
{
        if(e.which == 52)   // ASC(52) = "4"
            document.form1.Textbox.value = "Correct! 2 + 2 = 4"
        else
            document.form1.Textbox.value = "Sorry, try again!"         ⇐
}

</SCRIPT>
</HTML>
```

---

**Listing 4.8 keysj.htm**

```
<HTML>

<HEAD>
<TITLE>Key reading example</TITLE>
</HEAD>

<BODY>

<CENTER>

<FORM NAME = "form1">
<BR>
<H1>How much is 2 + 2?</H1>
<BR>
<INPUT NAME = Textbox TYPE = TEXT SIZE = 20>
</FORM>

</CENTER>

</BODY>
```

---

Open this page in Netscape Navigator now and answer the $2 + 2$ question. As we can see in Fig 4.11 ref, $2 + 2 = 4$. Now we're doing high-powered math with Dynamic HTML!

The code for this example, keysj.htm, appears in Listing 4.8.

**Figure 4.11 Reading keys from the keyboard in Netscape Navigator.**

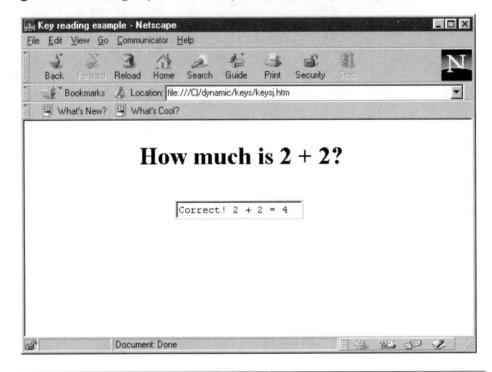

**Listing 4.8 Continued**

```
    <SCRIPT LANGUAGE = JavaScript>

document.onKeyPress = KeyPressHandler

function KeyPressHandler(e)
{
        if(e.which == 52)    // ASC(52) = "4"
            document.form1.Textbox.value = "Correct! 2 + 2 = 4"
        else
            document.form1.Textbox.value = "Sorry, try again!"
}
```

**Listing 4.8 Continued**

```
</SCRIPT>

</HTML>
```

We've seen quite a lot about using and handling text so far in this chapter. Now we'll take a look at *how* we display our text when we work with style sheets.

# Using Style Sheets

Style sheets are something relatively new to HTML. We've already seen how to change the color of text in Internet Explorer by referring to its style *attribute* like this:

```
link1.style.color="magenta"
```

This is not quite the same as using style sheets, as we'll see here.

A *style sheet* is just a collection of styles; the possible styles we can work with in Internet Explorer appear in Table 4.1, and the styles for Netscape Navigator in Table 4.2. As you might notice, the names of the styles for use in style sheets are incompatible between browsers—for example, font-size versus fontSize—so you'll have to target your styles sheets specifically by browser. One thing to note is that Internet Explorer uses the same kind of styles as Netscape Navigator when you use a tag's STYLE *attribute* (note the use of fontSize, not font-size, here):

```
sub link4_onMouseOver
    link4.style.color="magenta"
    link4.style.fontSize=24                          ⇐
End Sub
```

But Internet Explorer uses the styles in Table 4.2 when working with the <STYLE> *tag*, as we'll see (like font-size here, not fontSize):

```
<STYLE>
 H1 {font-size = 52pt; font-family = arial; text-decoration = under-
line} ⇐
 H2 {font-size = 36pt; font-family = arial}
</STYLE>
```

Let's see how to put some of this to work. We'll start with Internet Explorer as we create a new example named styles.htm in which we underline text when the user brings the mouse near that text—and we'll do that using a style sheet.

**Table 4.2 Internet Explorer's Style Sheet Styles**

| | | |
|---|---|---|
| background | background-attachment | background-color |
| background-image | background-position | background-repeat |
| border | border-bottom | border-bottom-width |
| border-color | border-left | border-left-width |
| border-right | border-right-width | border-style |
| border-top | border-top-width | border-width |
| color | display | font |
| font-family | font-size | font-style |
| font-variant | font-weight | height |
| left | letter-spacing | line-height |
| margin | margin-bottom | margin-left |
| margin-right | margin-top | overflow |
| position | text-align | text-decoration |
| text-indent | text-transform | top |
| vertical-align | visibility | width |
| z-index | | |

**Table 4.3 Netscape Navigator's Style Sheet Styles**

| | | |
|---|---|---|
| align | backgroundColor | backgroundImage |
| borderBottomWidth | borderColor | borderLeftWidth |
| borderRightWidth | borderStyle | borderTopWidth |
| borderWidths() | clear | color |
| display | fontFamily | fontSize |
| fontStyle | fontWeight | height |
| lineHeight | listStyleType | marginBottom |
| marginLeft | marginRight | margins() |
| marginTop | paddingBottom | paddingLeft |
| paddingRight | paddings() | paddingTop |
| textAlign | textDecoration | textTransform |
| verticalAlign | whiteSpace | width |

# Setting Up a Style Sheet in Internet Explorer

We start styles.htm by setting up our style sheet using the <STYLE> tag, which you use like this:

| Internet Explorer | Netscape Navigator |
|---|---|
| `<STYLE` | `<STYLE` |
| `TITLE=string` | `TITLE=string` |
| `TYPE=string` | `TYPE=string` |

We'll define two *classes* in this style sheet: underlinedText and normalText. We set up the styles we want in each class and then apply those classes to Web page elements. For example, we set the text-decoration attribute to "underline" in the underlinedText class, and to "none" in the normalText class (the keyword "classes" is optional in Internet Explorer; we could just as well have named the underlinedText class ".underlinedText"):

```
<HTML>

<HEAD>
<TITLE>Dynamic style example</TITLE>
</HEAD>

<STYLE>                                                          ⇐
  classes.underlinedText {text-decoration = underline}          ⇐
  classes.normalText {text-decoration = none}                   ⇐
</STYLE>                                                         ⇐
      .
      .
      .
```

Now we've set up our style sheet. All that remains is to apply the correct style to the text in our Internet Explorer page when the user moves the mouse. For this example, we'll set up an <H1> header that will underline itself when the user brings the mouse near it and appear normally when the user moves the mouse away. To do that, we'll use the onMouseOver and onMouseOut events in Internet Explorer. To underline the text, we only have to change the <H1> tag's className attribute to "underlinedText"; to change it back to normal, we just switch the className to "normalText":

```
<HTML>

<HEAD>
<TITLE>Dynamic style example</TITLE>
</HEAD>
<STYLE>
```

```
    classes.underlinedText {text-decoration = underline}
    classes.normalText {text-decoration = none}
</STYLE>

<BODY>

<CENTER>

<H1 onMouseOver = "className = 'underlinedText'"                          ⇐
onMouseOut = "className = 'normalText'">                                  ⇐
Underline this text with the mouse...                                    ⇐
</H1>                                                                     ⇐

<CENTER>
</BODY>
```

**Figure 4.12 We change an <H1> tag's style with the mouse.**

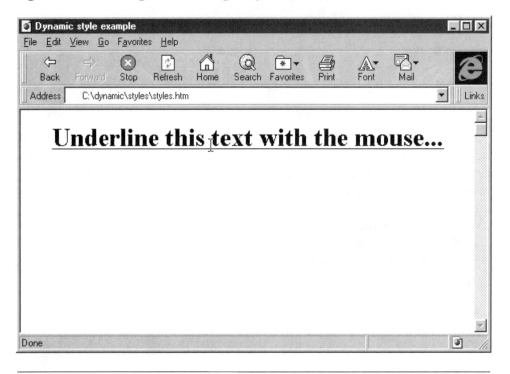

```
</HTML>
```

That's it—the Web page is ready to run.

You might notice that we used a time-saving device of VBScript here. For simple scripts, you can embed the code in the tag itself. That is, instead of connecting the onMouseOver event to a subroutine like this:

```
onMouseOver = HandleMouse()
```

we simply placed the code we want to execute right into the tag:

```
onMouseOver = "className = 'underlinedText'"
```

Open the page now in Internet Explorer and bring the mouse near the header. When you do, the header automatically underlines itself, as shown in Figure 4.12. Our first style sheet example is a success.

The code for this page, styles.htm, appears in Listing 4.9.

**Listing 4.9 styles.htm**

```
<HTML>
<HEAD>
<TITLE>Dynamic style example</TITLE>
</HEAD>

<STYLE>
  classes.underlinedText {text-decoration = underline}
  classes.normalText {text-decoration = none}
</STYLE>

<BODY>

<CENTER>

<H1 onMouseOver = "className = 'underlinedText'"
onMouseOut = "className = 'normalText'">
Underline this text with the mouse...
</H1>

<CENTER>

</BODY>
</HTML>
```

Let's take a look at the same process in Netscape Navigator.

## Setting Up a Style Sheet in Netscape Navigator

We can define our underlinedText class in the Netscape Navigator example stylesj.htm, but Navigator pages won't respond dynamically in the same way as Internet Explorer pages, so we just apply this new class to an <H1> heading this way, making sure it appears underlined when we first load the page (note that we use the "textDecoration" style here for Navigator, not the "text-decoration" style we would use with Internet Explorer):

```
<HTML>

<HEAD>
<TITLE>Style example</TITLE>
</HEAD>

<STYLE TYPE="text/javascript">
    classes.underlinedText.all.textDecoration = "underline"          ⇐
</STYLE>
<BODY>
<CENTER>

<H1 CLASS=underlinedText>This heading is underlined</H1>             ⇐

</CENTER>
</BODY>

</HTML>
```

Now open the page in Netscape Navigator. The headers appear as we have designed them, as shown in Figure 4.13. As you can see, we have created a new style class and applied it to our Web page. Now we're using style sheets in Netscape Navigator.

The code for this example, stylesj.htm, appears in Listing 4.10.

### Listing 4.10 stylesj.htm

```
<HTML>

<HEAD>
```

**Figure 4.13 A new style class defined in Netscape Navigator.**

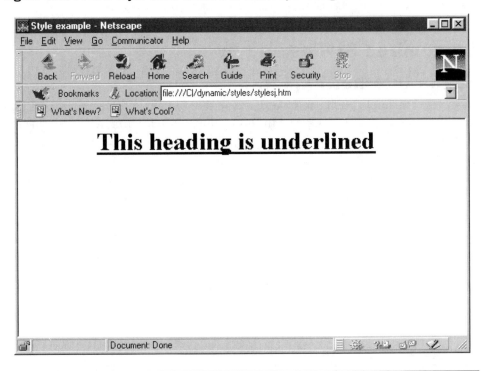

**Listing 4.10 Continued**

```
<TITLE>Style example</TITLE>
</HEAD>

<STYLE TYPE="text/javascript">
    classes.underlinedText.all.textDecoration = "underline"
</STYLE>

<BODY>
<CENTER>

<H1 CLASS=underlinedText>This heading is underlined</H1>

</CENTER>
</BODY>
</HTML>
```

We've gotten an introduction to using styles at this point. Let's continue on now as we see how to *redefine* tags in a Web page using style sheets.

# Customized Styling Tag by Tag in Internet Explorer

In our next example, we'll use style sheets to redefine the <H1> and <H2> tags in an Internet Explorer Web page. In this example, hstyles.htm, we'll redefine the <H1> tag to use underlined 52-point Arial text, and the <H2> tag to use 36-point Arial.

We'll start with Internet Explorer, creating an example named hstyles.htm by setting up our style sheet. In that style sheet, we set the <H1> and <H2> tags' font sizes, font type, and text decoration this way:

```
<HTML>

<HEAD>
<TITLE>Specific tag styling example</TITLE>
</HEAD>

<STYLE>
                                                              ⇐
  H1 {font-size = 52pt; font-family = arial; text-decoration = under-
line}                                                         ⇐
  H2 {font-size = 36pt; font-family = arial}
                                                              ⇐
</STYLE>
                                                              ⇐

<BODY>
    .
    .
    .
```

That's all we need . Now we can place an <H1> tag and an <H2> tag into our page, and they'll use the new styles:

```
<HTML>

<HEAD>
<TITLE>Specific tag styling example</TITLE>
```

```
</HEAD>

<STYLE>
 H1 {font-size = 52pt; font-family = arial; text-decoration = under-
line}
 H2 {font-size = 36pt; font-family = arial}
</STYLE>

<BODY>

<CENTER>

<H1>A styled H1 tag.</H1>                                            ⇐
<BR>
<H2>Here's a styled H2 tag!</H2>                                     ⇐
</CENTER>
</BODY>

</HTML>
```

---

**Listing 4.11 hstyles.htm**

```
<HTML>

<HEAD>
<TITLE>Specific tag styling example</TITLE>
</HEAD>

<STYLE>
 H1 {font-size = 52pt; font-family = arial; text-decoration = under-
line}
 H2 {font-size = 36pt; font-family = arial}
</STYLE>

<BODY>

<CENTER>

<H1>A styled H1 tag.</H1>
<BR>
<H2>Here's a styled H2 tag!</H2>

</CENTER>
```

*Continued*

---

Open the Web page in Internet Explorer now. As you can see in Fig 4.14 ref, we have redefined the <H1> and <H2> tags, and our new example is a success.

The code for this page, hstyles.htm, appears in Listing 4.11.

**Figure 4.14 The redefined <H1> and <H2> tags.**

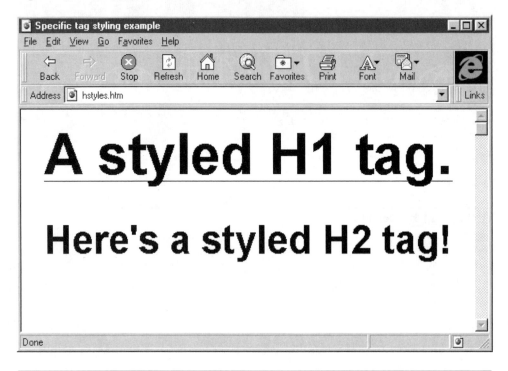

**Listing 4.11 Continued**

```
</BODY>

</HTML>
```

We can also redefine tags in Netscape Navigator, and we'll do that next.

# Customized Styling Tag by Tag in Netscape Navigator

To redefine the <H1> tag in Netscape Navigator, we use the tags keyword (as opposed to the classes keyword that we used in the last example, where we were

defining a new class). Here's how we set the <H1> tag's style to 52-point underlined Arial text, and the <H2> tag to 36-point Arial:

```
<HTML>

<HEAD>
<TITLE>Specific tag styling example</TITLE>
</HEAD>

<STYLE TYPE = "text/javascript">
 tags.H1.fontSize = "52"                              ⇐
 tags.H1.fontFamily = "arial"                         ⇐
 tags.H1.textDecoration = "underline"                 ⇐
 tags.H2.fontSize = "36"                              ⇐
 tags.H1.fontFamily = "arial"                         ⇐
</STYLE>

<BODY>
    .
    .
    .
```

Then we can use our new <H1> and <H2> tags this way:

```
<HTML>

<HEAD>
<TITLE>Specific tag styling example</TITLE>
</HEAD>

<STYLE TYPE = "text/javascript">
 tags.H1.fontSize = "52"
 tags.H1.fontFamily = "arial"
 tags.H1.textDecoration = "underline"
 tags.H2.fontSize = "36"
 tags.H1.fontFamily = "arial"
</STYLE>

<BODY>

<CENTER>

<H1>A styled H1 tag.</H1>
<BR>
```

**Figure 4.15 The redefined <H1> and <H2> tags in Netscape Navigator.**

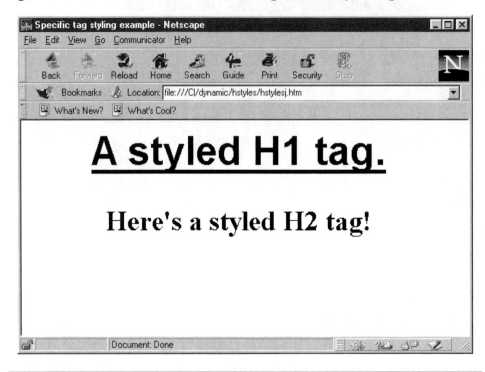

```
<H2>Here's a styled H2 tag!</H2>

</CENTER>

</BODY>

</HTML>
```

That's how you redefine a tag in the Netscape Navigator: Use the tags keyword first to indicate that you want to redefine a tag. Open the page in Netscape Navigator now. As you can see in Figure 4.15, we've redefined the <H1> and <H2> tags successfully.

The code for this example, hstylesj.htm, appears in Listing 4.12.

**Listing 4.12 hstylesj.htm**

```html
<HTML>
<HEAD>
<TITLE>Specific tag styling example</TITLE>
</HEAD>

<STYLE TYPE = "text/javascript">
 tags.H1.fontSize = "52"
 tags.H1.fontFamily = "arial"
 tags.H1.textDecoration = "underline"
 tags.H2.fontSize = "36"
 tags.H1.fontFamily = "arial"
</STYLE>

<BODY>

<CENTER>

<H1>A styled H1 tag.</H1>
<BR>
<H2>Here's a styled H2 tag!</H2>

</CENTER>

</BODY>

</HTML>
```

The last example we'll look at in this chapter will show us how style inheritance works.

# Inheriting Styles in Internet Explorer

The styles sheets we use are *cascading style sheets* (CSS). This means that when we define a style for an element, all the elements inside that element *inherit* the surrounding element's styles. To see how this works, we'll look at an example in Internet Explorer and then an example in Netscape Navigator. In this first example, we'll see how to define a new class that is to be used only with <DIV> tags. Then we'll see how tags inside such <DIV> tags will inherit this new class.

We start this new example, classes.htm, with a style sheet. In this style sheet, we'll define a new class, class1, which can be used only with the <DIV> tag. Defining that class works like this in Internet Explorer:

```
<HTML>
<HEAD>
<TITLE>Class inheritance example</TITLE>
</HEAD>

<STYLE>
  DIV.class1 {font-size = 24; margin-left = 15%}              ⇐
</STYLE>
        .
        .
        .
```

Note that here we use a new style attribute: margin-left, which lets us indent Web page elements. (This style is marginLeft in Navigator style sheets.) Here we specify that <DIV> elements using the class class1 should be indented 15 percent from the left edge of the page.

We have defined this new class to work only with <DIV> tags. We'll use this new class in a <DIV> tag and then place *another* <DIV> tag that *doesn't* use this class inside the first <DIV> tag:

```
<DIV CLASS = "class1">

    <DIV>

    </DIV>

<DIV>
```

Normally, the second <DIV> tag would not have access to class1, but because it's enclosed in the surrounding <DIV> tag—which *does* use class1—the inner <DIV> will use class1 as well. In this way, the inner <DIV> tag has inherited class1 from the outer, enclosing <DIV> tag.

In code, we start with the outer <DIV>, connecting class1 to it this way:

```
<HTML>

<HEAD>
<TITLE>Class inheritance example</TITLE>
</HEAD>

<STYLE>
  DIV.class1 {font-size = 24; margin-left = 15%}
```

```
</STYLE>
<BODY>

<CENTER>
<H1>Class inheritance...</H1>
</CENTER>

<DIV CLASS = "class1">                                              ⇐
This is text in the <I>outer</I> DIV.
<BR>
<BR>
   .
   .
   .
```

The inner **<DIV>** will have no explicit class reference:

```
<HTML>

<HEAD>
<TITLE>Class inheritance example</TITLE>
</HEAD>

<STYLE>
DIV.class1 {font-size = 24; margin-left = 15%}
</STYLE>

<BODY>

<CENTER>
<H1>Class inheritance...</H1>
</CENTER>

<DIV CLASS = "class1">
This is text in the <I>outer</I> DIV.
<BR>
<BR>

<DIV>                                                              ⇐
This is text in the <I>inner</I> DIV which has inherited the outer
DIV's
styles, so it looks just the same.
</DIV>                                                            ⇐
```

**Figure 4.16 Example showing how classes can be inherited.**

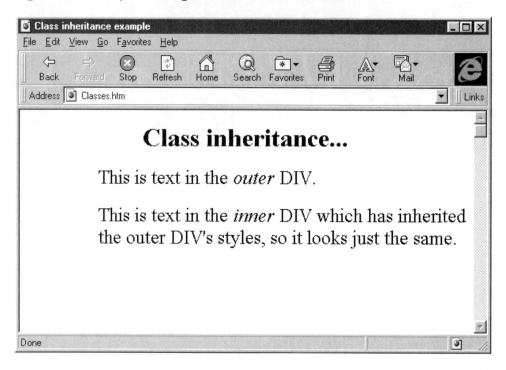

```
</DIV>

</BODY>

</HTML>
```

However, when we open the Web page, it's clear that the inner <DIV> has inherited class1 from the outer <DIV>, as we see in Figure 4.16. Now we're using cascading style sheets.

The code for this page, classes.htm, appears in Listing 4.13.

**Listing 4.13 classes.htm**

```
<HTML>

<HEAD>
```

**Listing 4.13 Continued**

```
<TITLE>Class inheritance example</TITLE>
</HEAD>

<STYLE>
  DIV.class1 {font-size = 24; margin-left = 15%}
</STYLE>

<BODY>

<CENTER>
<H1>Class inheritance...</H1>
</CENTER>

<DIV CLASS = "class1">
This is text in the <I>outer</I> DIV.
<BR>
<BR>

<DIV>
This is text in the <I>inner</I> DIV which has inherited the outer DIV's
styles, so it looks just the same.
</DIV>

</DIV>

</BODY>

</HTML>
```

Our next step will be to take a look at this example in Netscape Navigator, so let's turn to that now.

# Inheriting Styles in Netscape Navigator

To see how class inheritance works in Netscape Navigator, we'll create a new example, classesj.htm, which defines a new class, class1, with a font size of 24 points and a left margin of 15 percent:

```
<HTML>

<HEAD>
```

```
<TITLE>Class inheritance example</TITLE>
</HEAD>

<STYLE TYPE="text/javascript">
   classes.class1.all.fontSize = 24                    ⇐
   classes.class1.all.marginLeft = "15%"               ⇐
</STYLE>

<BODY>
     .
     .
     .
```

The we simply apply that class to our outer <DIV>, but not to the inner <DIV>:

```
<HTML>

<HEAD>
<TITLE>Class inheritance example</TITLE>
</HEAD>

<STYLE TYPE="text/javascript">
   classes.class1.all.fontSize = 24
   classes.class1.all.marginLeft = "15%"
</STYLE>

<BODY>

<CENTER>
<H1>Class inheritance...</H1>
</CENTER>

<DIV CLASS = class1>                                    ⇐
This is text in the <I>outer</I> DIV.
<BR>
<BR>

<DIV>                                                   ⇐
This is text in the <I>inner</I> DIV which has inherited the outer
DIV's
styles, so it looks just the same.
```

**Figure 4.17 Class inheritance in Netscape Navigator.**

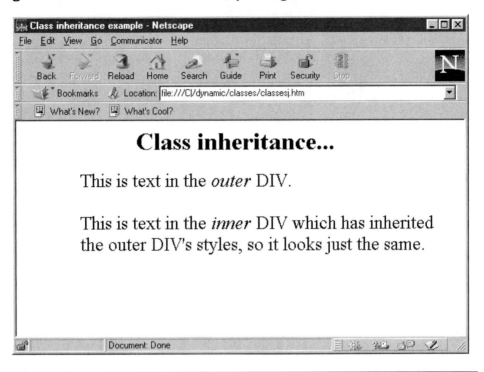

```
</DIV>

</DIV>
</BODY>

</HTML>
```

And that's it. When you open this new page in Netscape Navigator, as shown in Figure 4.17, we see the same class-inheritance behavior we saw in Internet Explorer. Our Netscape Navigator class-inheritance example is a success.

The code for this example, classesj.htm, appears in Listing 4.13.

**Listing 4.13 classesj.htm**

```
<HTML>

<HEAD>
```

*Continued*

**Listing 4.13 Continued**

```
<TITLE>Class inheritance example</TITLE>
</HEAD>

<STYLE TYPE="text/javascript">
  classes.class1.all.fontSize = 24
  classes.class1.all.marginLeft = "15%"
</STYLE>

<BODY>
<CENTER>
<H1>Class inheritance...</H1>
</CENTER>

<DIV CLASS = class1>
This is text in the <I>outer</I> DIV.
<BR>
<BR>
<DIV>
This is text in the <I>inner</I> DIV which has inherited the outer
DIV's
styles, so it looks just the same.
</DIV>

</DIV>

</BODY>

</HTML>
```

The last topic we'll look at in this chapter is how to use dynamic fonts in Netscape Navigator.

# Using Dynamic Fonts in Netscape Navigator

One new aspect of Netscape Navigator is dynamic fonts. Dynamic fonts allow you to download fonts from the Web and use them in your pages. For example, if you wanted to download the (nonexistent) "bigtime" font from a (nonexistent) Web site named www.a_font_source.com, you use the <LINK> tag this way in Netscape Navigator:

```
<LINK REL="fontdef" SRC="http://www.a_font_source.com/bigtimefont.pfr">
```

Then you can use the downloaded font at any time with the <FONT> tag:

```
<FONT FACE="bigtimefont">This text is in bigtime font!</FONT>
```

Downloading fonts like this helps eliminate the differences between computer platforms, and when your Web page can be loaded into any of a dozen types of computers, that is a big help.

## What's Ahead

That's it for this chapter. We've come far here, seeing how to use the mouse and the keyboard, how to use the mouse with the text in our page, how to select text in a Web page, how to use style sheets and class inheritance, how to redefine HTML tags, and more. We've augmented our Dynamic HTML arsenal by seeing how the mouse can work with text and how better to handle text itself in our Web pages.

In the next chapter, we'll start working with a new Dynamic HTML topic: seeing how just about *every* tag in Internet Explorer has been made active, with properties you can change on the fly and methods you can call at any time. Let's turn to that now.

C H A P T E R   F I V E

# ACTIVE HTML TAGS

n this chapter, we'll explore the extraordinary new capabilities of Internet Explorer, which allow us to script *everything*, not just controls, in a Web page. What does this mean? It means that every object you see in a Web page in Internet Explorer can be manipulated in code. This is something Netscape Navigator can't do, but it's such a powerful device that we will cover it in some detail in this chapter (so this is an Internet Explorer-only chapter).

The way the new Internet Explorer capabilities work is by adding properties, methods, and events to *every* tag. The Internet Explorer Dynamic HTML doesn't add new tags—it makes the tags that already exist scriptable. For example, you can use the size property of a <FONT> tag to change the size of the font in your scripts. You can use the <IMG> tag's onClick event to handle mouse clicks on the image. You can also use a tag's *methods*—that is, its built-in subroutines. For example, you can use the <H1> tag's ScrollIntoView() method to scroll the Web page so that that <H1> tag's text is visible.

This chapter gives an overview of Internet Explorer's new HTML capabilities: the new properties, methods, and events now available in each HTML tag. In particular, we'll take a new look at the HTML tags that we worked with in Chapter 1 when we brought ourselves up to speed in HTML by creating our html.htm page:

```
  ------------------------------------------------------
  |<HTML>                                              |
  |                                                    |
  |   ------------------------------------------------   |
  |   |<HEAD>                                          | |
  |   |                                                | |
```

```
|  |<TITLE>                                                  |  |
|  |This is the title.                                       |  |
|  |</TITLE>                                                 |  |
|  |                                                         |  |
|  |</HEAD>                                                  |  |
|  -------------------------------------------------------   |
|                                                            |
|  -------------------------------------------------------   |
|  |<BODY>                                                   |  |
|  |                                                         |  |
|  |          <H1>This is our main heading</H1>              |  |
|  |                                                         |  |
|  |                  --------------------                   |  |
|  |                  |                  |                   |  |
|  |                  |                  |                   |  |
|  |                  |                  |                   |  |
|  |                  |      Image       |                   |  |
|  |                  |                  |                   |  |
|  |                  |                  |                   |  |
|  |                  --------------------                   |  |
|  |                                                         |  |
|  |  -----------------------------------------------        |  |
|  | |                                               |       |  |
|  | |                                               |       |  |
|  | |                   Text                        |       |  |
|  | |                                               |       |  |
|  |  -----------------------------------------------        |  |
|  |                                                         |  |
|  |  ---------   -----------------------------------        |  |
|  | |         | |                                   |       |  |
|  | |         | |                                   |       |  |
|  | | Image   | |              Text                 |       |  |
|  | |         | |                                   |       |  |
|  | |         | |                                   |       |  |
|  |  ---------   -----------------------------------        |  |
|  |                                                         |  |
|  |  -----------------------------------------------        |  |
|  | | Enlarged Text                                 |       |  |
|  |  -----------------------------------------------        |  |
|  |                                                         |  |
|  |                  ------------------                     |  |
|  |                  |                |                     |  |
```

```
| |                      |-----------------|              | |
| |                      |     |     |     |              | |
| |                      |-----------------|              | |
| |                      |     |     |     |              | |
| |                       -----------------               | |
| |                                                        | |
| |</BODY>                                                | |
|   ------------------------------------------------------   |
|                                                            |
|</HTML>                                                     |
  ----------------------------------------------------------
```

We'll see that all these tags have built into them a great deal of power that we haven't seen before. To start, we'll tackle the very first tag in our Web page: the <HTML> tag.

# The Internet Explorer <HTML> Tag

## Properties

*className, docHeight, docLeft, docTop, docWidth, id, parentElement, sourceIndex, tagName, title*

Looking at the very first tag in our Web page, the <HTML> tag, will give us a good introduction to the new capabilities of Internet Explorer Dynamic HTML. The <HTML> tag has a number of properties, ready for us to use. In our first example, we'll use the <HTML> tag's ID property. Using this property is much like using the NAME attribute that we saw in the last chapter, where we gave names to various controls; you can use the tag's ID as its name in code. In fact, the ID property is more general than the NAME attribute, because just about all tags have the ID property, but not all have the NAME attribute. In this example, we'll see how to display the ID value we've given to our page's <HTML> tag. When the user clicks a button, we'll display the ID value we've given to our example's <HTML> tag.

We start this example, HTMLtag.htm, with the <HTML> tag, giving it the ID "firstTag" (this is the ID value that the page will display when the user clicks a button):

```
<HTML ID = firstTag>                                          ⇐
     .
     .
     .
```

Next, we add to our Web page a text box in which to display the <HTML> tag's ID and a button with the caption, "Show HTML tag's ID":

```
<HTML ID = firstTag>

<TITLE>HTML Tag Example</TITLE>

<BODY>

<CENTER>
<INPUT TYPE = TEXT NAME = Textbox SIZE = 40>                       ⇐
<BR>                                                              ⇐
<BR>                                                              ⇐
<INPUT TYPE = BUTTON Value = "Show HTML tag's ID">                ⇐
</CENTER>

</BODY>
     .
     .
     .
```

When the user clicks the button, we want to show the HTML tag's ID value, so we connect that button to a new subroutine named ShowID() in VBScript:

```
<HTML ID = firstTag>

<TITLE>HTML Tag Example</TITLE>

<BODY>

<CENTER>
<INPUT TYPE = TEXT NAME = Textbox SIZE = 40>
<BR>
<BR>
<INPUT TYPE = BUTTON Value = "Show HTML tag's ID" onClick =
"ShowID()">                                                       ⇐
</CENTER>

</BODY>

<SCRIPT LANGUAGE = VBScript>                                      ⇐
        Sub ShowID()                                              ⇐
           .                                                      ⇐
```

```
          .
          .
     End Sub                                               ⇐
                                                           ⇐
</SCRIPT>                                                  ⇐

</HTML>
```

The next question is how to reach the <HTML> tag in code so we can find its
ID value. One way to reach the <HTML> tag is by using its ID value, but clearly
that defeats the purpose of the example—what good is retrieving the tag's ID
property when we use that property to refer to the tag in the first place? Instead,
we'll use one of the new collections of Web page elements now available in Internet
Explorer.

Now that every element in the Web page has become active (that is to say,
scriptable), Internet Explorer organizes those elements into various collections.
All the Internet Explorer collections available in Dynamic HTML appear in Table
5.1; the collections in Netscape Navigator appear in Table 5.2. These collections
are arrays of Web page elements, and they help organize Web pages and give you
far more control over what goes on; using them, it's easy to get an overview of your
page's organization.

### Table 5.1 The Internet Explorer Collections

| all | anchors | applets |
| areas | cells | elements |
| embeds | forms | frames |
| frames | images | links |
| options | plugins | rows |
| scripts | | |

### Table 5.2 The Netscape Navigator Collections

| anchors | applets | arguments |
| elements | embeds | forms |
| frames | history | images |
| links | mimeTypes | options |
| plugins | | |

We'll use the most inclusive collection in the Internet Explorer arsenal, the all collection. This collection is a member of the document object, and it holds every tag in the Web page. Because this collection is a member of the document object, we refer to it as document.all(), and because the <HTML> tag is the very first tag in the Web page, it's also the first in the all collection. This means that we can refer to the first tag in our Web page, the <HTML> tag, as document.all(0).

In our ShowID() subroutine, then, we can reach the <HTML> tag's ID property as document.all(0).ID, so we display that tag's ID value this way:

```
<HTML ID = firstTag>

<TITLE>HTML Tag Example</TITLE>

<BODY>
    .
    .
    .
</BODY>

<SCRIPT LANGUAGE = VBScript>
        Sub ShowID()
             TextBox.Value = "The HTML tag's ID = " &
document.all(0).ID                                          ⇐
        End Sub
</SCRIPT>

</HTML>
```

Now we're ready to run our example. When the user clicks the Show HTML tag's ID button, the page displays the ID of the <HTML> tag, "firstTag," as shown in Figure 5.1. Our first example is a success. Now we're using the new properties available to us in Internet Explorer.

The code for Figure5.1's Web page appears in Listing 5.1.

---

**Listing 5.1 HTMLtag.htm**

```
<HTML ID = firstTag>

<TITLE>HTML Tag Example</TITLE>

<BODY>

<CENTER>
```

---

**Figure 5.1 Reaching the <HTML> tag's ID property.**

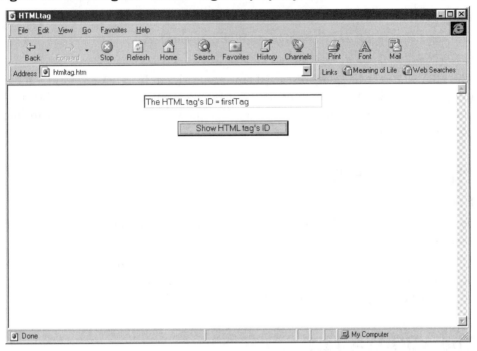

**Listing 5.1 Continued**

```
<INPUT TYPE = TEXT NAME = Textbox SIZE = 40>
<BR>
<BR>
<INPUT TYPE = BUTTON Value = "Show HTML tag's ID" onClick = "ShowID()">
</CENTER>

</BODY>

<SCRIPT LANGUAGE = VBScript>
      Sub ShowID()
            TextBox.Value = "The HTML tag's ID = " & document.all(0).ID
        End Sub
</SCRIPT>

</HTML>
```

The next tag in our Web page is the <HEAD> tag.

# The <HEAD> Tag

## Properties

*className, docHeight, docLeft, docTop, docWidth, parentElement, sourceIndex, tagName, id, style, title*

The <HEAD> tag has gained several new properties in Internet Explorer, such as the properties that hold the dimensions of the page—docHeight and docWidth—and others. We'll see several of these properties at work later, but in the meantime, we'll pass on to the next tag, the <TITLE> tag.

# The <TITLE> Tag

## Properties

*className, docHeight, docLeft, docTop, docWidth, id, parentElement, sourceIndex, tagName, title*

Like the <HEAD> tag, the <TITLE> tag has gained several new properties, but like the <HEAD> tag, there's not too much to it that's very exciting here, so let's go on to where the action is in our Web page: the <BODY> tag.

# The <BODY> Tag

## Properties

*className, docHeight, docLeft, docTop, docWidth, parentElement, sourceIndex, tagName, align, aLink, background, bgColor, bgProperties, id, leftMargin, link, scroll, style, text, title, topMargin, vLink*

## Methods

*removeMember, scrollIntoView, contains, getMember, setMember*

## Events

*onafterupdate, onbeforeupdate, onblur, onclick, ondblclick, onfocus, onhelp, onkeydown, onkeypress, onkeyup, onmousedown, onmousemove, onmouseout, onmouseover, onmouseup, onscroll*

The <BODY> tag is rich with new properties, methods, and events. You can work with and change the color of hyperlinks in the page using this tag's aLink, link, and vLink properties, or you can change the color of the background with the bgColor property, or you can change the image used to tile the background with the background property, and more.

Let's take a look at an example. One of the properties of the <BODY> tag is the title property. The body's title is displayed in a small box (also called a *tool tip*) when the user lets the mouse rest over the Web page's body, and we can even change that title as we like in our example. (Don't confuse the title property with the <TITLE> tag; an element's title is displayed when the mouse rests over that element, but the <TITLE> tag sets the whole page's title, which appears in the Web browser.) Let's see how to change the title property when the user clicks a button. We'll start the Web page with the title property "Default Text Here" and then change it to "This is the body" when the user clicks a button with the caption "Change the page's title."

We start this new example, body.htm, with the <BODY> tag, giving that tag the ID "BODY1" and setting its title property to "Default Text Here":

```
<HTML>

<HEAD>
<TITLE>Body Example</TITLE>
</HEAD>

<BODY ID = "BODY1" TITLE = "Default Text Here">
     .
     .
     .


<HTML>
```

Now when the user lets the mouse rest on our Web page, the text "Default Text Here" will appear in a small box next to the mouse cursor. Next, we add the button we'll need to change the body's title to our Web page, giving it the caption "Change the page's title" and connecting it to the subroutine ChangeTitle():

```
<HTML>

<HEAD>
<TITLE>Body Example</TITLE>
</HEAD>

<BODY ID = "BODY1" TITLE = "Default Text Here">
<CENTER>
<INPUT TYPE = BUTTON Value = "Change the page's title" onClick =
"ChangeTitle()">                                                    ⇐
```

```
</CENTER>

</BODY>

<SCRIPT LANGUAGE = VBScript>
        Sub ChangeTitle()                                            ⇐
          .
          .
          .
        End Sub                                                      ⇐
</SCRIPT>

</HTML>
```

When the user clicks this button, we want to change the body's title property to "This is the Body," and we do that with this line of VBScript code:

```
<HTML>

<HEAD>
<TITLE>Body Example</TITLE>
</HEAD>

<BODY ID = "BODY1" TITLE = "Default Text Here">
<CENTER>
<INPUT TYPE = BUTTON Value = "Change the page's title" onClick =
"ChangeTitle()">
</CENTER>

</BODY>

<SCRIPT LANGUAGE = VBScript>
        Sub ChangeTitle()
                BODY1.title = "This is the Body."                    ⇐
        End Sub
</SCRIPT>

</HTML>
```

That's all there is to it. When we look at this page in Internet Explorer, the body's title is "Default Text Here" at first, as shown in Figure 5.2.

After the user clicks the button, however, our page's title property becomes "This is the Body," as shown in Figure 5.3.

**Figure 5.2 The body default title for our Web page.**

Now we've been able to change a property, the title property, of our page's body on the fly. We're making progress in Dynamic HTML. The code for this Web page appears in Listing 5.2.

**Listing 5.2 body.htm**

```
<HTML>

<HEAD>
<TITLE>Body Example</TITLE>
</HEAD>

<BODY ID = "BODY1" TITLE = "Default Text Here">
<CENTER>
<INPUT TYPE = BUTTON Value = "Change the page's title" onClick =
"ChangeTitle()">
</CENTER>
```
*Continued*

**Figure 5.3 The new body title for our Web page.**

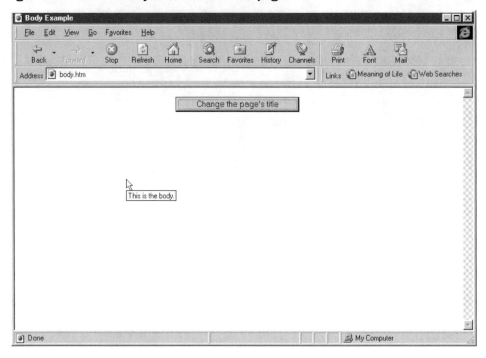

**Listing 5.2 Continued**

```
</BODY>

<SCRIPT LANGUAGE = VBScript>
        Sub ChangeTitle()
                BODY1.title = "This is the body."
        End Sub
</SCRIPT>

</HTML>
```

The next tag in our Web page is the <H1> tag.

# The <H1> Tag

## Properties

*className, docHeight, docLeft, docTop, docWidth, parentElement,
sourceIndex, tagName, align, id, style, title*

## Methods

*removeMember, scrollIntoView, contains, getMember, setMember*

Even the header tags like <H1> have become active in Dynamic HTML. In this case, we'll take a look at a Dynamic HTML method, not a property. Here, we'll use the Internet Explorer <H1> tag's scrollIntoView() method. (Note that all H# tags, from H1 to H6, share the same properties and methods.) This method will let us scroll the Web page in the browser so that this <H1> tag's text is in view. Let's see how this works.

We start this new example, H1.htm, with an <H1> tag to which we give the ID "H1tag":

```
<HTML>

<HEAD>
<TITLE>H1 Example</TITLE>
</HEAD>

<BODY>

<CENTER>
<H1 ID = H1tag>H1 Example</H1>                                    ⇐
    .
    .
    .
```

Next, we will add a button far down on the page with the caption "Scroll to H1 header." When the user clicks this button, the Web browser will scroll back to the <H1> heading automatically. We add that button far down the page by putting in a number of break tags, <BR>, and we connect the button to the subroutine ScrolltoH1() this way:

```
<HTML>

<HEAD>
<TITLE>H1 Example</TITLE>
</HEAD>

<BODY>

<CENTER>
<H1 ID = H1tag>H1 Example</H1>
```

```
<BR>                                                                         ⇐
<BR>
<BR>
<BR>
<BR>
<BR>
<BR>
<BR>
<BR>
<BR>
<BR>
<BR>
<BR>
<BR>
<BR>
<BR>
<BR>
<BR>
<BR>
<BR>
<BR>
<BR>
<BR>
<BR>
<INPUT TYPE = BUTTON Value = "Scroll to H1 header" onClick =
"ScrolltoH1()">                                                              ⇐
</CENTER>

</BODY>
     .
     .
     .
```

Next, we add the subroutine ScrolltoH1() itself:

```
<HTML>

<HEAD>
<TITLE>H1 Example</TITLE>
</HEAD>

<BODY>
     .
     .
```

```
      .
</BODY>

<SCRIPT LANGUAGE = VBScript>
        Sub ScrolltoH1()⇐
          .
          .
          .
        End Sub                                              ⇐
</SCRIPT>

</HTML>
```

When the user clicks the button, we want to scroll back to the <H1> tag that we have given the ID "H1tag." We do that with the scrollIntoView() method:

```
<HTML>

<HEAD>
<TITLE>H1 Example</TITLE>
</HEAD>

<BODY>
    .
    .
    .
</BODY>

<SCRIPT LANGUAGE = VBScript>
        Sub ScrolltoH1()
                H1tag.scrollIntoView()                       ⇐
        End Sub
</SCRIPT>

</HTML>
```

Now open this page in Internet Explorer and scroll down to the bottom of the page where the button is, as shown in Figure 5.4.

When you click the button, Internet Explorer automatically scrolls the page back up to the <H1> tag's text, as shown in Figure 5.5. Our example is a success: Now we're scrolling Web pages in response to the user's requests.

The code for this Web page, H1.htm, appears in Listing 5.3.

**Figure 5.4 Preparing to scroll a Web page automatically.**

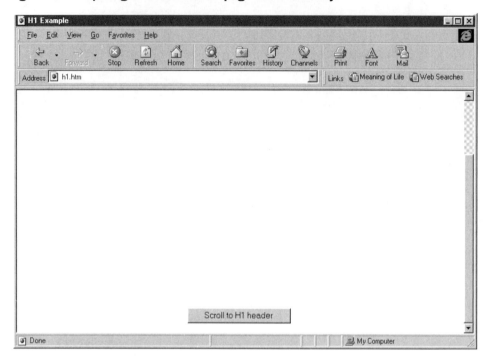

**Listing 5.3 H1.htm**

```
<HTML>

<HEAD>
<TITLE>H1 Example</TITLE>
</HEAD>

<BODY>

<CENTER>
<H1 ID = H1tag>H1 Example</H1>
<BR>
<BR>
<BR>
<BR>
```

**Figure 5.5 Scrolling a Web page automatically.**

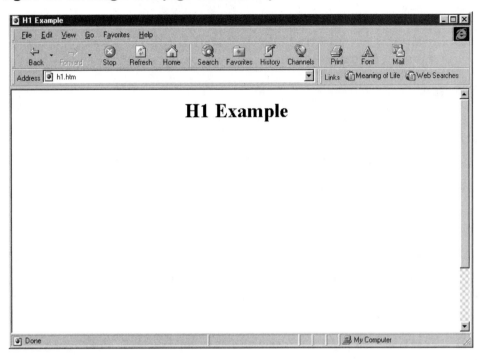

**Listing 5.3 Continued**

```
<BR>
<BR>
<BR>
<BR>
<BR>
<BR>
<BR>
<BR>
<BR>
<BR>
<BR>
<BR>
<BR>
<BR>
```

*Continued*

**Listing 5.3 Continued**

```
<BR>
<BR>
<BR>
<INPUT TYPE = BUTTON Value = "Scroll to H1 header" onClick =
"ScrolltoH1()">
</CENTER>

</BODY>

<SCRIPT LANGUAGE = VBScript>
        Sub ScrolltoH1()
                H1tag.scrollIntoView()
        End Sub
</SCRIPT>

</HTML>
```

We've covered the <HTML>, <HEAD>, <TITLE>, <BODY>, <H1> tags at this point; the next one in our Web page is the Internet Explorer <IMG> tag.

# The <IMG> Tag

## Properties

*dataFld, dataSrc, className, docHeight, docLeft, docTop, docWidth, parentElement, sourceIndex, tagName, align, alt, border, dynsrc, height, hspace, id, isMap, loop, lowsrc, name, src, style, title, useMap, vrml, vspace, width*

## Methods

*removeMember, scrollIntoView, contains, getMember, setMember*

## Events

*onabort, onafterupdate, onbeforeupdate, onblur, onclick, ondblclick, onerror, onfocus, onhelp, onkeydown, onkeypress, onkeyup, onload, onmousedown, onmousemove, onmouseout, onmouseover, onmouseup, onreadystatechange*

We've already seen the <IMG> tag, of course—that's the tag that we use to embed images (and videos) in the Web page. Now that we're using Dynamic HTML, however, there's even more to learn about this tag. For example, we can now *change* the image's border, alt text (displayed in browsers without graphics capabilities), its width or height, and, in fact, we can even change the image itself at any time using the <IMG> tag's SRC property.

Let's see how to change the image. In this example, img.htm, we will first display one image in Internet Explorer, but when the user clicks a button, the page will switch to a new image. The two images we'll use—image1.gif and image2.gif—appear in Figure 5.6.

Let's create this example Web page now. We start img.htm with an <IMG> tag, which we name IMG1 and which we use to display the image image1.gif:

```
<HTML>

<TITLE>IMG example</TITLE>

<BODY>

<CENTER>
<IMG NAME = IMG1 SRC = "gif/image1.gif" WIDTH = 236 HEIGHT = 118>    ⇐
<BR>
<BR>
    .
    .
    .
```

Next, we add the button that will allow the user to change the image, and we'll give that button the caption "Change Image," connecting it to a subroutine named ChangeImage():

---

**Figure 5.6 Our <IMG> example's images.**

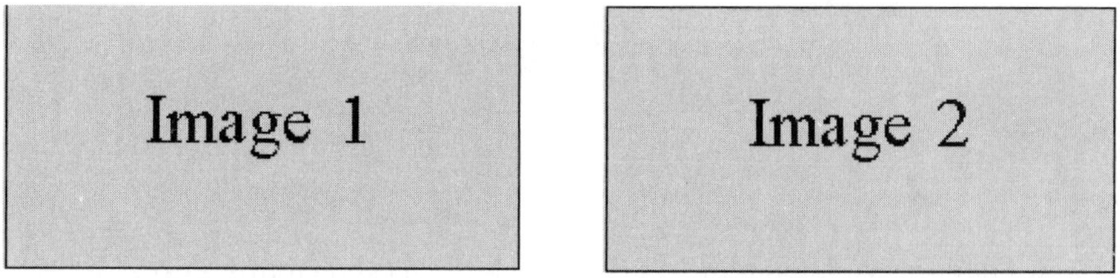

---

```
<HTML>

<TITLE>IMG example</TITLE>

<BODY>

<CENTER>
<IMG NAME = IMG1 SRC = "gif/image1.gif" WIDTH = 236 HEIGHT = 118>
<BR>
<BR>
<INPUT TYPE = BUTTON Value = "Change Image" onClick =
"ChangeImage()">                                                    ⇐
</CENTER>

</BODY>
    .
    .
    .
```

Now we add the subroutine ChangeImage(). In this subroutine, we simply reload the <IMG> tag's SRC property with the second image, image2.gif:

```
<HTML>

<TITLE>IMG example</TITLE>

<BODY>
    .
    .
    .
</BODY>

<SCRIPT LANGUAGE = VBScript>
        Sub ChangeImage()                                           ⇐
                IMG1.SRC = "gif/image2.gif"                         ⇐
        End Sub                                                     ⇐
</SCRIPT>

</HTML>
```

Now open the Web page in Internet Explorer, as shown in Figure 5.7.

When the user clicks the button, however, the page switches to the second image, as shown in Figure 5.8.

**Figure 5.7 Our &lt;IMG&gt; tag example's first image.**

As in this example, we're able to use the Dynamic HTML capabilities of the &lt;IMG&gt; tag to change the image we display at any time. Our img.htm Web page is a success. The code for this page appears in Listing 5.4.

**Listing 5.4 IMG.htm**

```
<HTML>

<TITLE>IMG example</TITLE>

<BODY>

<CENTER>
<IMG NAME = IMG1 SRC = "gif/image1.gif" WIDTH = 236 HEIGHT = 118>
<BR>
<BR>
```

*Continued*

**Figure 5.8 Our <IMG> tag example's second image.**

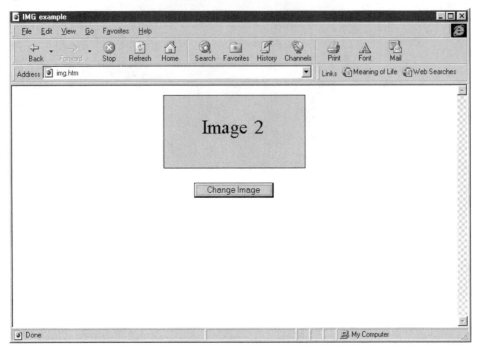

**Listing 5.4 Continued**

```
<INPUT TYPE = BUTTON Value = "Change Image" onClick = "ChangeImage()">
</CENTER>

</BODY>

<SCRIPT LANGUAGE = VBScript>
        Sub ChangeImage()
                IMG1.SRC = "gif/image2.gif"
        End Sub
</SCRIPT>

</HTML>
```

The next part of our Web page is made up of simple text:

```
-------------------------------------------------------
|<HTML>                                                |
```

```
|                                                              |
|   --------------------------------------------------  |
|  |<HEAD>                                            |  |
|  |                                                  |  |
|  |<TITLE>                                           |  |
|  |This is the title.                                |  |
|  |</TITLE>                                          |  |
|  |                                                  |  |
|  |</HEAD>                                           |  |
|   --------------------------------------------------  |
|                                                       |
|   --------------------------------------------------  |
|  |<BODY>                                            |  |
|  |                                                  |  |
|  |        <H1>This is our main heading</H1>         |  |
|  |                                                  |  |
|  |           --------------------                   |  |
|  |          |                    |                  |  |
|  |          |                    |                  |  |
|  |          |                    |                  |  |
|  |          |        Image       |                  |  |
|  |          |                    |                  |  |
|  |          |                    |                  |  |
|  |           --------------------                   |  |
|  |                                                  |  |
|  |   ---------------------------------------------  |  |
|  |  |                                            |  |  |
|  |  |                                            |  |  |    ⇐
|  |  |                  Text                      |  |  |
|  |  |                                            |  |  |
|  |   ---------------------------------------------  |  |
|  |                                                  |  |
|  |   ---------   ------------------------------     |  |
|  |  |         | |                              |    |  |
|  |  |         | |                              |    |  |
|  |  | Image   | |            Text              |    |  |
|  |  |         | |                              |    |  |
|  |  |         | |                              |    |  |
|  |   ---------   ------------------------------     |  |
|  |                                                  |  |
|  |   --------------------------------------------   |  |
|  | Enlarged Text                                    |  |
```

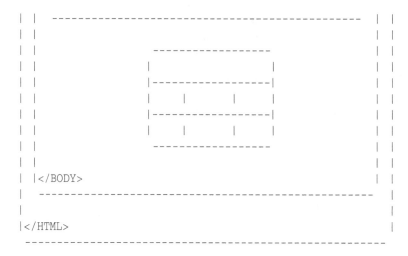

```
| |   --------------------------------------------    | |
| |                                                   | |
| |               ------------------                  | |
| |              |                  |                 | |
| |              |------------------|                 | |
| |              |   |       |      |                 | |
| |              |------------------|                 | |
| |              |   |       |      |                 | |
| |               ------------------                  | |
| |                                                   | |
| |</BODY>                                            | |
|  --------------------------------------------------   |
|                                                       |
|</HTML>                                                |
 -----------------------------------------------------
```

It's not easy to handle raw text with scripts unless we enclose it in HTML tags. The <DIV> tag is perfect for this; as we saw in the last chapter, DIV stands for division, and we use this tag to enclose segments of the Web page in convenient packages.

# The <DIV> Tag

### Properties

*dataFld, dataFormatAs, dataSrc, className, docHeight, docLeft, docTop, docWidth, parentElement, sourceIndex, tagName, align, id, style, title*

### Methods

*removeMember, scrollIntoView, contains, getMember, setMember*

### Events

*onafterupdate, onbeforeupdate, onblur, onclick, ondblclick, onfocus, onhelp, onkeydown, onkeypress, onkeyup, onmousedown, onmousemove*

The <DIV> tag can enclose any section of the Web page you want, not just text. Because that's the case, this tag is not specifically designed to work with text, and we'll have to make special provisions to do so. In our next example, let's see how to turn some text in the Web page blue when the user clicks a button. To do that, we'll set up a style sheet that we can apply to our text. In that style sheet, we'll set up two new classes, and it will be those classes that we actually apply to our <DIV> tag. (In fact, the <DIV> tag's most used property is probably the className property.) Let's see how all this works now.

We start by placing the text we will turn blue, "Here is the text you can color!" in a <DIV> tag to which we give the ID value "DIV1":

```
<HTML>

<HEAD>
<TITLE>DIV Example</TITLE>
</HEAD>

<BODY>

<CENTER>
<DIV ID = DIV1>                                               ⇐
Here is the text you can color!                              ⇐
</DIV>                                                       ⇐
    .
    .
    .
```

Next, we set up two buttons, one with the caption "Make text black" and one with the caption "Make text blue," connecting them to the subroutines MakeBlack() and MakeBlue() this way:

```
<HTML>

<HEAD>
<TITLE>DIV Example</TITLE>
</HEAD>

<BODY>

<CENTER>
<DIV ID = DIV1>
Here is the text you can color!
</DIV>
<BR>
<INPUT TYPE = BUTTON Value = "Make text black" onClick =
"MakeBlack()">                                               ⇐
<BR>
<BR>
<INPUT TYPE = BUTTON Value = "Make text blue" onClick = "MakeBlue()">⇐

</CENTER>
```

```
</BODY>
    .
    .
    .
```

Next, we will set up a style sheet with two classes in it: one for black text, one for blue. After these classes are set up, we'll be able to apply them to the <DIV> tag to turn the text the color we want. We set up the new style sheet with the <STYLE> tag:

```
<HTML>

<HEAD>
<TITLE>DIV Example</TITLE>
</HEAD>

<BODY>
    .
    .
    .
</BODY>

<STYLE>                                              ⇐
    .
    .
    .
</STYLE>                                              ⇐
    .
    .
    .
```

We define two new classes here, blackText and blueText:

```
<HTML>

<HEAD>
<TITLE>DIV Example</TITLE>
</HEAD>

<BODY>
    .
    .
    .
```

```
</BODY>

<STYLE>
 .blackText {color:Black}                                    ⇐
 .blueText {color:Blue}                                      ⇐
</STYLE>
      .
      .
      .
```

When the user clicks the Make text black button, our code will apply the
blackText class to the <DIV> tag, turning the text black. We do that by setting
the <DIV> tag's className property to blackText, which looks like this in the
MakeBlack() subroutine:

```
<HTML>

<HEAD>
<TITLE>DIV Example</TITLE>
</HEAD>

<BODY>
      .
      .
      .
</BODY>

<STYLE>
 .blackText {color:Black}
 .blueText {color:Blue}
</STYLE>

<SCRIPT LANGUAGE = VBScript>
        Sub MakeBlack()                                      ⇐
                DIV1.className = "blackText"                 ⇐
        End Sub                                              ⇐
         .
         .
         .

<HTML>
```

Similarly, the blueText class makes the text blue with when the user clicks the Make text blue button:

```
<HEAD>
<TITLE>DIV Example</TITLE>
</HEAD>

<BODY>
    .
    .
    .
</BODY>

<STYLE>
 .blackText {color:Black}
 .blueText {color:Blue}
</STYLE>

<SCRIPT LANGUAGE = VBScript>
        Sub MakeBlack()
                DIV1.className = "blackText"
        End Sub

        Sub MakeBlue()                                      ⇐
                DIV1.className = "blueText"                 ⇐
        End Sub                                             ⇐
</SCRIPT>

</HTML>
```

Now open Internet Explorer in the browser, as shown in Figure 5.9. When the user clicks the two buttons, the text color will change from black to blue and back again.

The code for Figure 5.9's Web page appears in Listing 5.5.

**Listing 5.5 div.htm**

```
<HTML>

<HEAD>
<TITLE>DIV Example</TITLE>
</HEAD>
```

**Figure 5.9 Changing the color of text in a <DIV> section.**

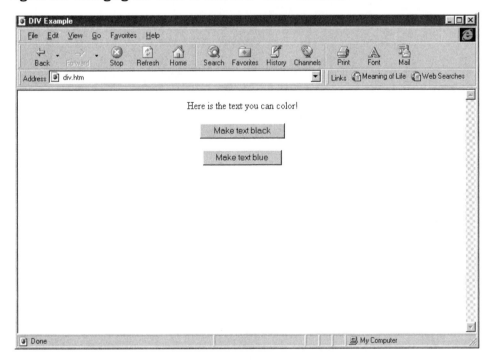

## Listing 5.5 Continued

```
<BODY>

<CENTER>
<DIV ID = DIV1>
Here is the text you can color!
</DIV>
<BR>
<INPUT TYPE = BUTTON Value = "Make text black" onClick =
"MakeBlack()">
<BR>
<BR>
<INPUT TYPE = BUTTON Value = "Make text blue" onClick = "MakeBlue()">

</CENTER>
```

*Continued*

**Listing 5.5 Continued**
```
</BODY>

<STYLE>
 .blackText {color:Black}
 .blueText {color:Blue}
</STYLE>

<SCRIPT LANGUAGE = VBScript>
        Sub MakeBlack()
                DIV1.className = "blackText"
        End Sub

        Sub MakeBlue()
                DIV1.className = "blueText"
        End Sub
</SCRIPT>

</HTML>
```

The next tag in our Web page is the <FONT> tag, which we used to display enlarged text in our Web page:

```
      -------------------------------------------------
      |<HTML>                                           |
      |                                                 |
      |  ------------------------------------------- |  |
      |  |<HEAD>                                   |  |  |
      |  |                                         |  |  |
      |  |<TITLE>                                  |  |  |
      |  |This is the title.                       |  |  |
      |  |</TITLE>                                 |  |  |
      |  |                                         |  |  |
      |  |</HEAD>                                  |  |  |
      |  ------------------------------------------- |  |
      |                                                 |
      |  ------------------------------------------- |  |
      |  |<BODY>                                   |  |  |
      |  |                                         |  |  |
      |  |         <H1>This is our main heading</H1> |  |  |
      |  |                                         |  |  |
      |  |              --------------------       |  |  |
      |  |                  |                 |     |  |  |
```

```
| |                    |                      |                    | |
| |                    |                      |                    | |
| |                    |          Image       |                    | |
| |                    |                      |                    | |
| |                    |                      |                    | |
| |              ---------------------                              | |
| |                                                                 | |
| |    --------------------------------------------------          | |
| | |                                                     |         | | |
| | |                                                     |         | | |
| | |                     Text                            |         | | |
| | |                                                     |         | | |
| |    --------------------------------------------------          | |
| |                                                                 | |
| |    ---------     --------------------------------------        | |
| | |           | |                                        |       | | |
| | |           | |                                        |       | | |
| | |   Image   | |               Text                     |       | | |
| | |           | |                                        |       | | |
| | |           | |                                        |       | | |
| |    ---------     --------------------------------------        | |
| |                                                                 | |
| |    --------------------------------------------------          | |
| | | Enlarged Text                                       |         | | |    ⇐
| |    --------------------------------------------------          | |
| |                                                                 | |
| |                  -----------------                              | |
| |                 |                 |                             | |
| |                 |-----------------|                             | |
| |                 |      |       |      |                         | |
| |                 |-----------------|                             | |
| |                 |      |       |      |                         | |
| |                  -----------------                              | |
| |                                                                 | |
| |</BODY>                                                          | |
|    --------------------------------------------------------       |
|                                                                   |
|</HTML>                                                            |
 -------------------------------------------------------------
```

Let's take a guided tour of the Internet Explorer <FONT> tag's new capabilities.

# The <FONT> Tag

## Properties

*className, docHeight, docLeft, docTop, docWidth, parentElement, sourceIndex, tagName, color, face, id, size, style, title*

## Methods

*removeMember, scrollIntoView, contains, getMember, setMember*

## Events

*onclick, ondblclick, onhelp, onmousedown, onmousemove, onmouseout, onmouseover, onmouseup*

Using the <FONT> tag, we can modify the font face (that is, the font itself), the color of the font, the font's size, and its style. For example, we can display some text and allow the user to enlarge the text with the click of a button by using the <FONT> tag's size property.

We start this new example, font.htm, with the text that we will enlarge—"Here is the text!"—enclosed in a <FONT> tag with the ID Font1:

```
<HTML>

<HEAD>
<TITLE>Font Example</TITLE>
</HEAD>

<BODY>

<CENTER>
<FONT ID = Font1>Here is the text!</FONT>          ⇐
    .
    .
    .
```

Next, we add a button with the caption "Enlarge text," connecting that button to the subroutine EnlargeText():

```
<HTML>

<HEAD>
<TITLE>Font Example</TITLE>
</HEAD>
```

```
<BODY>

<CENTER>
<FONT ID = Font1>Here is the text!</FONT>
<BR>
<BR>
<INPUT TYPE = BUTTON Value = "Enlarge text" onClick =
"EnlargeText()">                                              ⇐
</CENTER>

</BODY>
        .
        .
        .
```

Now we can write the EnlargeText() subroutine. In this subroutine, we want to enlarge the text, so we simply set Font1's font size to 36 points:

```
<HTML>

<HEAD>
<TITLE>Font Example</TITLE>
</HEAD>

<BODY>

<CENTER>
<FONT ID = Font1>Here is the text!</FONT>
<BR>
<BR>
<INPUT TYPE = BUTTON Value = "Enlarge text" onClick = "EnlargeText()">
</CENTER>

</BODY>

<SCRIPT LANGUAGE = VBScript>
        Sub EnlargeText()
                Font1.size = 36                              ⇐
        End Sub
</SCRIPT>

</HTML>
```

Notice in particular that the font size we place in the <FONT> tag's size property is measured in points, not in the standard HTML font sizes, which range from only 1 to 7. Using point sizes is far more useful (not least because they support larger text than the standard HTML sizes) and is yet another benefit of Dynamic HTML.

When we open the page in Internet Explorer, we see the text we've placed in the page. When the user clicks the button in the page, that text enlarges automatically, as shown in Figure 5.10. Our font.htm example is a success.

The code for Figure 5.10's page appears in Listing 5.6.

## Listing 5.6 font.htm

```
<HTML>

<HEAD>
```

**Figure 5.10 Enlarging text with the <FONT> tag's size property.**

**Listing 5.6 Continued**

```
<TITLE>Font Example</TITLE>
</HEAD>

<BODY>

<CENTER>
<FONT ID = Font1>Here is the text!</FONT>
<BR>
<BR>
<INPUT TYPE = BUTTON Value = "Enlarge text" onClick = "EnlargeText()">
</CENTER>

</BODY>

<SCRIPT LANGUAGE = VBScript>
        Sub EnlargeText()
                Font1.size = 36
        End Sub
</SCRIPT>

</HTML>
```

We've taken a look at a good number of tags already, but there are more to come. Next in our Web page is the <TABLE> tag.

# The <TABLE> Tag

## Properties

*dataSrc, className, docHeight, docLeft, docTop, docWidth, parentElement, sourceIndex, tagName, align, background, bgColor, border, borderColor, borderColorDark, borderColorLight, cellPadding, cellSpacing, cols, frame, height, id, rules, style, title, width*

## Methods

*removeMember, scrollIntoView, contains, getMember, setMember*

## Events

*onafterupdate, onbeforeupdate, onclick, ondblclick, onhelp, onkeydown, onkeypress, onkeyup, onmousedown, onmousemove, onmouseout, onmouseover, onmouseup*

We can change many aspects of a table dynamically. We can change its colors, its width, height, cell padding, and more. We can even change the contents of the cells by working with the <TD> tag. One of the Dynamic HTML properties of the <TABLE> tag is the border property, and using that property, we can set the width of a table's border. In this example, we'll set the border of a table to a new, thicker value when the user clicks a button.

We start our new example, setbord.htm, by setting up a table with some entries in it. In this example, we'll set up a tic-tac-toe board this way, giving the table the ID "Table":

```
<HTML>

<HEAD>
<TITLE>Set a table's border</TITLE>
</HEAD>

<BODY>

<CENTER>
<TABLE BORDER ID = Table>                                           ⇐
<TR><TD>X</TD><TD>O</TD><TD>O</TD>                                   ⇐
<TR><TD>O</TD><TD>X</TD><TD>X</TD>                                   ⇐
<TR><TD>O</TD><TD>O</TD><TD>X</TD>                                   ⇐
</TABLE>                                                             ⇐
      .
      .
      .
```

Next, we add to our Web page a button that the user can click; when the user clicks this button, the table's border will thicken. Here's how we add that button:

```
<HTML>

<HEAD>
<TITLE>Set a table's border</TITLE>
</HEAD>

<BODY>

<CENTER>
<TABLE BORDER ID = Table>
<TR><TD>X</TD><TD>O</TD><TD>O</TD>
```

```
<TR><TD>O</TD><TD>X</TD><TD>X</TD>
<TR><TD>O</TD><TD>O</TD><TD>X</TD>
</TABLE>

<BR>
<BR>
<INPUT TYPE = BUTTON Value = "Thicken table's border" onClick =
SetBorder()>⇐
</CENTER>

</BODY>
    .
    .
    .
```

When the user clicks the button, we can cause the border to increase with the table's border property in the SetBorder() subroutine:

```
<HTML>

<HEAD>
<TITLE>Set a table's border</TITLE>
</HEAD>

<BODY>
    .
    .
    .
</BODY>

<SCRIPT LANGUAGE = VBScript>
        Sub SetBorder()
                Table.border = 10                                        ⇐
        End Sub
</SCRIPT>

</HTML>
```

Now open this page in Internet Explorer and click the button. When you do, the table's border thickens, as shown in Figure 5.11. Our <TABLE> example is a success. We're able to use the <TABLE> tag's properties and methods in our Web pages now.

The listing for Figure 5.11's Web page appears in Listing 5.7.

**Figure 5.11 Increasing a table's border width using the border property.**

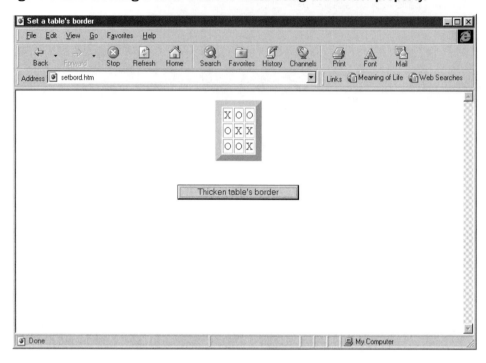

**Listing 5.7 setbord.htm**

```
<HTML>

<HEAD>
<TITLE>Set a table's border</TITLE>
</HEAD>

<BODY>

<CENTER>
<TABLE BORDER ID = Table>
<TR><TD>X</TD><TD>O</TD><TD>O</TD>
<TR><TD>O</TD><TD>X</TD><TD>X</TD>
<TR><TD>O</TD><TD>O</TD><TD>X</TD>
</TABLE>
```

**Listing 5.7 Continued**

```
<BR>
<BR>
<INPUT TYPE = BUTTON Value = "Thicken table's border" onClick =
SetBorder()>
</CENTER>

</BODY>

<SCRIPT LANGUAGE = VBScript>
        Sub SetBorder()
                Table.border = 10
        End Sub
</SCRIPT>

</HTML>
```

Besides the tags we've covered, another tag that we've seen deserves another look: the <INPUT> tag.

# The <INPUT> Tag

## Properties

*dataFld, dataSrc, className, docHeight, docLeft, docTop, docWidth, parentElement, sourceIndex, tagName, accessKey, align, disabled, id, language, maxLength, name, readOnly, size, style, tabIndex, title, type, value*

## Methods

*removeMember, scrollIntoView, contains, getMember, setMember*

## Events

*onafterupdate, onbeforeupdate, onblur, onchange, onclick, ondblclick, onfocus, onhelp, onkeydown, onkeypress, onkeyup, onmousedown, onmousemove, onmouseout, onmouseover, onmouseup , onselect*

Even the <INPUT> tag has become dynamic. Let's take a look at this tag in an example. In this case, we'll call the new Web page resizer.htm and let the user simply click a button to resize a text box.

We start with the text box, giving it an initial size of 20 characters and a name of "Textbox" as well as a button with the caption "Resize text box" that connects the button to a subroutine named ResizeTextbox():

```
<HTML>

<HEAD>
<TITLE>Resize Text Box</TITLE>
</HEAD>

<BODY>

<CENTER>
<INPUT TYPE = TEXT NAME = Textbox SIZE = 20 VALUE = "You can resize
this box.">                                                          ⇐
<BR>
<BR>
<INPUT TYPE=BUTTON Value="Resize text box" onClick =
"ResizeTextbox()">                                                   ⇐
</CENTER>

</BODY>
     .
     .
     .
```

Now we add the ResizeTextbox() method, resizing the text box to a width of
40 characters in that subroutine:

```
<HTML>

<HEAD>
<TITLE>Resize Text Box</TITLE>
</HEAD>

<BODY>

<CENTER>
<INPUT TYPE = TEXT NAME = Textbox SIZE = 20 VALUE = "You can resize
this box.">
<BR>
<BR>
<INPUT TYPE = BUTTON Value = "Resize text box" onClick =
"ResizeTextbox()">
</CENTER>
```

```
</BODY>

<SCRIPT LANGUAGE = VBScript>
        Sub ResizeTextbox()                              ⇐
                TextBox.Size = 40                        ⇐
        End Sub                                          ⇐
</SCRIPT>

</HTML>
```

When you open the page in Internet Explorer, you see the text box with the text "You can resize this box." in it, as shown in Figure 5.12. When you click the button marked "Resize text box," the button increases in size. Our resizing Web page is a success.

The code for Figure 5.12's Web page, resizer.htm, appears in Listing 5.8.

**Figure 5.12 Resizing a text box on demand.**

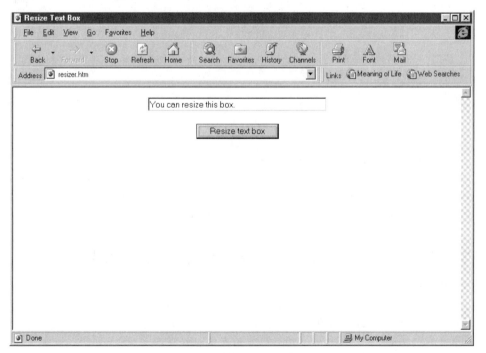

**Listing 5.8 resizer.htm**

```html
<HTML>

<HEAD>
<TITLE>Resize Text Box</TITLE>
</HEAD>

<BODY>

<CENTER>
<INPUT TYPE = TEXT NAME = Textbox SIZE = 20 VALUE = "You can resize
this box.">
<BR>
<BR>
<INPUT TYPE = BUTTON Value = "Resize text box" onClick =
"ResizeTextbox()">
</CENTER>

</BODY>

<SCRIPT LANGUAGE = VBScript>
        Sub ResizeTextbox()
                TextBox.Size = 40
        End Sub
</SCRIPT>

</HTML>
```

Besides the tags we've seen in this chapter, we also have access to several new properties and methods in the standard Internet Explorer objects that we can use with scripts. We'll look at one of these new properties, activeElement, now. This new property is a member of the document object.

# The Document Object and Event Bubbling

## Properties

*alinkColor, linkColor, vlinkColor, mimeType, title, bgColor, link, vLink, aLink, cookie, lastModified, charset, location, referrer, fgColor, activeElement, strReadyState, domain, URL, fileSize, fileCreatedDate, fileModifiedDate, fileUpdatedDate,*

## Collections

*anchors, forms, links, all, scripts, images, applets, frames, embeds, plugins*

## Methods

*close, open, clear, write, writeln, rangeFromText, rangeFromElement, execCommand, queryCommandEnabled, queryCommandText, elementFromPoint, queryCommandSupported, queryCommandState, queryCommandIndeterm, createElement*

## Events

*onclick, onmouseover, ondblclick, onkeypress, onmousedown,*

*onmousemove, onmouseup, onkeydown, onkeyup, onmouseout,*

*onreadystatechange, onhelp, onbeforeupdate, onafterupdate*

One very useful new property of the document object is the activeElement property; this property holds the Web page element that has the current focus. Let's take advantage of this property to create an example. In this case, we can place two controls in an Internet Explorer Web page: a text box and a button. When the user clicks one of these controls, we can determine which control was clicked with the activeElement property and place the text "Hello from Dynamic HTML" into that control. Let's create this example, activelm.htm, now.

We begin by displaying the text box and button:

```
<HTML>

<HEAD>
<TITLE>Active Element Example</TITLE>
</HEAD>

<BODY>

<CENTER>
Click either control...
<BR>
<BR>
<INPUT TYPE = TEXT SIZE = 30>                              ⇐
<BR>
<BR>
<INPUT TYPE = BUTTON Value = "Click to change my caption">   ⇐
</CENTER>
```

```
</BODY>
        .
        .
        .
```

Next, we will set up code to handle mouse clicks in our document, which we'll handle in the document_OnClick() subroutine. You might ask the following question: The user is clicking controls, not the document itself, so why does the browser call the document_OnClick() subroutine? The answer is *event bubbling*, which we'll investigate now.

Even though the user clicks a control, the document's OnClick event handler is still called because of an Internet Explorer feature called event bubbling. We'll see more about event bubbling soon, but what it means is that if an element receives an event, but doesn't explicitly handle that event, the event is sent on to the element that contains the element that originally got the event. In our case, that means that when the user clicks the text box, that click event will eventually be passed on to the document_OnClick() subroutine. For that reason, we can set the text in a control to "Hello from Dynamic HTML" this way in document_OnClick() when the user clicks any control in our Web page simply by referring to the control with the focus document.activeElement:

```
<HTML>

<HEAD>
<TITLE>Active Element Example</TITLE>
</HEAD>

<BODY>
        .
        .
        .
</BODY>

<SCRIPT LANGUAGE = VBScript>
        Sub document_OnClick                                    ⇐
                document.activeElement.Value = "Hello from Dynamic
HTML"                                                           ⇐
        End Sub                                                 ⇐
</SCRIPT>

</HTML>
```

That's all we need. Open the Web page in Internet Explorer, which will look like Figure 5.13, now.

When you click either control (not the document itself behind the controls, because the document itself does not support a Value attribute), the text in that control changes to "Hello from Dynamic HTML," as shown in Figure 5.13. In this way, we're able to determine which control in the Web page has the focus.

The listing for this Web page, activelm.htm, is shown in Listing 5.9.

## Listing 5.9 activelm.htm

```
<HTML>

<HEAD>
<TITLE>Active Element Example</TITLE>
</HEAD>
```

*Continued*

**Figure 5.13 Setting the active element's text.**

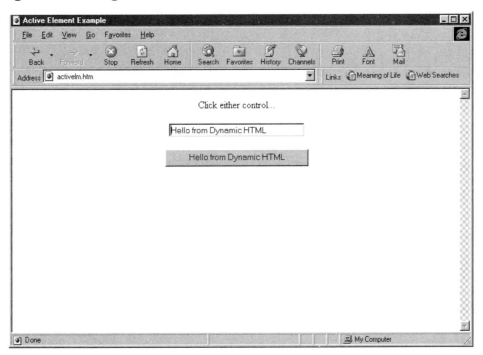

**Listing 5.9 Continued**

```
<BODY>

<CENTER>
Click either control...
<BR>
<BR>
<INPUT TYPE = TEXT SIZE = 30>
<BR>
<BR>
<INPUT TYPE = BUTTON Value = "Click to change my caption">
</CENTER>

</BODY>

<SCRIPT LANGUAGE = VBScript>
        Sub document_OnClick
                document.activeElement.Value = "Hello from Dynamic
HTML"
        End Sub
</SCRIPT>

</HTML>
```

# What's Ahead

That's it for this chapter. We've come far here, exploring the new properties and methods that we now have access to in Internet Explorer. We've explored quite a number of the newly active tags in that browser in this chapter: the <HTML> tag, the <HEAD> tag, the <TITLE> tag, the <BODY> tag, the <IMG> tag, the <DIV> tag, the <FONT> tag, the <INPUT> tag, and others. We've made progress, adding a great deal of Dynamic HTML power to our arsenal.

That's just the beginning, though. In the next chapter, we'll continue our exploration by examining the new graphics effects we can create. For some programmers, this is what Dynamic HTML is all about.

# C H A P T E R  6

# AMAZING
# GRAPHICS EFFECTS

I n this chapter, we start working with a new topic that many people consider to be the whole rationale of the Web: working with and handling graphics. Here, we'll see graphics effects beyond the ordinary as we probe what Internet Explorer and Netscape Navigator have to offer us. Knowing the importance of graphics, both Microsoft and Netscape have strengthened their graphics capabilities in their new releases of these popular browsers.

To start, we'll see how to work with text—in a graphics environment, text is considered graphics too. We will see that we can now place text where we want it, including making text overlap other text.

Next, we'll explore some of the new capabilities of Internet Explorer's multimedia controls. Microsoft has added several new multimedia controls, and although Netscape doesn't support them yet, they are too important to overlook, and we'll get started looking at them here. The new Internet Explorer multimedia controls appear in Table 6.1.

We'll take a look at these controls in this and the next chapter.

In this chapter, we'll see how to apply graphics *filters* to our Web pages. We'll see that filters allow us to alter the way we present graphics to the user; in particular, we'll see that we can blur, distort, flip, and easily apply many other such effects to graphics.

In addition, we'll use the Internet Explorer multimedia controls to see how to make text and images in a Web page fade in and out dynamically, supporting dissolves, wipes, and fades as the user watches. This is a powerful effect and one that can really bring Web pages to life, as we'll see.

**Table 6.1 The Internet Explorer Multimedia Controls**

| Multimedia Control | Does this |
| --- | --- |
| Sequencer | Easily controls timing of events on pages |
| Structured graphics | Provides high-quality, lightweight, scalable, rotatable graphics |
| Sprite | Creates animated movable images |
| Path | Easily moves objects across a two-dimensional path |
| DirectAnimation | Supports complex animation |
| DirectShow ActiveMovie | Supports movies and sound mixing |

We'll also take a look at another Internet Explorer multimedia control in this chapter: the structured graphics control. Using this control, you can draw complex graphics figures via commands you send to the control.

In addition, we'll see that Netscape has come up with something Internet Explorer doesn't have: layers. Layers are just what they sound like; you can apply graphics to your Web pages in layers and address graphics in each layer separately. In this chapter, we'll see how this feature is useful for creating graphics effects; in the next chapter, we'll see how it's useful for creating animation.

There's a lot of graphics power coming up in this chapter. Let's start now by working with overlapping text in Web pages.

# Overlapping Text in Web Pages

In our first example, we'll see how to create overlapping text in both Internet Explorer and Netscape Navigator. We'll see how we can position text anywhere we like in Web pages—a powerful new feature of Dynamic HTML. In this case, we'll just place the text "This is a demonstration of overlapping text. The colored text will appear on top of this text...." into our Web page, and then we'll cover that text with large green text reading simply "Text."

We start by giving our Web page a black background:

```
<HTML>

<HEAD>
<TITLE>Overlapping text example</TITLE>
</HEAD>
```

```
<BODY BGCOLOR=BLACK>                                                    ⇐
    .
    .
    .
```

Next, we add a <DIV> with the underlying text, "This is a demonstration of overlapping text. The colored text will appear on top of this text...." To position this <DIV> in our Web page, we use the STYLE attribute and the styles LEFT, TOP, WIDTH, and HEIGHT, giving the coordinates of those locations in pixels. We also indicate that all our measurements are "absolute" with respect to the top left of the Web page:

```
<HTML>

<HEAD>
<TITLE>Overlapping text example</TITLE>
</HEAD>

<BODY BGCOLOR=BLACK>

<DIV STYLE="POSITION:ABSOLUTE; LEFT:100; TOP:30; WIDTH:250;
HEIGHT:280">                                                           ⇐
    .
    .
    .
```

Now we display the underlying text in white Arial font:

```
<HTML>

<HEAD>
<TITLE>Overlapping text example</TITLE>
</HEAD>

<BODY BGCOLOR=BLACK>

<DIV STYLE="POSITION:ABSOLUTE; LEFT:100; TOP:30; WIDTH:250;
HEIGHT:280">
<FONT SIZE = 4 FACE = "ARIAL" COLOR = WHITE>                            ⇐
This is a demonstration of overlapping text. The colored text will
appear on top of this text....                                         ⇐
</FONT>
</DIV>
```

.
.
.

At this point, we're free to create a new <DIV> that overlaps the old one, displaying the word "Text" twice in large green Verdana font:

```
<HTML>

<HEAD>
<TITLE>Overlapping text example</TITLE>
</HEAD>

<BODY BGCOLOR=BLACK>

<DIV STYLE="POSITION:ABSOLUTE; LEFT:100; TOP:30; WIDTH:250;
HEIGHT:280">
<FONT SIZE = 4 FACE = "ARIAL" COLOR = WHITE>
This is a demonstration of overlapping text. The colored text will
appear on top of this text....
</FONT>
</DIV>

<DIV STYLE="POSITION:ABSOLUTE; LEFT:100; TOP:0; WIDTH:250; HEIGHT:200">  ⇐
<FONT SIZE = 7 FACE = "VERDANA" COLOR = GREEN>                            ⇐
<CENTER>
Text
<BR>
Text

</CENTER>

</FONT>
</DIV>

</BODY>
</HTML>
```

Open the Web page now. As you can see in Figure 6.1, the text we have placed into our Web page does indeed overlap, just as we planned. Using absolute placements of <DIV>s, our overlapping text example is a success.

**Figure 6.1 Creating overlapping text.**

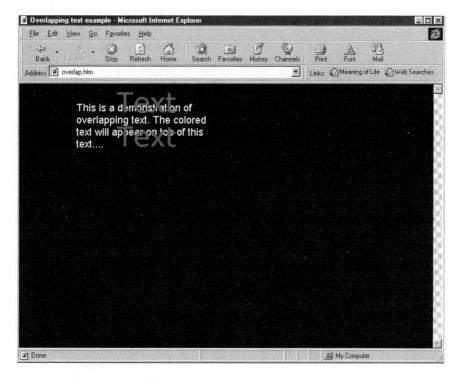

The code for this example, overlap.htm, appears in Listing 6.1.

**Listing 6.1 overlap.htm**

```
<HTML>

<HEAD>
<TITLE>Overlapping text example</TITLE>
</HEAD>

<BODY BGCOLOR=BLACK>

<DIV STYLE="POSITION:ABSOLUTE; LEFT:100; TOP:30; WIDTH:250;
HEIGHT:280">
<FONT SIZE = 4 FACE = "ARIAL" COLOR = WHITE>
```

*Continued*

**Listing 6.1 Continued**

```
This is a demonstration of overlapping text. The colored text will
appear on top of this text....
</FONT>
</DIV>

<DIV STYLE="POSITION:ABSOLUTE; LEFT:100; TOP:0; WIDTH:250; HEIGHT:200">
<FONT SIZE = 7 FACE = "VERDANA" COLOR = GREEN>
<CENTER>
Text
<BR>
Text

</CENTER>

</FONT>
</DIV>

</BODY>
</HTML>
```

Now let's press on to working with the new multimedia capabilities in Internet Explorer. The first such effect we'll work with is the application of *filters*.

# Using Graphics Filters

Because handling graphics has become more and more important in Web pages, browsers like Internet Explorer and Netscape Navigator have responded to demand. One new technique that Internet Explorer supports is the use of *filters*. Filters can be applied to any object on the HTML page that supports the Filter property, such as <DIV>, <IMG>, or <OBJECT> tags; the filters we'll look at in this example include the Blur, Gray, Flip Horizontal, Flip Vertical, Invert, Shadow, Wave, and Xray filters.

In this new example, filters.htm, we'll display eight buttons, one for each of the filters we will let the user use:

```
-----------------------------------------------------------------
|                                                               |
|---------------------------------------------------------------|
|                Click a button to apply a filter...            |
```

```
|                                                                      |
|                                                                      |
|   ----  -------------  ----------  ----  ------  ------  ----  ----   |
|  |Blur||Flip Vertical||Flip Horiz||Gray||Invert||Shadow||Wave||XRay|  |
|   ----  -------------  ----------  ----  ------  ------  ----  ----   |
|                                                                      |
|                                                                      |
|           You can use filters on text, controls, or images!          |
|                                                                      |
|                                                                      |
|                                                                      |
|                                                                      |
|                                                                      |
----------------------------------------------------------------------
```

When the user clicks a button, the associated filter will be applied to the text "You can use filters on text, controls, or images!" that appears under the buttons. Via the associated filter, we'll be able to blur, flip, gray, wave that text, and more. We begin our filter.htm Web page with a title:

```
<HTML>

<HEAD>
<TITLE>Using filters...</TITLE>
</HEAD>
    .
    .
    .
```

Next, we'll give our page blue text so the various color effects will stand out more when you look at the Web page in Internet Explorer (although those effects won't be so obvious in the figures in this book, of course):

```
<HTML>

<HEAD>
<TITLE>Using filters...</TITLE>
</HEAD>

<BODY text = "#0000ff">                                          ⇐
    .
    .
    .
```

We can also add a new prompt to the user, asking him or her to apply a filter by clicking a button:

```
<HTML>

<HEAD>
<TITLE>Using filters...</TITLE>
</HEAD>

<BODY text = "#0000ff">

<CENTER>                                                            ⇐
<H1>                                                                ⇐
Click a button to apply a filter...                                 ⇐
</H1>                                                               ⇐
</CENTER>                                                           ⇐
    .
    .
    .
```

We add some text—"You can use filters on text, controls, or images!"—to which we will apply the filters:

```
<HTML>

<HEAD>
<TITLE>Using filters...</TITLE>
</HEAD>

<BODY text = "#0000ff">

<CENTER>
<H1>
Click a button to apply a filter...
</H1>
</CENTER>
    .
    .
    .
<CENTER>
<p>
<DIV ID=Div1 style ="WIDTH:95%" style="font-size:24pt;font-family:ver-
dana;font-style:bold" >
```

```
You can use filters on text, controls, or images!                    ⇐
</DIV>
</CENTER>

</BODY>
</HTML>
```

Notice that we put that text into a <DIV> section so we can refer to the <DIV>—and the text in it—by ID: Div1. At this point, we're ready to apply filters to that text.

## Applying Graphics Filters

The first filter we'll apply to the target text in our Web page is the *Blur* filter; this filter blurs the text or image to which you apply it. In Internet Explorer, you apply a filter using an HTML element's filter style. Let's see how this works now; we start by adding a new button with the caption "Blur":

```
<HTML>

<HEAD>
<TITLE>Using filters...</TITLE>
</HEAD>

<BODY text = "#0000ff">

<CENTER>
<H1>
Click a button to apply a filter...
</H1>
</CENTER>

<CENTER>
<input value="Blur" type=button>                                     ⇐
    .
    .
    .
```

When the user clicks that button, we can apply a new filter to Div1 by setting the Div1.style.filter property. To apply a blur filter, we must specify the direction we want the text to be blurred in (we use a value of 45 degrees), specify the strength of the blurring, and set an enabled flag to 1 (we must set the enabled flag to 1 every time we want to use a filter):

---

```
<HTML>

<HEAD>
<TITLE>Using filters...</TITLE>
</HEAD>

<BODY text = "#0000ff">

<CENTER>
<H1>
Click a button to apply a filter...
</H1>
</CENTER>

<CENTER>
<input value="Blur" type=button onclick="Div1.style.filter =
'blur(direction=45, strength=10, enabled=1)'">                    ⇐
    .
    .
    .
```

That's all there is to it.

Let's take a look at another type of filter now: the *flip* filters, which let us flip elements vertically or horizontally. The methods for these filters are flipv() and fliph(), and we apply those filters this way:

```
<HTML>

<HEAD>
<TITLE>Using filters...</TITLE>
</HEAD>

<BODY text = "#0000ff">

<CENTER>
<H1>
Click a button to apply a filter...
</H1>
</CENTER>

<CENTER>
<input value="Blur" type=button onclick="Div1.style.filter =
'blur(direction=45, strength=10, enabled=1)'">
```

```
<input value="Flip Vertical" type=button onclick="Div1.style.filter =
'flipv(enabled=1)'">                                                    ⟸
<input value="Flip Horiz" type=button onclick="Div1.style.filter =
'fliph(enabled=1)'">                                                    ⟸
    .
    .
    .
```

Now we're able to flip the target text vertically or horizontally, providing a powerful effect (we'll see the horizontal flip filter at work in a minute).

We can also "gray" text (i.e., display it in monotone gray) with the *Gray* filter this way:

```
<HTML>
    .
    .
    .

<CENTER>
<input value="Blur" type=button onclick="Div1.style.filter =
'blur(direction=45, strength=10, enabled=1)'">
<input value="Flip Vertical" type=button onclick="Div1.style.filter =
'flipv(enabled=1)'">
<input value="Flip Horiz" type=button onclick="Div1.style.filter =
'fliph(enabled=1)'">
<input value="Gray" type=button onclick="Div1.style.filter =
'gray(enabled=1)'">                                                     ⟸
    .
    .
    .

</BODY>
</HTML>
```

There are other filters available as well. We can color invert the target text with the *invert* filter. Applying this filter to the blue text in our Web page turns it yellow, for example:

```
<HTML>
    .
    .
    .

<CENTER>
<input value="Blur" type=button onclick="Div1.style.filter =
'blur(direction=45, strength=10, enabled=1)'">
```

```
<input value="Flip Vertical" type=button onclick="Div1.style.filter =
'flipv(enabled=1)'">
<input value="Flip Horiz" type=button onclick="Div1.style.filter =
'fliph(enabled=1)'">
<input value="Gray" type=button onclick="Div1.style.filter =
'gray(enabled=1)'">
<input value="Invert" type=button onclick="Div1.style.filter =
'invert(enabled=1)'">                                                    ⇐
        .
        .
        .

</BODY>
</HTML>
```

We can also add a shadow to the text with the *Shadow* filter. We indicate the color we want the shadow to be and its direction in degrees this way:

```
<HTML>
        .
        .
        .

<CENTER>
<input value="Blur" type=button onclick="Div1.style.filter =
'blur(direction=45, strength=10, enabled=1)'">
<input value="Flip Vertical" type=button onclick="Div1.style.filter =
'flipv(enabled=1)'">
<input value="Flip Horiz" type=button onclick="Div1.style.filter =
'fliph(enabled=1)'">
<input value="Gray" type=button onclick="Div1.style.filter =
'gray(enabled=1)'">
<input value="Invert" type=button onclick="Div1.style.filter =
'invert(enabled=1)'">
<input value="Shadow" type=button onclick="Div1.style.filter = 'shad-
ow(color=#5500AA, direction=300, enabled=1)'">                          ⇐
        .
        .
        .

</BODY>
</HTML>
```

Applying a shadow filter results in a striking effect, although it's not exactly what you might expect from the term "shadow," as we'll see in a moment. The effect is a little more like providing the text with a backswept, colored corona or halo. If you want to provide a more traditional shadow, use the dropshadow() method, specifying an *x* and *y* offset for the shadow of each letter and the color of that shadow like this:

```
dropshadow(offx=10, offy=10, color=#5500AA, enabled=1)
```

We can also apply a sine-like wave to the target text with the *Wave* filter. The text is waved vertically; You supply a wave frequency (the number of vertical sine-line cycles) and a strength for the wave (the amplitude of the sine-like distortion) like this:

```
<HTML>
     .
     .
     .
<CENTER>
<input value="Blur" type=button onclick="Div1.style.filter =
'blur(direction=45, strength=10, enabled=1)'">
<input value="Flip Vertical" type=button onclick="Div1.style.filter =
'flipv(enabled=1)'">
<input value="Flip Horiz" type=button onclick="Div1.style.filter =
'fliph(enabled=1)'">
<input value="Gray" type=button onclick="Div1.style.filter =
'gray(enabled=1)'">
<input value="Invert" type=button onclick="Div1.style.filter =
'invert(enabled=1)'">
<input value="Shadow" type=button onclick="Div1.style.filter = 'shad-
ow(color=#5500AA, direction=300, enabled=1)'">
<input value="Wave" type=button onclick="Div1.style.filter =
'wave(freq=1, strength=5, enabled=1)'">                              ⇐
     .
     .
     .
</BODY>
</HTML>
```

The last filter we'll apply is the *Xray* filter. This filter acts much like the Gray filter, turning the target black and white in a passable representation of an Xray negative:

```
<HTML>
     .
     .
     .
<CENTER>
```

```
<input value="Blur" type=button onclick="Div1.style.filter =
'blur(direction=45, strength=10, enabled=1)'">
<input value="Flip Vertical" type=button onclick="Div1.style.filter =
'flipv(enabled=1)'">
<input value="Flip Horiz" type=button onclick="Div1.style.filter =
'fliph(enabled=1)'">
<input value="Gray" type=button onclick="Div1.style.filter =
'gray(enabled=1)'">
<input value="Invert" type=button onclick="Div1.style.filter =
'invert(enabled=1)'">
<input value="Shadow" type=button onclick="Div1.style.filter = 'shad-
ow(color=#5500AA, direction=300, enabled=1)'">
<input value="Wave" type=button onclick="Div1.style.filter =
'wave(freq=1, strength=5, enabled=1)'">
<input value="XRay" type=button onclick="Div1.style.filter =
'xray(enabled=1)'">                                                    ⇐
</CENTER>
      .
      .
      .

</BODY>
</HTML>
```

That's it—our filters.htm page is ready to go. Open the page in Internet Explorer and click a button to see the matching filter applied to the text. For example, in Figure 6.2, you see the Flip Horizontal filter at work.

In Figure 6.3, we've used the Shadow filter. You can see how the letters appear with a shadow swept behind them. As you can see, these effects are very powerful, and you can also apply them dynamically as the Web page appears on the user's screen.

The code for this example, filters.htm, appears in Listing 6.2.

---

### Listing 6.2 filters.htm

```
<HTML>

<HEAD>
<TITLE>Using filters...</TITLE>
</HEAD>

<BODY text = "#0000ff">
```

**Figure 6.2 Applying the Flip Horizontal filter to a Web page.**

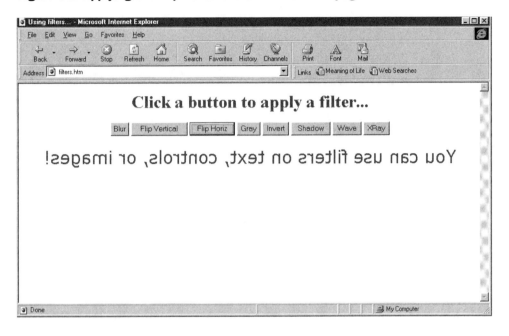

**Listing 6.2 Continued**

```
<CENTER>
<H1>
Click a button to apply a filter...
</H1>
</CENTER>

<CENTER>
<input value="Blur" type=button onclick="Div1.style.filter =
'blur(direction=45, strength=10, enabled=1)'">
<input value="Flip Vertical" type=button onclick="Div1.style.filter =
'flipv(enabled=1)'">
<input value="Flip Horiz" type=button onclick="Div1.style.filter =
'fliph(enabled=1)'">
<input value="Gray" type=button onclick="Div1.style.filter =
'gray(enabled=1)'">
```

*Continued*

**Figure 6.3 Applying the Shadow filter to a Web page.**

**Listing 6.2 Continued**

```
<input value="Invert" type=button onclick="Div1.style.filter =
'invert(enabled=1)'">
<input value="Shadow" type=button onclick="Div1.style.filter = 'shad-
ow(color=#5500AA, direction=300, enabled=1)'">
<input value="Wave" type=button onclick="Div1.style.filter =
'wave(freq=1, strength=5, enabled=1)'">
<input value="XRay" type=button onclick="Div1.style.filter =
'xray(enabled=1)'">
</CENTER>

<CENTER>
<p>
<DIV ID=Div1 style ="WIDTH:95%" style="font-size:24pt;font-family:ver-
dana;font-style:bold" >
You can use filters on text, controls, or images!
```

**Listing 6.2 Continued**

```
</DIV>
</CENTER>

</BODY>
</HTML>
```

We've gotten a good introduction to filters now, but there's more to see. In our next example, we'll see how to make text fade in and out as the user watches.

## Dissolving In and Out with Transitions

In this example, fader.htm, we'll see how to fade, wipe, and dissolve text as the user watches. These effects are called *transitions*. In particular, when the user clicks a button marked with the name of a transition, we'll apply that transition to the text in our Web page. The transitions we'll take a look at here are the dissolve, split vertical in, split vertical out, split horizontal in, split horizontal out, wipe left down (a "wipe" acts something like a washcloth wiping in the indicated direction), and wipe left up.

```
 -----------------------------------------------------------------
|                                                                 |
| --------------------------------------------------------------- |
|                                                                 |
|                                                                 |
|                   With filters, you                             |
|                   can create wipes                              |
|                   and dissolves and                             |
|                   many additional                               |
|                   visual effects.                               |
|                                                                 |
|                                                                 |
| -------- ---------- ------------ -------- --------- --------- ------- |
||Dissolve|Vertical In|Vertical Out|Horiz In|Horiz Out|Left Down|Left Up||
| -------- ---------- ------------ -------- --------- --------- ------- |
|                                                                 |
|                                                                 |
|                                                                 |
 -----------------------------------------------------------------
```

When the user clicks a button, our script will apply the corresponding transition in our Web page. Because transitions let you alternate between different text elements (or images) in your page, we'll use these two strings, alternating between them with visual dissolves, wipes, and fades: "Using filters, you can fade images and text in and out." and "With filters, you can create wipes and dissolves and many additional visual effects."

We start our new example, fader.htm, with the buttons we'll use to support the transitions. When the user clicks one of these buttons, it will call a new subroutine, ApplyEffect(), passing it the transition we want to display. The available transitions are numbered from 0 to 23, and they all appear in Table 6.2.

Here's how we add the buttons to support the transitions we'll use:

```
<HTML>

<HEAD>
<TITLE>Fader Example</TITLE>
</HEAD>

<BODY>

<DIV STYLE="POSITION:ABSOLUTE;WIDTH:800;HEIGHT:100;TOP:400;LEFT:0">
<CENTER>
<input value="Dissolve" type=button onMouseDown="ApplyEffect(12)">      ⇐
<input value="Vertical In" type=button onMouseDown="ApplyEffect(13)"> ⇐
<input value="Vertical Out" type=button onMouseDown="ApplyEffect(14)">  ⇐
<input value="Horizontal In" type=button onMouseDown="ApplyEffect(15)"> ⇐
<input value="Horizontal Out" type=button
onMouseDown="ApplyEffect(16)">                                         ⇐
<input value="Left Down" type=button onMouseDown="ApplyEffect(17)">    ⇐
<input value="Left Up" type=button onMouseDown="ApplyEffect(18)">      ⇐
</CENTER>
</DIV>
        .
        .
        .
```

(You may wonder why we use the onMouseDown event rather than onClick for button clicks; the reason is that in Preview 2 of Internet Explorer 4.0, there is a bug that causes the button itself to be drawn in the transition <DIV> if you use onClick for buttons.)

Next, we add two <DIV>s with the two text blocks we'll alternate between, named targetText1 and targetText2. Note that we enclose those <DIV>s in an surrounding <DIV> and that we set that <DIV>'s filter property to: revealTrans

**Table 6.2 The Internet Explorer Multimedia Controls**

| Transition Number | Does this |
|---|---|
| 0 | Box In |
| 1 | Box Out |
| 2 | Circle In |
| 3 | Circle Out |
| 4 | Wipe Up |
| 5 | Wipe Down |
| 6 | Wipe Right |
| 7 | Wipe Left |
| 8 | Vertical Blinds |
| 9 | Horizontal Blinds |
| 10 | Checker Board Across |
| 11 | Checker Board Down |
| 12 | Random Dissolve |
| 13 | Split Vertical In |
| 14 | Split Vertical Out |
| 15 | Split Horizontal In |
| 16 | Split Horizontal Out |
| 17 | Strips Left Down |
| 18 | Strips Left Up |
| 19 | Strips Right Down |
| 20 | Strips Right Up |
| 21 | Random Bars Horizontal |
| 22 | Random Bars Vertical |
| 23 | Random |

(the filter for dissolve, fade, and wipe transitions), giving the transition a two-second duration:

```
<HTML>

<HEAD>
<TITLE>Fader Example</TITLE>
```

```
</HEAD>

<BODY>

<DIV STYLE="POSITION:ABSOLUTE;WIDTH:800;HEIGHT:100;TOP:400;LEFT:0">
<CENTER>
<input value="Dissolve" type=button onMouseDown="ApplyEffect(12)">
<input value="Vertical In" type=button onMouseDown="ApplyEffect(13)">
<input value="Vertical Out" type=button onMouseDown="ApplyEffect(14)">
<input value="Horizontal In" type=button onMouseDown="ApplyEffect(15)">
<input value="Horizontal Out" type=button
onMouseDown="ApplyEffect(16)">
<input value="Left Down" type=button onMouseDown="ApplyEffect(17)">
<input value="Left Up" type=button onMouseDown="ApplyEffect(18)">
</CENTER>
</DIV>

<DIV      ID="Div1"
    STYLE="POSITION:ABSOLUTE; WIDTH:250; HEIGHT:200; Left:200; Top:100;
    FILTER:revealTrans(Duration=2.0)">                              ⇐

    <DIV ID="targetText1"
        STYLE="POSITION:ABSOLUTE;WIDTH:250;HEIGHT:210;TOP:0;LEFT:0">
        <FONT SIZE=6 FACE="Arial">
        Using filters, you can fade images and text in and out.    ⇐
    </DIV>

    <DIV ID="targetText2"
        STYLE="POSITION:ABSOLUTE;WIDTH:250;HEIGHT:210;TOP:0;LEFT:0">
        <FONT SIZE=6 FACE="Arial">
        With filters, you can create wipes and dissolves and many
        additional visual effects.                                 ⇐
    </DIV>

</DIV>
```

We're ready to make our transitions active. We start by hiding one of the text blocks, targetText1, when the page first loads (so we can alternate between targetText1 and targetText2) by setting that text block's visibility style to hidden:

```
<SCRIPT LANGUAGE="VBScript">
Sub Window_onLoad()
    targetText1.style.visibility = "hidden"                        ⇐
```

```
End Sub
    .
    .
    .
```

Now when the page first loads, it will display the second text block to the user. The next step is to initialize the filter for the transition we want. That transition's number is passed to us as the value Transition, and we can reach Div1's filters with its filters collection, so we install our new transition this way in ApplyTransition():

```
<SCRIPT LANGUAGE="VBScript">
Sub Window_onLoad()
    targetText1.style.visibility = "hidden"
End Sub

Sub ApplyEffect(Transition)

    call Div1.filters(0).Apply()                        ⇐
    Div1.filters(0).Transition = Transition             ⇐
    .
    .
    .

End Sub
```

Next we'll make sure we alternate between the two text blocks, using a flag named useText1. If this flag is true, we'll use text block 1, if it is false, we'll use text block 2, making those blocks alternately visible and invisible so that when a transition repaints the text, we'll alternate between those blocks of text:

```
<SCRIPT LANGUAGE="VBScript">
Dim useText1                                            ⇐
useText1 = true                                         ⇐

Sub Window_onLoad()
    targetText1.style.visibility = "hidden"
End Sub

Sub ApplyEffect(Transition)

    call Div1.filters(0).Apply()
    Div1.filters(0).Transition = Transition

    If (useText1) = true then                           ⇐
        targetText1.style.visibility = ""               ⇐
```

```
        targetText2.style.visibility = "hidden"        ⇐
        useText1 = false                               ⇐
    else                                               ⇐
        targetText2.style.visibility = ""              ⇐
        targetText1.style.visibility = "hidden"        ⇐
        useText1 = true                                ⇐
    end if                                             ⇐
        .
        .
        .
End Sub
```

Finally, we apply the transition itself, using its play() method:

```
<SCRIPT LANGUAGE="VBScript">
Dim useText1
useText1 = true

Sub Window_onLoad()
    targetText1.style.visibility = "hidden"
End Sub

Sub ApplyEffect(Transition)

    call Div1.filters(0).Apply()
    Div1.filters(0).Transition = Transition

    If (useText1) = true then
        targetText1.style.visibility = ""
        targetText2.style.visibility = "hidden"
        useText1 = false
    else
        targetText2.style.visibility = ""
        targetText1.style.visibility = "hidden"
        useText1 = true
    end if

    Div1.filters(0).play(2.0)                          ⇐

End Sub
```

And that's it. Open the page in Internet Explorer now, as shown in Figure 6.4, and click a button, such as the Left Down button, which causes a wipe transition moving down and to the left. That's all there is to it. Our transitions example is a success!

The code for this example, fader.htm, appears in Listing 6.3.

---

**Listing 6.3 fader.htm**

```
<HTML>

<HEAD>
<TITLE>Fader Example</TITLE>
</HEAD>

<BODY>

<DIV STYLE="POSITION:ABSOLUTE;WIDTH:800;HEIGHT:100;TOP:400;LEFT:0">
<CENTER>
<input value="Dissolve" type=button onMouseDown="ApplyEffect(12)">
```

*Continued*

---

**Figure 6.4 Using a left-down transition on text in a Web page.**

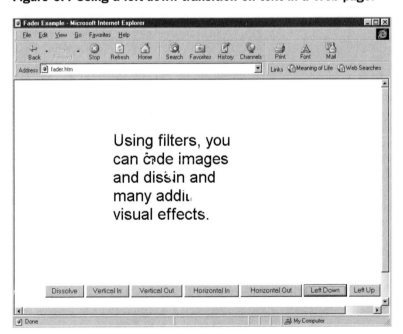

**Listing 6.3 Continued**

```
<input value="Vertical In" type=button onMouseDown="ApplyEffect(13)">
<input value="Vertical Out" type=button onMouseDown="ApplyEffect(14)">
<input value="Horizontal In" type=button onMouseDown="ApplyEffect(15)">
<input value="Horizontal Out" type=button
onMouseDown="ApplyEffect(16)">
<input value="Left Down" type=button onMouseDown="ApplyEffect(17)">
<input value="Left Up" type=button onMouseDown="ApplyEffect(18)">
</CENTER>
</DIV>

<DIV     ID="Div1"
    STYLE="POSITION:ABSOLUTE; WIDTH:250; HEIGHT:200; Left:200; Top:100;
    FILTER:revealTrans(Duration=2.0)">

    <DIV ID="targetText1"
        STYLE="POSITION:ABSOLUTE;WIDTH:250;HEIGHT:210;TOP:0;LEFT:0">
        <FONT SIZE=6 FACE="Arial">
        Using filters, you can fade images and text in and out.
    </DIV>

    <DIV ID="targetText2"
        STYLE="POSITION:ABSOLUTE;WIDTH:250;HEIGHT:210;TOP:0;LEFT:0">
        <FONT SIZE=6 FACE="Arial">
        With filters, you can create wipes and dissolves and many
        additional visual effects.
    </DIV>

</DIV>

</BODY>

<SCRIPT LANGUAGE="VBScript">
Dim useText1
useText1 = true

Sub Window_onLoad()
    targetText1.style.visibility = "hidden"
End Sub

Sub ApplyEffect(Transition)
```

**Listing 6.3 Continued**

```
call Div1.filters(0).Apply()
Div1.filters(0).Transition = Transition

If (useText1) = true then
    targetText1.style.visibility = ""
    targetText2.style.visibility = "hidden"
    useText1 = false
else
    targetText2.style.visibility = ""
    targetText1.style.visibility = "hidden"
    useText1 = true
end if

Div1.filters(0).play(2.0)
```

```
End Sub
```

```
</SCRIPT>
```

```
</HTML>
```

We've seen how to use filters in Internet Explorer for various effects. Next, we'll take a look at an important multimedia control: the Internet Explorer structured graphics control.

## Using the Structured Graphics Control

The Internet Explorer structured graphics control lets us draw graphics, such as arcs, pies, rectangles, ovals, and more, using the various methods shown in Table 6.3. This is one of the most powerful new techniques in Internet Explorer. In this example, graphics.htm, we'll use the structured graphics control to draw a complex figure from code.

To use a multimedia control like the structured graphics control in Internet Explorer, we use the <OBJECT> tag:

```
<OBJECT
ACCESSKEY=string
ALIGN=ABSBOTTOM | ABSMIDDLE | BASELINE | BOTTOM | LEFT | MIDDLE |
RIGHT | TEXTTOP | TOP
CLASSID=string
```

```
CODE=string
CODEBASE=string
CODETYPE=string
DATA=string
DATAFLD=string
DATASRC=string
DISABLED
HEIGHT=string
ID=string
NAME=string
STYLE=string
TABINDEX=integer
TITLE=string
TYPE=string
WIDTH=string
event = script
>
```

**Table 6.3 The Structured Graphics Control's Methods**

| Method | Does this |
| --- | --- |
| Arc | Creates a single circular or elliptical arc. |
| Clear | Clears the control. |
| Oval | Creates an ellipse. |
| Pie | Creates a single circular or elliptical arc closed at the center of the bounding rectangle to form a wedge (pie) shape. |
| Polygon | Creates a closed polygon. |
| PolyLine | Creates a segmented line. |
| Rect | Creates a rectangle. |
| Rotate | Sets the rotation of the world. |
| RoundRect | Creates a rounded rectangle. |
| Scale | Sets the current scaling in the X, Y, Z axis for the world. |
| SetFillColor | Sets the foreground and background colors for graphic fills. |
| SetFillStyle | Sets the type of fill. |
| SetFont | Sets the font for the control. |
| SetGradientFill | Specifies the start and end points for a gradient fill. |
| SetHatchFill | Specifies whether the hatch fill is transparent. |

**Table 6.3 Continued**

| Method | Does this |
|---|---|
| SetIdentity | Set the object to its original state. |
| SetLineColor | Sets the line color for drawing graphics. |
| SetLineStyle | Changes the line style for the current shape. |
| SetGradientShape | Sets the shape of a gradient to be an outline of a polygon shape. |
| Text | Creates a string with the current font and color. |
| Transform4x4 | Sets scaling, rotating, and translation information all at once, using a transform matrix. |
| Translate | Sets the X, Y, Z location of the world. |

When you load Internet Explorer into your computer, it installs the various multimedia controls in your system, and you reach them by referring to them by their control class ID. The structured graphics control's class ID is 369303C2-D7AC-11d0-89D5-00A0C90833E6, and we use that ID in the <OBJECT> tag this way:

```
<OBJECT ID=object
CLASSID="CLSID:369303C2-D7AC-11d0-89D5-00A0C90833E6">                    ⇐
<PARAM NAME=LINEnnnn VALUE=property | method>
</OBJECT>
```

Here, the parameter *name* for the first figure we want to draw is Line0001, the next is Line0002, and so on, as we'll see. The *value* of the parameter is the method we want to use to draw the figure, such as arc() or oval().

We should note that although we will pass method names to the structured graphics control as parameters, Microsoft also lets programmers call graphics methods directly, using the name you've given to the control, like this:

```
structuredGraphics1.SetFillStyle(1)
```

Let's take a look at the structured graphics control now.

## Drawing with the Structured Graphics Control

We start by creating our structured graphics control in our graphics.htm example:

```
<HTML>
<HEAD>
<TITLE>The structured graphics control</TITLE>
</HEAD>
<BODY>
```

```
<CENTER>
<H1>Using the structured graphics control...</H1>

<OBJECT ID="graphics"
    CLASSID="CLSID:369303C2-D7AC-11d0-89D5-00A0C90833E6"
    STYLE="WIDTH:150; HEIGHT:150">                                    ⇐
    .
    .
    .
```

We've given the graphics control a space 150 × 150 pixels in the Web page. Next, we draw a circle in that space, which we can make blue with a red border.

## Drawing Circles

To draw our circle, we first set the color lines will be drawn to red with SetLineColor(), the color figures that will be filled with to blue with SetFillColor(), and the fill style to solid with SetFillStyle():

```
<HTML>
<HEAD>
<TITLE>The structured graphics control</TITLE>
</HEAD>
<BODY>

<CENTER>
<H1>Using the structured graphics control...</H1>

<OBJECT ID="graphics"
    CLASSID="CLSID:369303C2-D7AC-11d0-89D5-00A0C90833E6"
    STYLE="WIDTH:150; HEIGHT:150">
    <PARAM NAME="Line0001" VALUE="SetLineColor(255, 0, 0)">          ⇐
    <PARAM NAME="Line0002" VALUE="SetFillColor(0, 0, 255)">         ⇐
    <PARAM NAME="Line0003" VALUE="SetFillStyle(1)">                ⇐
    .
    .
    .
```

Now we draw the circle with the Oval() method, which looks like this:

```
Oval(x, y, width, height, rotation)
```

Here, $x, y$ are the $x$ and y coordinates for the oval, *width* is the width of its enclosing rectangle, *height* is the height of the enclosing rectangle, and *rotation* the degree of rotation for the oval (from the 0 degrees position). That looks like this in our example:

```
<HTML>
<HEAD>
<TITLE>The structured graphics control</TITLE>
</HEAD>
<BODY>

<CENTER>
<H1>Using the structured graphics control...</H1>

<OBJECT ID="graphics"
    CLASSID="CLSID:369303C2-D7AC-11d0-89D5-00A0C90833E6"
    STYLE="WIDTH:150; HEIGHT:150">
    <PARAM NAME="Line0001" VALUE="SetLineColor(255, 0, 0)">
    <PARAM NAME="Line0002" VALUE="SetFillColor(0, 0, 255)">
    <PARAM NAME="Line0003" VALUE="SetFillStyle(1)">
    <PARAM NAME="Line0004" VALUE="Oval(-75, -75, 80, 80, 0)">          ⇐
     .
     .
     .
```

That's it—now we're drawing circles! Next, let's take a look at drawing pie shapes.

## Drawing Pie Shapes

We use the Pie() method to draw pie slices:

```
Pie(x, y, width, height, startAngle, arcAngle, rotation)
```

Here, *x* is the *x* coordinate of the center of the pie, *y* is the *y* coordinate, *width* is the width of the enclosing rectangle, *height* is the height of the enclosing rectangle, *startAngle* is the beginning angle of the pie slice (in degrees), *arcAngle* is the angle of the pie slice's arc (relative to *startAngle*, in degrees), and *rotation* is the degree of rotation from the 0 degrees position.

In our example, we can draw three red pie sections. First, we set the drawing color to red:

```
<HTML>
<HEAD>
<TITLE>The structured graphics control</TITLE>
</HEAD>
```

```
<BODY>

<CENTER>
<H1>Using the structured graphics control...</H1>

<OBJECT ID="graphics"
    CLASSID="CLSID:369303C2-D7AC-11d0-89D5-00A0C90833E6"
    STYLE="WIDTH:150; HEIGHT:150">
    <PARAM NAME="Line0001" VALUE="SetLineColor(255, 0, 0)">
    <PARAM NAME="Line0002" VALUE="SetFillColor(0, 0, 255)">
    <PARAM NAME="Line0003" VALUE="SetFillStyle(1)">
    <PARAM NAME="Line0004" VALUE="Oval(-75, -75, 80, 80, 0)">
    <PARAM NAME="Line0005" VALUE="SetFillColor(255, 0, 0)">          ⇐
    .
    .
    .
```

Next, we draw three pie sections inside the circle:

```
<HTML>
<HEAD>
<TITLE>The structured graphics control</TITLE>
</HEAD>
<BODY>

<CENTER>
<H1>Using the structured graphics control...</H1>

<OBJECT ID="graphics"
    CLASSID="CLSID:369303C2-D7AC-11d0-89D5-00A0C90833E6"
    STYLE="WIDTH:150; HEIGHT:150">
    <PARAM NAME="Line0001" VALUE="SetLineColor(255, 0, 0)">
    <PARAM NAME="Line0002" VALUE="SetFillColor(0, 0, 255)">
    <PARAM NAME="Line0003" VALUE="SetFillStyle(1)">
    <PARAM NAME="Line0004" VALUE="Oval(-75, -75, 80, 80, 0)">
    <PARAM NAME="Line0005" VALUE="SetFillColor(255, 0, 0)">
    <PARAM NAME="Line0006" VALUE="Pie(-75, -75, 80, 80, 0, 55, 0)">     ⇐
    <PARAM NAME="Line0007" VALUE="Pie(-75, -75, 80, 80, 0, 55, 120)">   ⇐
    <PARAM NAME="Line0008" VALUE="Pie(-75, -75, 80, 80, 0, 55, 240)">   ⇐
</OBJECT>
```

Now when you open the Web page in Internet Explorer, you'll see our circle
with the three pie sections, as shown in Figure 6.5. Our structured graphics con-

trol example works as planned. As you can see, the structured graphics control is a powerful one, allowing you to draw circles, rectangles, and more. You can also draw graphics on the fly, passing various parameters to the structured graphics control as you wish.

The code for this example, graphics.htm, appears in Listing 6.4.

**Listing 6.4 graphics.htm**

```
<HTML>
<HEAD>
<TITLE>The structured graphics control</TITLE>
</HEAD>
<BODY>

<CENTER>
```

*Continued*

**Figure 6.5 Using the structured graphics control.**

**Listing 6.4 Continued**

```
<H1>Using the structured graphics control...</H1>

<OBJECT ID="graphics"
    CLASSID="CLSID:369303C2-D7AC-11d0-89D5-00A0C90833E6"
    STYLE="WIDTH:150; HEIGHT:150">
    <PARAM NAME="Line0001" VALUE="SetLineColor(255, 0, 0)">
    <PARAM NAME="Line0002" VALUE="SetFillColor(0, 0, 255)">
    <PARAM NAME="Line0003" VALUE="SetFillStyle(1)">
    <PARAM NAME="Line0004" VALUE="Oval(-75, -75, 80, 80, 0)">
    <PARAM NAME="Line0005" VALUE="SetFillColor(255, 0, 0)">
    <PARAM NAME="Line0006" VALUE="Pie(-75, -75, 80, 80, 0, 55, 0)">
    <PARAM NAME="Line0007" VALUE="Pie(-75, -75, 80, 80, 0, 55, 120)">
    <PARAM NAME="Line0008" VALUE="Pie(-75, -75, 80, 80, 0, 55, 240)">
</OBJECT>

</CENTER>

</BODY>
</HTML>
```

That completes our overview of the Internet Explorer structured graphics control. There are more graphics to come, however. In the next example, we'll see how to use *layers* in Netscape Navigator.

# Using Layers in Netscape Navigator

A new addition to Netscape Navigator is the use of layers. The <LAYER> tag looks like this in Netscape Navigator:

```
LAYER
NAME="name"
ID="ID"
LEFT="pixel"
TOP="pixel"
PAGEX="pixel"
PAGEY="pixel"
SRC="URL"
Z-INDEX="z-index"
ABOVE="z-index"
BELOW="z-index"
WIDTH="pixel"
```

```
HEIGHT="pixel"
CLIP="clip"
VISIBILITY="visibility"
BGCOLOR="color"
BACKGROUND"color"
>
```

Let's see an example. In layers.htm, we'll first create one layer and display an image, Image 1, in that layer:

```
 -----------------------------------------------------------------
|                                                                 |
|---------------------------------------------------------------- |
|    -------------------------                                     |
|  |                           |                                  |
|  |                           |                                  |
|  |        Image 1            |                                  |
|  |                           |                                  |
|  |                           |                                  |
|  |                           |                                  |
|    -------------------------                                     |
|                                                                 |
|                                                                 |
|                                                                 |
|                                                                 |
|                                                                 |
 -----------------------------------------------------------------
```

Next, we'll create another layer and place a new image, Image 2, in that layer. This new layer will be offset from the first, so we'll see Image 2 overlap Image 1 slightly:

```
 -----------------------------------------------------------------
|                                                                 |
|---------------------------------------------------------------- |
|    -------------------------                                     |
|  |                       -----------------------------          |
|  |                     |                           |            |
|  |      Image 1         |                           |           |
|  |                     |       Image 2              |           |
|  |                     |                           |            |
|  |                     |                           |            |
|    ----------------- |                             |           |
```

```
|                  - - - - - - - - - - - - - - - - - - - - - - - - - -                    |
|                                                                                          |
|                                                                                          |
|                                                                                          |
|                                                                                          |
|                                                                                          |
- - - - - - - - - - - - - - - - - - - - - - - - - - - - - - - - - - - - - - - - - - - - - -
```

Let's create this example now. To start, we create the first layer, layer1, using the <Layer> tag:

```
<HTML>

<HEAD>
<TITLE>Working with layers</TITLE>
</HEAD>

<BODY>

<LAYER NAME="layer1">                                                      ⇐
    .
    .
    .
```

Next, we add the first image, Image 1, and label it:

```
<HTML>

<HEAD>
<TITLE>Working with layers</TITLE>
</HEAD>

<BODY>

<LAYER NAME="layer1">
   <IMG NAME = IMG1 SRC = "image1.gif" WIDTH = 236 HEIGHT = 118>          ⇐
   <P>Image 1</P>                                                         ⇐
   <BR>
   <H1>Working with layers...</H1>
   <BR>
</LAYER>
```

That completes the first layer. We should note here that this layer will start at the upper left of the Web page because we have used the <LAYER> tag, but you can also use the Netscape <ILAYER> tag, which creates an "in-flow" layer, which will "flow" naturally with the rest of the page contents, as the contents in Web pages normally do.

## Offsetting Layers

Let's add the second layer. We will offset that layer a little from the first layer so we can see the two images in those layers overlap. To offset a layer, we use its LEFT and TOP attributes. In this case, we'll offset the second layer, layer2, by 200 pixels horizontally and 20 pixels vertically:

```
<HTML>

<HEAD>
<TITLE>Working with layers</TITLE>
</HEAD>

<BODY>

<LAYER NAME="layer1">
  <IMG NAME = IMG1 SRC = "image1.gif" WIDTH = 236 HEIGHT = 118>
  <P>Image 1</P>
  <BR>
  <H1>Working with layers...</H1>
  <BR>
</LAYER>

<LAYER NAME="layer2"                                              ⇐
  LEFT=200;                                                       ⇐
  TOP=20>                                                         ⇐
```

You can also offset layers easily with respect to each other. To find the location of the top left point of a layer named layer1, you use the layer[ ] array this way:

```
window.document.layers["layer1"].left
```

and

```
window.document.layers["layer1"].top
```

After you have the location of other layers, you can set the TOP and LEFT attributes of the layer you want to position.

In our layers.htm example, we display the second image, Image 2, and label it:

```
<HTML>
```

```
<HEAD>
<TITLE>Working with layers</TITLE>
</HEAD>

<BODY>

<LAYER NAME="layer1">
  <IMG NAME = IMG1 SRC = "image1.gif" WIDTH = 236 HEIGHT = 118>
  <P>Image 1</P>
  <BR>
  <H1>Working with layers...</H1>
  <BR>
</LAYER>

<LAYER NAME="layer2"
  LEFT=200;
  TOP=20>
  <IMG NAME = IMG1 SRC = "image2.gif" WIDTH = 236 HEIGHT = 118>          ⇐
  <P>Image 2</P>                                                        ⇐
</LAYER>

</BODY>

</HTML>
```

Open this example in Netscape Navigator. As you can see in Figure 6.6, there are two layers, each with a graphic image, offset from each other. In this way, we can layer our Web pages, placing graphics on top of graphics. This technique is useful in working with animation, as we'll see in the next chapter.

The code for this example, layers.htm, appears in Listing 6.5.

**Listing 6.5 layers.htm**

```
<HTML>

<HEAD>
<TITLE>Working with layers</TITLE>
</HEAD>

<BODY>

<LAYER NAME="layer1">
```

**Figure 6.6 Using layers in Netscape Navigator.**

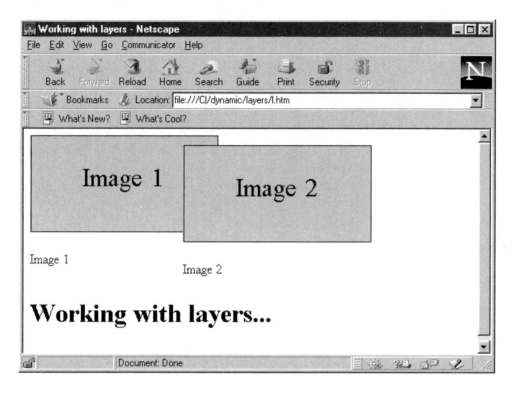

**Listing 6.5 Continued**

```
<IMG NAME = IMG1 SRC = "image1.gif" WIDTH = 236 HEIGHT = 118>
<P>Image 1</P>
<BR>
<H1>Working with layers...</H1>
<BR>
</LAYER>

<LAYER NAME="layer2"
  LEFT=200;
  TOP=20>
  <IMG NAME = IMG1 SRC = "image2.gif" WIDTH = 236 HEIGHT = 118>
  <P>Image 2</P>
```

*Continued*

**Listing 6.5 Continued**

```
</LAYER>

</BODY>

</HTML>
```

## What's Ahead

This chapter has begun our overview of the new graphics techniques available with the two browsers. We'll continue that overview in the next chapter, when we work with graphics animation, one of the most popular techniques on the Web.

# CHAPTER 7

# GRAPHICS ANIMATION

I n this chapter, we'll see how to create graphics animation, bringing our Web pages to life as we rotate, translate, and animate graphics shapes. Graphics animation is one of the most powerful techniques in Web programming today, and there have been significant advancements in Dynamic HTML. We'll look into those advancements in this chapter.

To start, we'll see how to let users animate a Web page themselves as they move objects around with the mouse. That is, we'll see how to support dragging and dropping with the mouse. In this way, users can animate Web page objects themselves, moving them around as they like.

Then we'll see how to use the *DirectAnimation* control to create animation. This powerful control is quite complex, and covering it thoroughly could take a book in itself, but we'll get an introduction to that control here.

Next, we'll see how to work with the new *sequencer* multimedia control in Internet Explorer to create true animation. We'll draw some colored shapes on the screen and see how to animate them by translating them across the screen and rotating them. (The sequencer control even lets you rotate graphics objects in the *z*-direction, which is off the screen.) This is a powerful control that actually runs other controls, as we'll see.

Then we'll see how to use layers in Netscape Navigator to support graphics animation. It turns out that we can move layers around on the fly, which means that we can place a graphics object in a layer and then move it at will, under program control. By placing various images in different layers, you can animate selected layers and move only the images you want. This is a powerful technique.

Finally, we'll see how to use the new *path* multimedia control in Internet Explorer to construct a path on the screen that a graphics object will follow. When we play that path, the browser will move the graphics object we select along that path. In fact, we'll do more than that—we'll also adjust the size of the graphics image as it moves along the path so that it appears to grow as it comes closer to the user.

As you can see, there's a lot of graphics power coming up in this chapter, so let's get started at once with dragging and dropping.

## Dragging and Dropping

In our first example, we'll see how to let the user drag and drop a graphics image using the mouse. We'll use Internet Explorer in this example, because it's easy to position objects in an Internet Explorer page with style attributes, something you can't do with Netscape Navigator yet. (However, it's not difficult to modify the Netscape Navigator animation ex*ampl*e that's coming up to use the mouse, letting the user drag and drop graphics images.)

This new example will be called dragdrop.htm. When the Web page opens, we'll present two images to the user, Image 1 and Image 2:

```
 ------------------------------------------------------------------
|                                                                  |
|                                                                  |
|------------------------------------------------------------------|
|                                                                  |
|    ----------------------                                        |
|                                                                  |
|   |                      |                                       |
|                                                                  |
|   |                      |                                       |
|                                                                  |
|   |      Image 1         |                                       |
|                                                                  |
|   |                      |                                       |
|                                                                  |
|   |                      |                                       |
|                                                                  |
|    ----------------------                                        |
|                                                                  |
|                            ----------------------                |
|                                                                  |
```

Image 2

The user can drag Image 1 as they like, using the mouse:

Image 2

```
|   |           Image 1              |         |                          |              |
|                                                                                       |
|   |                               |         |                          |              |
|                                                                                       |
|   |                               |          ------------------------   |              |
|                                                                                       |
|    ----------------------                                                |              |
 -------------------------------------------------------------------------------
```

However, let's keep Image 2 stationary; we'll see how to do that as well here.

We start dragdrop.htm with a <DIV>, Div1, in which we'll place the two images, image1 and image2. Note that we set the style of both images to "CONTAINER:POSITIONED; POSITION: ABSOLUTE"; this will allow us to move these images around with the mouse (although we'll see how to cancel such movements in Image 2's case):

```
<HTML>

<HEAD>
<TITLE>Drag and drop...</TITLE>
</HEAD>

<BODY>

<CENTER>
<H1>Drag and drop...</H2>
</CENTER>

<DIV ID = Div1 STYLE = "position:relative;width:100%; height:500px">

  <IMG ID = "image2" STYLE = "CONTAINER:POSITIONED; POSITION:ABSOLUTE;
TOP:80px; LEFT:150px; WIDTH: 236px; HEIGHT = 118PX;"
SRC="images/image2.gif">                                                 ⇐

  <IMG STYLE = "CONTAINER:POSITIONED; POSITION:ABSOLUTE; TOP:0pt;
LEFT:0pt; WIDTH:236px; HEIGHT:118px;" SRC="images/image1.gif">
                                                                         ⇐

</DIV>

</BODY>
```

Now let's start the scripting portion of the page.

## Dragging and Dropping with the Mouse

When users want to move an image, they will drag it with the mouse. It will be easiest to handle all such drag-and-drop operations for all graphics objects in one subroutine, so we'll use the document_onMouseMove() subroutine:

```
<SCRIPT LANGUAGE = VBScript>

Sub document_onMouseMove()                                              ⇐
   .
   .
   .
end Sub

</SCRIPT>
```

The first step is to determine the type of object that the user is trying to drag. We do that by checking the event object's srcElement object, which we'll call the source object. If source's type is "IMG" and the left mouse button is down, then the user is trying to drag an image:

```
<SCRIPT LANGUAGE = VBScript>

Sub document_onMouseMove()

   Dim source                                                          ⇐
   Set source = Window.event.srcElement                                ⇐
   If source.tagName="IMG" And window.event.Button = 1 Then            ⇐
      .
      .
      .
   End If

end Sub

</SCRIPT>
```

In this case, we're ready to drag and drop the image. Let's see how that works.

## Implementing Drag and Drop

We know the user is trying to drag an image, so we will position the image, making sure the mouse cursor is right in the middle of it. We do that by first finding the new left and top positions for the image and setting the image's style attributes pixelLeft and pixelTop to that position, moving the image to match the mouse position. We also return a value of FALSE from the onMouseMove() subroutine by setting the event object's returnValue property to FALSE, because if we don't return a value of FALSE, the browser will assume we handled the mouse move event, and it will not send us any subsequent mouse movements until the mouse button goes up:

```
<SCRIPT LANGUAGE = VBScript>

Sub document_onMouseMove()

    Dim source, left, top
    Set source = Window.event.srcElement
    If source.tagName="IMG" And window.event.Button = 1 Then

        left = window.event.X - source.width/2 -
document.all.Div1.offsetLeft                                        ⇐
        top = window.event.X - source.height/2 -
document.all.Div1.offsetTop                                         ⇐

        source.style.pixelLeft= left                               ⇐
        source.style.pixelTop= top                                 ⇐

        window.event.returnValue = FALSE                           ⇐

    End If

end Sub
```

We've implemented dragging and dropping for both Image 1 and Image 2. But we wanted to keep Image 2 stationary. How do we do that?

## Cancelling Drag and Drop

The next step will be to cancel drag-and-drop operations for Image 2. When the user drags Image 2 with the mouse, an image2_onMouseMove() event is generated. If we don't handle that event, the event *bubbles* up to the document_onMouseMove() event. To make sure that doesn't happen in Image 2's case, we cancel the event bubbling in image2_onMouseMove():

```
Sub image2_onMouseMove()

    window.event.cancelBubble = TRUE                               ⇐
```

**Figure 7.1 Dragging and dropping Web page objects.**

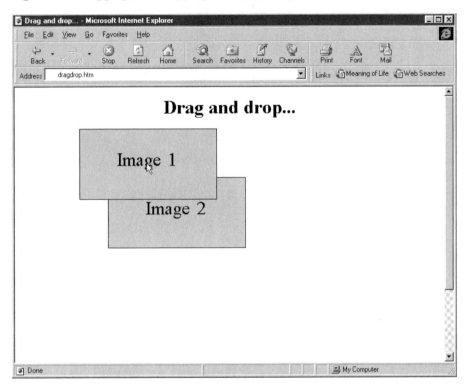

```
end Sub
```

Now Image 2 will not move, even if the user tries to drag it.

Let's give this Web page a try. Open it now and use the mouse to drag Image 1 around, as shown in Figure 7.1. Now we've implemented dragging and dropping in our Web pages.

The code for this example appears in Listing 7.1.

**Listing 7.1 dragdrop.htm**

```
<HTML>

<HEAD>
```

*Continued*

**Listing 7.1 Continued**

```
<TITLE>Drag and drop...</TITLE>
</HEAD>

<BODY>

<CENTER>
<H1>Drag and drop...</H2>
</CENTER>

<DIV ID = Div1 STYLE = "position:relative;width:100%; height:500px">

  <IMG ID = "image2" STYLE = "CONTAINER:POSITIONED; POSITION:ABSOLUTE;
TOP:80px; LEFT:150px; WIDTH: 236px; HEIGHT = 118PX;"
SRC="images/image2.gif">

  <IMG STYLE = "CONTAINER:POSITIONED; POSITION:ABSOLUTE; TOP:0pt;
LEFT:0pt; WIDTH:236px; HEIGHT:118px;" SRC="images/image1.gif">

</DIV>

</BODY>


<SCRIPT LANGUAGE = VBScript>

Sub document_onmousemove()

    Dim source, left, top
    Set source = Window.event.srcElement
    If source.tagName="IMG" And window.event.Button = 1 Then

        left = window.event.X - source.Width/2 -
document.all.Div1.offsetLeft
        top = window.event.Y - source.Height/2 -
document.all.Div1.offsetTop

        source.style.pixelLeft= left
        source.style.pixelTop= top

        window.event.returnValue = FALSE
```

**Listing 7.1 Continued**

```
    End If

end Sub

Sub image2_onmousemove()

    window.event.cancelBubble = TRUE

end Sub

</SCRIPT>

</HTML>
```

Although dragging and dropping is a powerful technique, sometimes we want the movement of graphics objects to follow program control. There's a new way of doing that in Internet Explorer: the DirectAnimation multimedia control, which we'll take a look at now.

# Creating Graphics Animation with the DirectAnimation Control

You use the Internet Explorer DirectAnimation control to create complex animations—in fact, as mentioned at the beginning of the chapter, the DirectAnimation control is so complex it would take a book to explore it thoroughly. We'll take a look at it here to get an introduction to this powerful control.

In our DirectAnimation example, we'll create a graphics figure made up of a colored square and circle and send it spinning across the Web page, rotating not only in the plane of the screen but also giving the appearance of rotating out of the screen as it moves along.

We start this new example, animate.htm, by adding a new DirectAnimation control we'll name DAControl; that control's ID is B6FFC24C-7E13-11D0-9B47-00C04FC2F51D:

```
<HTML>

<HEAD>
```

```
<TITLE>Animation Example</TITLE>
</HEAD>

<BODY>

<CENTER>
<H1>
Animation example...
</H1>
<OBJECT ID="DAControl"
        STYLE="position:absolute; left:10%; top:10; width:800;
height:400"
        CLASSID="CLSID:B6FFC24C-7E13-11D0-9B47-00C04FC2F51D">     ⇐
   </OBJECT>

<CENTER>
   .
   .
   .
```

Now we're ready to write the script for our new DirectAnimation control.

## Scripting DirectAnimation Controls

We start working with the DirectAnimation control by creating a *meter library* object. This object holds a library of DirectAnimation routines that measure all dimensions in meters. (The other common DirectAnimation object is the pixel library, PixelLibrary, in which all measurements are pixels.)

We use the library method NewDrawingSurface() to create a new drawing surface, which we'll simply name drawingSurface. This is the surface on which we'll draw the graphics we'll animate:

```
<SCRIPT LANGUAGE="VBScript">

Set MeterLibrary = DAControl.MeterLibrary                      ⇐
Set drawingSurface = MeterLibrary.NewDrawingSurface()          ⇐
   .
   .
   .
```

Now we'll create the graphics figure itself.

---

## Drawing Graphics on Drawing Surfaces

The graphics figure we'll animate consists of a red circle and a blue square. We'll fill the circle and square in with solid color by setting the drawing surface's fill style to 1. You specify drawing colors with the ColorRgb() method, passing values (0-1) for the red, green, and blue color components. Here's how we create the circle, using the drawing surface Oval() method:

```
<SCRIPT LANGUAGE="VBScript">
Set MeterLibrary = DAControl.MeterLibrary
Set drawingSurface = MeterLibrary.NewDrawingSurface()

drawingSurface.FillStyle(1)                                        ⇐
drawingSurface.FillColor MeterLibrary.ColorRgb(1, 0, 0)            ⇐
drawingSurface.FillPath MeterLibrary.Oval(400, 400)               ⇐
    .
    .
    .
```

Next, we'll draw the square using the Polyline() method, which lets you specify the points to connect to create a figure of arbitrary shape (there is also a Rect() method we could use, but PolyLine() is more powerful because you can draw arbitrary shapes with it,). Then, using the drawing surface's Image object, we create a new image object named figure to hold the image we've created:

```
<SCRIPT LANGUAGE="VBScript">
Set MeterLibrary = DAControl.MeterLibrary
Set drawingSurface = MeterLibrary.NewDrawingSurface()

drawingSurface.FillStyle(1)
drawingSurface.FillColor MeterLibrary.ColorRgb(1, 0, 0)
drawingSurface.FillPath MeterLibrary.Oval(400, 400)

drawingSurface.FillColor MeterLibrary.ColorRgb(0, 0, 1)           ⇐
drawingSurface.FillPath MeterLibrary.Polyline(Array(0, 0, 400, 0, 400,
400, 0, 400, 0, 0))                                               ⇐

Set figure = drawingSurface.Image                                 ⇐
    .
    .
    .
```

At this point, we have the graphics figure we'll use, displaying both a circle and a square. Now we're ready to animate that figure.

## Displaying Graphics with the DirectAnimation Control

We start the display process by setting up the start and end points of the line we want to move the figure along when we send it spinning across the screen, as well as the three-dimensional axis we want to rotate the figure around this way:

```
<SCRIPT LANGUAGE="VBScript">
Set MeterLibrary = DAControl.MeterLibrary
Set drawingSurface = MeterLibrary.NewDrawingSurface()

drawingSurface.FillStyle(1)
drawingSurface.FillColor MeterLibrary.ColorRgb(1, 0, 0)
drawingSurface.FillPath MeterLibrary.Oval(400, 400)

drawingSurface.FillColor MeterLibrary.ColorRgb(0, 0, 1)
drawingSurface.FillPath MeterLibrary.Polyline(Array(0, 0, 400, 0, 400,
400, 0, 400, 0, 0))

Set figure = drawingSurface.Image

Set RotationStartPosition = MeterLibrary.Point2(-1500, 0)          ⇐
Set RotationEndPosition = MeterLibrary.Point2(1500, 0)             ⇐
Set RotationAxis = MeterLibrary.Vector3(10, 20, -10)              ⇐
     .
     .
     .
```

Now we'll set up the two actions we'll take: rotating and translating the graphics figure.

## Rotating a Figure

We'll start with the rotation, using the DirectAnimation Rotate3RateDegrees() method, which rotates the figure around a given axis. We'll give this rotation a five-second period, then project the resulting three-dimensional object into the *x*-*y* plane with the ParallelTransform2 method:

```
<SCRIPT LANGUAGE="VBScript">
Set MeterLibrary = DAControl.MeterLibrary
Set drawingSurface = MeterLibrary.NewDrawingSurface()
     .
     .
     .

Set RotationStartPosition = MeterLibrary.Point2(-1500, 0)
```

```
Set RotationEndPosition = MeterLibrary.Point2(1500, 0)
Set RotationAxis = MeterLibrary.Vector3(10, 20, -10)
Set Rotation = MeterLibrary.Rotate3RateDegrees(RotationAxis,
180).Duration(5).ParallelTransform2                          ⇐
   .
   .
   .
```

Next comes the translation of the figure across the screen, left to right.

## Translating Graphics Figures

To set up the translation, we use the DirectAnimation FollowPath() method, creating a DirectAnimation line with the Line() method and giving this translation a period of five seconds this way:

```
<SCRIPT LANGUAGE="VBScript">
Set MeterLibrary = DAControl.MeterLibrary
Set drawingSurface = MeterLibrary.NewDrawingSurface()
   .
   .
   .
Set RotationStartPosition = MeterLibrary.Point2(-1500, 0)
Set RotationEndPosition = MeterLibrary.Point2(1500, 0)
Set RotationAxis = MeterLibrary.Vector3(10, 20, -10)

Set Rotation = MeterLibrary.Rotate3RateDegrees(RotationAxis,
180).Duration(5).ParallelTransform2

Set Translation =
MeterLibrary.FollowPath(MeterLibrary.Line(RotationStartPosition,
RotationEndPosition), 5)                                     ⇐
   .
   .
   .
```

Now our rotation and translation are both set up. We create a new object, figure1, which concatenates the two actions we want to take, rotating and translating the figure, this way:

```
<SCRIPT LANGUAGE="VBScript">
Set MeterLibrary = DAControl.MeterLibrary
Set drawingSurface = MeterLibrary.NewDrawingSurface()
   .
```

```
    .
    .
Set RotationStartPosition = MeterLibrary.Point2(-1500, 0)
Set RotationEndPosition = MeterLibrary.Point2(1500, 0)
Set RotationAxis = MeterLibrary.Vector3(10, 20, -10)

Set Rotation = MeterLibrary.Rotate3RateDegrees(RotationAxis,
180).Duration(5).ParallelTransform2

Set Translation =
MeterLibrary.FollowPath(MeterLibrary.Line(RotationStartPosition,
RotationEndPosition), 5)

Set figure1 = figure.Transform(Rotation).Transform(Translation)      ⇐
    .
    .
    .
```

Because we've been using meters as our measurements, we scale the drawing down to screen size with the Transform() and Scale2() methods, then display the animation with the DirectAnimation control's start() method:

```
<SCRIPT LANGUAGE="VBScript">
Set MeterLibrary = DAControl.MeterLibrary
Set drawingSurface = MeterLibrary.NewDrawingSurface()
    .
    .
    .
Set RotationStartPosition = MeterLibrary.Point2(-1500, 0)
Set RotationEndPosition = MeterLibrary.Point2(1500, 0)
Set RotationAxis = MeterLibrary.Vector3(10, 20, -10)

Set Rotation = MeterLibrary.Rotate3RateDegrees(RotationAxis,
180).Duration(5).ParallelTransform2

Set Translation =
MeterLibrary.FollowPath(MeterLibrary.Line(RotationStartPosition,
RotationEndPosition), 5)

Set figure1 = figure.Transform(Rotation).Transform(Translation)      ⇐

DAControl.Image = figure1.Transform(MeterLibrary.Scale2(1.0/10000.0,
1.0/10000.0                                                          ⇐
```

```
DAControl.start                                                    ⇐

</SCRIPT>

</BODY>
</HTML>
```

That's it for our DirectAnimation example. Load it into Internet Explorer
now. The graphics figure we've created spins across the screen, as shown in Figure
7.2. Our DirectAnimation example is a success.

There's a great deal more to the DirectAnimation control: 3D modeling,
sound, and advanced image handling. If you need powerful animation, this is the
place to go. You can find documentation for this control in the Microsoft Internet
Software Development kit (InetSDK), available free at www.microsoft.com.

---

**Figure 7.2 Animating Web page objects with DirectAnimation.**

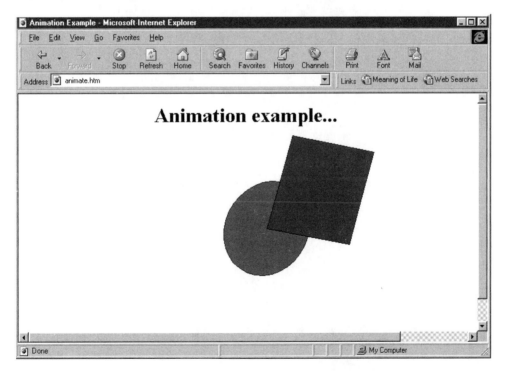

---

The code for this example, animate.htm, appears in Listing 7.2.

**Listing 7.2 animate.htm**

```
<HTML>

<HEAD>
<TITLE>Animation Example</TITLE>
</HEAD>

<BODY>

<CENTER>
<H1>
Animation example...
</H1>
<OBJECT ID="DAControl"
        STYLE="position:absolute; left:10%; top:10; width:800;
height:400"
        CLASSID="CLSID:B6FFC24C-7E13-11D0-9B47-00C04FC2F51D">
</OBJECT>

<CENTER>

<SCRIPT LANGUAGE="VBScript">

Set MeterLibrary = DAControl.MeterLibrary
Set drawingSurface = MeterLibrary.NewDrawingSurface()

drawingSurface.FillStyle(1)
drawingSurface.FillColor MeterLibrary.ColorRgb(1, 0, 0)
drawingSurface.FillPath MeterLibrary.Oval(400, 400)

drawingSurface.FillColor MeterLibrary.ColorRgb(0, 0, 1)
drawingSurface.FillPath MeterLibrary.Polyline(Array(0, 0, 400, 0, 400,
400, 0, 400, 0, 0))

Set figure = drawingSurface.Image

Set RotationStartPosition = MeterLibrary.Point2(-1500, 0)
Set RotationEndPosition = MeterLibrary.Point2(1500, 0)
Set RotationAxis = MeterLibrary.Vector3(10, 20, -10)

Set Rotation = MeterLibrary.Rotate3RateDegrees(RotationAxis,
```

**Listing 7.2 Continued**

```
180).Duration(5).ParallelTransform2

Set Translation =
MeterLibrary.FollowPath(MeterLibrary.Line(RotationStartPosition,
RotationEndPosition), 5)

Set figure1 = figure.Transform(Rotation).Transform(Translation)

DAControl.Image = figure1.Transform(MeterLibrary.Scale2(1.0/10000.0,
1.0/10000.0))

DAControl.start

</SCRIPT>

</BODY>
</HTML>
```

There are easier ways to create simple animations with Internet Explorer, and we'll take a look at them now, using the *sequencer* control.

# Creating Graphics Animation with Internet Explorer's Sequencer Control

You can use an Internet Explorer sequencer control to manipulate other multimedia or ActiveX controls (in fact, like the other multimedia controls, the sequencer control is part of the DirectAnimation package and is really a subset of the DirectAnimation control). For that reason, the sequencer control is one multimedia control you can use to support animation. Here's the way it works: We'll create a graphics figure with the structured graphics control, then we'll use the sequencer control to call the structured graphics control's Rotate() method to animate the figure.

Here's how you use the sequencer control:

```
<OBJECT ID=object
    CLASSID="CLSID:369303C2-D7AC-11d0-89D5-00A0C90833E6">
</OBJECT>
```

Let's put this to work in an Internet Explorer Web page named seq.htm. In this page, we can display the tricolor disk we developed with the structured graphics control in the last chapter, and then animate that disk by spinning it around an axis set at 45 degrees in the *x-y* plane.

We start with the usual title and message to the user:

```
<HTML>

<HEAD>
<TITLE>Sequencer example</TITLE>
</HEAD>

<BODY>

<CENTER>
<H1>Using a sequencer control...</H1>
</CENTER>
          .
          .
          .
```

Next, we add a structured graphics control we'll name graphics to display the colored disk and the sequencer control we'll use, which we'll name sequencer:

```
<HTML>

<HEAD>
<TITLE>Sequencer example</TITLE>
</HEAD>

<BODY>

<CENTER>
<H1>Using a sequencer control...</H1>
</CENTER>

<OBJECT ID=graphics
STYLE="POSITION: ABSOLUTE;
HEIGHT:300;WIDTH:450;TOP:100;LEFT:60;VISIBILITY:VISIBLE; ZINDEX:-1"
CLASSID="CLSID:369303C2-D7AC-11d0-89D5-00A0C90833E6">
    <PARAM NAME="Line0001" VALUE="SetLineColor(255, 0, 0)">
    <PARAM NAME="Line0002" VALUE="SetFillColor(0, 0, 255)">
    <PARAM NAME="Line0003" VALUE="SetFillStyle(1)">
    <PARAM NAME="Line0004" VALUE="Oval(-75, -75, 80, 80, 0)">
    <PARAM NAME="Line0005" VALUE="SetFillColor(255, 0, 0)">
    <PARAM NAME="Line0006" VALUE="Pie(-75, -75, 80, 80, 0, 55, 0)">
    <PARAM NAME="Line0007" VALUE="Pie(-75, -75, 80, 80, 0, 55, 120)">
```

```
    <PARAM NAME="Line0008" VALUE="Pie(-75, -75, 80, 80, 0, 55, 240)">
</OBJECT>                                                              ⇐

<OBJECT ID="Sequencer"
        CLASSID="CLSID:B0A6BAE2-AAF0-11d0-A152-00A0C908DB96"
        STYLE="WIDTH:2;HEIGHT:2">                                      ⇐
</OBJECT>
    .
    .
    .
```

At this point, then, we're ready to use the sequencer control to create the animation.

## Using a Sequencer to Control a Graphics Control

Sequencer controls work with *action sets*, and we'll set up our sequencer control to call a subroutine named rotateGraphic() every tenth second this way:

```
<SCRIPT LANGUAGE=VBSCRIPT>

Sub Sequencer_oninit
        call Sequencer("ActionSet1").At(0.000, "rotateGraphic", -1,
0.100, 1)                                                              ⇐
    .
    .
    .
```

Then we start the animation by calling the sequencer control's Play() method:

```
<SCRIPT LANGUAGE=VBSCRIPT>

Sub Sequencer_oninit
        call Sequencer("ActionSet1").At(0.000, "rotateGraphic", -1,
0.100, 1)
        Call Sequencer("ActionSet1").Play                             ⇐
End Sub
    .
    .
    .
```

All that's left is to set up the rotateGraphic() subroutine and to rotate the graphics figure in that method. We rotate the graphics figure with the structured graphics Rotate() method this way:                                    *Continued*

---

GRAPHICS ANIMATION  369

```
<SCRIPT LANGUAGE=VBSCRIPT>

Sub Sequencer_oninit
        call Sequencer("ActionSet1").At(0.000, "rotateGraphic", -1,
0.100, 1)
        Call Sequencer("ActionSet1").Play
End Sub

Sub rotateGraphic                                              ⇐
        Call graphics.Rotate(10, 10, 0)                        ⇐
End Sub                                                        ⇐

</SCRIPT>
```

Now our sequencer Web page is complete. Open the page in Internet Explorer now. When you do, the tricolor graphics image will rotate around the 45-degree axis in an intriguing twist, as represented in Figure 7.3.

Our sequencer control example is a success. As we've seen, you use the sequencer control to call other controls' methods at a set interval, making it perfect for animation. The code for this example, seq.htm, appears in Listing 7.3.

---

**Listing 7.3 seq.htm**

```
<HTML>

<HEAD>
<TITLE>Sequencer example</TITLE>
</HEAD>

<BODY>

<CENTER>
<H1>Using a sequencer control...</H1>
</CENTER>

<OBJECT ID=graphics
STYLE="POSITION: ABSOLUTE;
HEIGHT:300;WIDTH:450;TOP:100;LEFT:60;VISIBILITY:VISIBLE; ZINDEX:-1"
CLASSID="CLSID:369303C2-D7AC-11d0-89D5-00A0C90833E6">
    <PARAM NAME="Line0001" VALUE="SetLineColor(255, 0, 0)">
    <PARAM NAME="Line0002" VALUE="SetFillColor(0, 0, 255)">
    <PARAM NAME="Line0003" VALUE="SetFillStyle(1)">
```

---

**Figure 7.3 Animating Web page objects with a sequencer control.**

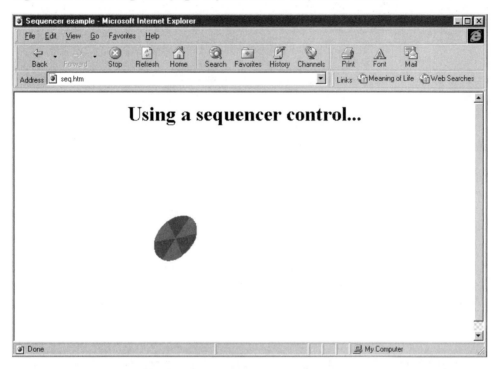

**Listing 7.3 Continued**

```
    <PARAM NAME="Line0004" VALUE="Oval(-75, -75, 80, 80, 0)">
    <PARAM NAME="Line0005" VALUE="SetFillColor(255, 0, 0)">
    <PARAM NAME="Line0006" VALUE="Pie(-75, -75, 80, 80, 0, 55, 0)">
    <PARAM NAME="Line0007" VALUE="Pie(-75, -75, 80, 80, 0, 55, 120)">
    <PARAM NAME="Line0008" VALUE="Pie(-75, -75, 80, 80, 0, 55, 240)">
</OBJECT>

<OBJECT ID="Sequencer"
        CLASSID="CLSID:B0A6BAE2-AAF0-11d0-A152-00A0C908DB96"
        STYLE="WIDTH:2;HEIGHT:2">
</OBJECT>

<SCRIPT LANGUAGE=VBSCRIPT>
```

*Continued*

**Listing 7.3 Continued**

```
Sub Sequencer_oninit
        call Sequencer("ActionSet1").At(0.000, "rotateGraphic", -1,
0.100, 1)
        Call Sequencer("ActionSet1").Play
End Sub

Sub rotateGraphic
        Call graphics.Rotate(10, 10, 0)
End Sub

</SCRIPT>

</BODY>
</HTML>
```

Although Netscape Navigator doesn't support the structured graphics and sequencer controls, it does support something Internet Explorer doesn't: layers. We can move layers around under program control, creating graphics animation. Let's see how this works.

# Animation Using Netscape Navigator's Layers

We can create animation in Netscape Navigator using layers. For example, we might place an image, Image 1, into a layer like this:

```
 ---------------------------------------------------------------------
|                                                                     |
|                                                                     |
|--------------------------------------------------------------------|
|                                                                     |
|     ---------------------                                           |
|                                                                     |
|   |                         |                                       |
|                                                                     |
|   |                         |                                       |
|                                                                     |
|   |         Image 1         |                                       |
|                                                                     |
|   |                         |                                       |
|                                                                     |
```

Then, we can move the whole layer itself down this way, making it appear to the user that the image itself is moving downward:

```
|    ----------------------                                        |
|                                                                  |
|   |                         |                                    |
|                                                                  |
|   |                         |                                    |
|                                                                  |
|   |       Image 1           |                                    |
|                                                                  |
|   |                         |                                    |
|                                                                  |
|   |                         |                                    |
|                                                                  |
|    ----------------------                                        |
----------------------------------------------------------------------
```

Let's call this Netscape Navigator example animate2.htm. We start the example in the usual way:

```
<HTML>

<HEAD>
<TITLE>Animation using layers</TITLE>
</HEAD>

<CENTER>
<H1>Animation using layers</H1>
</CENTER>
        .
        .
        .
```

Now we add the layer that will contain the image, calling that layer Image1:

```
<HTML>

<HEAD>
<TITLE>Animation using layers</TITLE>
</HEAD>

<CENTER>
<H1>Animation using layers</H1>
</CENTER>

<LAYER NAME="Image1">                                              ⇐
```

.
.
.

Now we add the image, image1.gif, to that layer:

```
<HTML>

<HEAD>
<TITLE>Animation using layers</TITLE>
</HEAD>

<CENTER>
<H1>Animation using layers</H1>
</CENTER>

<LAYER NAME="Image1">

<IMG SRC="image1.gif" WIDTH=236 HEIGHT=118>                    ⇐

</LAYER>
```
.
.
.

At this point, then, we have set up our layer with the image in it. Next, we'll start working with that layer in code.

## Moving Layers from JavaScript

In JavaScript, we first set aside an object for our new layer, naming that object Image1. Next, we use the layer's moveTo() method to place the image in its starting position in the Web page:

```
<HTML>

<HEAD>
<TITLE>Animation using layers</TITLE>
</HEAD>

<CENTER>
<H1>Animation using layers</H1>
</CENTER>
```

```
<LAYER NAME="Image1">

<IMG SRC="image1.gif" WIDTH=236 HEIGHT=118>

</LAYER>

<SCRIPT LANGUAGE="JavaScript">

    Image1 = document.layers['Image1'];                          ⇐
    Image1.moveTo(25, 20);                                        ⇐
    .
    .
    .
```

Now we're ready to start the animation by moving the layer downward.

## Supporting Layer Animations

To support animation, we'll use the setInterval() method. Here, we indicate that
we want the function animateImage() called every 25 milliseconds. Note that we
also save the return value from setInterval(), which we'll use later:

```
<HTML>

<HEAD>
<TITLE>Animation using layers</TITLE>
</HEAD>

<CENTER>
<H1>Animation using layers</H1>
</CENTER>

<LAYER NAME="Image1">

<IMG SRC="image1.gif" WIDTH=236 HEIGHT=118>

</LAYER>

<SCRIPT LANGUAGE="JavaScript">

    Image1 = document.layers['Image1'];
    Image1.moveTo(25, 20);
    animateInterval = setInterval(animateImage, 25);             ⇐
```

.
.
.

Besides calling the new function animateImage() every 25 milliseconds, we'll need some way of keeping track of how far down the screen we've moved the image. We don't want to move it down forever, so we set up a variable named counter to keep track of the number of times we've moved the image, initializing that variable to 1:

```
<HTML>

<HEAD>
<TITLE>Animation using layers</TITLE>
</HEAD>

<CENTER>
<H1>Animation using layers</H1>
</CENTER>

<LAYER NAME="Image1">

<IMG SRC="image1.gif" WIDTH=236 HEIGHT=118>

</LAYER>

<SCRIPT LANGUAGE="JavaScript">

    Image1 = document.layers['Image1'];
    Image1.moveTo(25, 20);
    counter = 1;                                        ⇐
    animateInterval = setInterval(animateImage, 25);
    .
    .
    .
```

Next, we will write the animateImage() function. We start by checking if the counter variable is less than 10. If it is, we increment that variable by 1 and move the layer down by 10 pixels simply by adding 10 to its Top property:

```
<HTML>

<HEAD>
```

```
<TITLE>Animation using layers</TITLE>
</HEAD>

<CENTER>
<H1>Animation using layers</H1>
</CENTER>

<LAYER NAME="Image1">

<IMG SRC="image1.gif" WIDTH=236 HEIGHT=118>

</LAYER>

<SCRIPT LANGUAGE="JavaScript">

    Image1 = document.layers['Image1'];
    Image1.moveTo(25, 20);
    counter = 1;
    animateInterval = setInterval(animateImage, 25);

function animateImage() {                                    ⇐
    if (counter < 10) {                                      ⇐
        counter++;                                           ⇐
        Image1.top += 10;                                    ⇐
    .
    .
    .
```

On the other hand, if the counter variable is greater than 10, we should terminate the animation, and we do that with clearInterval(), passing that method the value we got from setInterval():

```
<HTML>

<HEAD>
<TITLE>Animation using layers</TITLE>
</HEAD>

<CENTER>
<H1>Animation using layers</H1>
</CENTER>

<LAYER NAME="Image1">
```

```
<IMG SRC="image1.gif" WIDTH=236 HEIGHT=118>

</LAYER>

<SCRIPT LANGUAGE="JavaScript">

    Image1 = document.layers['Image1'];
    Image1.moveTo(25, 20);
    counter = 1;
    animateInterval = setInterval(animateImage, 25);

function animateImage() {
    if (counter < 10) {
        counter++;
        Image1.top += 10;
    } else {                                              ⇐
        clearInterval(animateInterval);                   ⇐
    }
}

</SCRIPT>

</BODY>

</HTML>
```

That completes the example. Open this Web page now in Netscape Navigator. When you do, the image appears near the top of the page and then slides down toward the bottom, as shown in Figure 7.4. Now we're supporting animation using Netscape Navigator layers.

The code for this example, animate2.htm, appears in Listing 7.4.

---

### Listing 7.4 animate2.htm

```
<HTML>

<HEAD>
<TITLE>Animation using layers</TITLE>
</HEAD>

<CENTER>
<H1>Animation using layers</H1>
```

*Continued*

---

**Figure 7.4 Animating Web page objects with layers.**

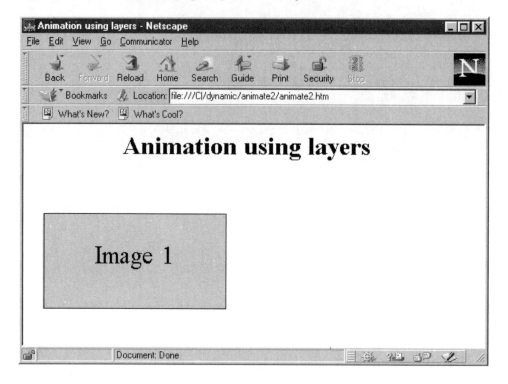

**Listing 7.4 Continued**

```
</CENTER>

<LAYER NAME="Image1">

<IMG SRC="image1.gif" WIDTH=236 HEIGHT=118>

</LAYER>

<SCRIPT LANGUAGE="JavaScript">

    Image1 = document.layers['Image1'];
    Image1.moveTo(25, 20);
```

```
        counter = 1;
        animateInterval = setInterval(animateImage, 25);

function animateImage() {
    if (counter < 10) {
        counter++;
        Image1.top += 10;
    } else {
        clearInterval(animateInterval);
    }
}

</SCRIPT>

</BODY>

</HTML>
```

That's it for using layers for the moment. Now let's turn to another Internet Explorer multimedia control: the path control.

# Using the Path Control in Internet Explorer

You use the path multimedia control to move objects around in an Internet Explorer Web page. That's very useful in graphics animation, because we can use the path control to move an image around as we like. We'll define the path the image will take in parameters we pass to the path control.

You use the path control this way in Internet Explorer:

```
<OBJECT ID=object
    CLASSID="CLSID:D7A7D7C3-D47F-11d0-89D3-00A0C90833E6">
    [<PARAM NAME=property VALUE=setting>]
</OBJECT>
```

The *object* parameter is a string identifying the object to move along the path, the *property* parameter is one of the properties from Table 7.1, and the *setting* parameter is a value for that property.

We'll use the path control to move an image, Image1, in our new example, which we name mover.htm. We start that Web page out as usual, with a title and description:

```
<HTML>
```

## Table 7.1 The Path Control's Properties

| Property | Description |
| --- | --- |
| AutoStart | Indicates if the path control should start when first displayed. |
| Bounce | Sets the path behavior to either reverse direction and return to the beginning, or stop at the end. |
| Direction | Sets the direction of the path playback. |
| Duration | Sets the duration of the path playback. |
| PlayState | Returns the path's current playback state. |
| Repeat | Sets the number of times the path loops during playback. |
| Shape | The shape of the path itself |
| Target | Sets the object that is to follow the path. |
| Time | Returns the elapsed playback time |

```
<HEAD>
<TITLE>Path control example</TITLE>
</HEAD>

<CENTER>
<H1>Path control example</H1>
</CENTER>
    .
    .
    .
```

Then we display the image we'll use—image1.gif—using an <IMG> tag. Note that we make its position style absolute so we can move the image as we like:

```
<HTML>
<HEAD>
<TITLE>Path example</TITLE>
</HEAD>

<BODY>

<IMG ID=image SRC="Image1.gif" STYLE="position:absolute">          ⇐
    .
    .
    .
Next, we add the path control, which we'll name path:
```

```
<HTML>
<HEAD>
<TITLE>Path example</TITLE>
</HEAD>

<BODY>

<IMG ID=image SRC="Image1.gif" STYLE="position:absolute">

<OBJECT ID="path"
CLASSID = "CLSID:D7A7D7C3-D47F-11D0-89D3-00A0C90833E6">          ⇐
   .
   .
   .
```

Now we're ready to configure the path control by passing parameters to it, using the <PARAM> tag.

## Passing Parameters to a Path Control

The first parameter we'll use is the path control's AutoStart parameter, and we'll pass a value of -1, which means that we want the path control to start moving the image as soon as the page is loaded:

```
<HTML>
<HEAD>
<TITLE>Path example</TITLE>
</HEAD>

<BODY>

<IMG ID=image SRC="Image1.gif" STYLE="position:absolute">

<OBJECT ID="path"
CLASSID = "CLSID:D7A7D7C3-D47F-11D0-89D3-00A0C90833E6">
   <PARAM NAME="AutoStart" VALUE="-1">                         ⇐
   .
   .
   .
```

Next, we indicate that we want to move the image along the path we'll set up repeatedly by setting the Repeat parameter to -1, which makes it repeat forever:

```
<HTML>
<HEAD>
```

```
<TITLE>Path example</TITLE>
</HEAD>

<BODY>

<IMG ID=image SRC="Image1.gif" STYLE="position:absolute">

<OBJECT ID="path"
CLASSID = "CLSID:D7A7D7C3-D47F-11D0-89D3-00A0C90833E6">
    <PARAM NAME="AutoStart" VALUE="-1">
    <PARAM NAME="Repeat" VALUE="-1">                        ⇐
    .
    .
    .
```

We indicate that we want the image to "bounce" along the path, forward and back, by setting the Bounce parameter to 1:

```
<HTML>
<HEAD>
<TITLE>Path example</TITLE>
</HEAD>

<BODY>

<IMG ID=image SRC="Image1.gif" STYLE="position:absolute">

<OBJECT ID="path"
CLASSID = "CLSID:D7A7D7C3-D47F-11D0-89D3-00A0C90833E6">
    <PARAM NAME="AutoStart" VALUE="-1">
    <PARAM NAME="Repeat" VALUE="-1">
    <PARAM NAME="Bounce" VALUE="1">                         ⇐
    .
    .
    .
```

We can also set how long it should take the image to move along the path by setting the Duration parameter; here, we set that to 10 seconds:

```
<HTML>
<HEAD>
<TITLE>Path example</TITLE>
</HEAD>
```

```
<BODY>

<IMG ID=image SRC="Image1.gif" STYLE="position:absolute">

<OBJECT ID="path"
CLASSID = "CLSID:D7A7D7C3-D47F-11D0-89D3-00A0C90833E6">
    <PARAM NAME="AutoStart" VALUE="-1">
    <PARAM NAME="Repeat" VALUE="-1">
    <PARAM NAME="Bounce" VALUE="1">
    <PARAM NAME="Duration" VALUE="10">                          ⇐
    .
    .
    .
```

We're ready to define the path itself. Here, we use the PolyLine() method to define a parabolic-like path that we can move the image along, and we pass that path as the Shape parameter:

```
<HTML>
<HEAD>
<TITLE>Path example</TITLE>
</HEAD>

<BODY>

<IMG ID=image SRC="Image1.gif" STYLE="position:absolute">

<OBJECT ID="path"
CLASSID = "CLSID:D7A7D7C3-D47F-11D0-89D3-00A0C90833E6">
    <PARAM NAME="AutoStart" VALUE="-1">
    <PARAM NAME="Repeat" VALUE="-1">
    <PARAM NAME="Bounce" VALUE="1">
    <PARAM NAME="Duration" VALUE="10">
    <PARAM NAME="Shape" VALUE="PolyLine(9, 300,185, 275,150, 250,125,
225,90, 200,70, 180,90, 163,135, 138,165, 118,207)">          ⇐
    .
    .
    .
```

Finally, we indicate to the path control that we want it to move the object we've named image along the path by making that object the path control's *target*:

```
<HTML>
<HEAD>
```

```
<TITLE>Path example</TITLE>
</HEAD>

<BODY>

<IMG ID=image SRC="Image1.gif" STYLE="position:absolute">

<OBJECT ID="path"
CLASSID = "CLSID:D7A7D7C3-D47F-11D0-89D3-00A0C90833E6">
    <PARAM NAME="AutoStart" VALUE="-1">
    <PARAM NAME="Repeat" VALUE="-1">
    <PARAM NAME="Bounce" VALUE="1">
    <PARAM NAME="Duration" VALUE="10">
    <PARAM NAME="Shape" VALUE="PolyLine(9, 300,185, 275,150, 250,125,
225,90, 200,70, 180,90, 163,135, 138,165, 118,207)">
    <PARAM NAME="Target" VALUE="image">                      ⇐
</OBJECT>

</BODY>
</HTML>
```

Now open the Web page in Internet Explorer. The image moves along the path, bouncing back and forth. Figure 7.5 shows the image in the process of moving along the path. In this way, we're able to make complex graphic animations easy.

The code for this example, mover.htm, appears in Listing 7.5.

---

**Listing 7.5 mover.htm**

```
<HTML>
<HEAD>
<TITLE>Path example</TITLE>
</HEAD>

<BODY>

<IMG ID=image SRC="Image1.gif" STYLE="position:absolute">

<OBJECT ID="path"
CLASSID = "CLSID:D7A7D7C3-D47F-11D0-89D3-00A0C90833E6">
    <PARAM NAME="AutoStart" VALUE="-1">
    <PARAM NAME="Repeat" VALUE="-1">
    <PARAM NAME="Bounce" VALUE="1">
```

---

**Figure 7.5 Animating Web page objects with the path control.**

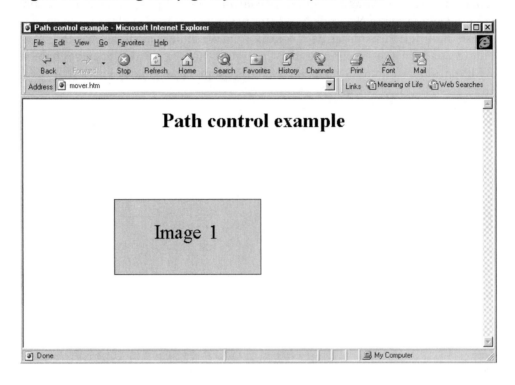

**Listing 7.5 Continued**

```
    <PARAM NAME="Duration" VALUE="10">
    <PARAM NAME="Shape" VALUE="PolyLine(9, 300,185, 275,150, 250,125,
225,90, 200,70, 180,90, 163,135, 138,165, 118,207)">
    <PARAM NAME="Target" VALUE="image">
</OBJECT>

</BODY>
</HTML>
```

# What's Ahead

We've come far in this chapter. We've seen what new graphics animation capabilities are available to us: dragging and dropping, using the Internet Explorer

DirectAnimation control to create powerful animations, using the sequencer control along with the structured graphics control to create programmed animation, creating animation in Netscape Navigator using layers, and finally, we've seen how to use the Internet Explorer path control to move images along a set path. All in all, we've added a lot of power to our arsenal in this chapter. In the next chapter, we'll continue with another popular Web page topic: using dialog boxes that seem to jump right out of the browser.

# C H A P T E R   E I G H T

# WORKING WITH DIALOG
## *Boxes and Windows*

In this chapter, we take a look at all kinds of dialog boxes. Just about everyone knows what dialog boxes are: They're those little on-screen boxes that pass information to the user or receive user input. We'll see the full range of dialog boxes at work in this chapter, from the simplest to the most complex. We'll also see how to open a simple window on the screen to display a Web page. Opening dialog boxes or windows from a Web page is an impressive piece of technology; it's still unusual for Web pages to be able to open new windows and dialog boxes entirely separate from the browser.

To start, we'll see a simple alert box, designed to pass on some warning information that the user should know, and message boxes, which also pass information on to the user, but not quite so dramatically. The main difference between alert and message boxes is that alert boxes support a warning icon with an exclamation point in it.

Next, we'll start getting some input from the user. To start, we'll display a confirm dialog box, which simply supports a message we pass to the user and two buttons: OK and Cancel. We'll see how the user responds by determining which button is pushed. Then we'll continue on to input and prompt boxes. These boxes get a string of text from the user. These dialog boxes are very similar, and their main difference is that input boxes are part of VBScript, while prompt boxes are supported by the window object.

After that, we'll take more responsibility for designing what appears on the screen when we work with windows. In our example, we'll see how to open a Web page by opening a new copy of the Web browser with that page in it.

Then we'll continue on to dialog boxes that we design ourselves. We'll see how to design a dialog box that returns information to us in our script. In our example, we'll have the dialog box return a string that the user has typed. Finally, we'll see how to pass information to a dialog box when we open it as well as how to pass information back to us that the user has entered.

There's a lot of dialog box and window work coming up in this chapter, so let's start with alert boxes.

## Using Alert Boxes

*Alert boxes* alert the user to some circumstance; besides displaying a warning message, they display a warning icon. Let's take a look at alert boxes now in a new example named alerts.htm. We'll write this example first in VBScript, then in JavaScript.

In this example, we'll cause an alert box to open when the user clicks a button with the caption "Display alert box." We add that button to our example and a prompt to the user:

```
<HTML>

<HEAD>
<TITLE>Alert dialog box example</TITLE>
</HEAD>

<BODY>

<CENTER>

<H1>Click the button to see an alert box...</H1>
<BR>
<BR>
<INPUT TYPE=BUTTON VALUE="Display alert box" NAME="AlertButton">

</CENTER>

</BODY>
        .
        .
        .
```

When the user clicks the button, the page will display the alert box, with the message "This is an alert box.":

```
<HTML>

<HEAD>
<TITLE>Alert dialog box example</TITLE>
</HEAD>

<BODY>
    .
    .
    .
</BODY>

<SCRIPT LANGUAGE=VBScript>
        Sub AlertButton_OnClick
                window.Alert("This is an alert box.")              ⇐
        End Sub
</SCRIPT>

</BODY>

</HTML>
```

Now open the page in Internet Explorer and click the button, opening the alert box. You can see our message in Figure 8.1 as well as the warning icon in the alert box. Our alert box example is a success.

The code for Figure 8.1, alerts.htm, appears in Listing 8.1.

---

**Listing 8.1 alerts.htm**

```
<HTML>

<HEAD>
<TITLE>Alert dialog box example</TITLE>
</HEAD>

<BODY>

<CENTER>
```

*Continued*

---

**Figure 8.1 Using an alert box.**

**Listing 8.1 Continued**

```
<H1>Click the button to see an alert box...</H1>
<BR>
<BR>
<INPUT TYPE=BUTTON VALUE="Display alert box" NAME="AlertButton">

</CENTER>

</BODY>

<SCRIPT LANGUAGE=VBScript>
        Sub AlertButton_OnClick
                window.Alert("This is an alert box.")
        End Sub
</SCRIPT>
```

**Listing 8.1 Continued**

```
</BODY>

</HTML>
```

It's very easy to convert this example to JavaScript for Netscape Navigator, because the Navigator window object also has an alert() method. That code looks like this:

```
<HTML>

<HEAD>
<TITLE>Alert dialog box example</TITLE>
</HEAD>

<BODY>

<FORM>
<CENTER>

<H1>Click the button to see an alert box...</H1>
<BR>
<BR>
<INPUT TYPE=BUTTON VALUE="Display alert box" onClick =
"AlertButton_OnClick()">

</CENTER>
</FORM>

</BODY>

<SCRIPT LANGUAGE = JavaScript>
        function AlertButton_OnClick()               ⇐
        {                                            ⇐
                window.alert("This is an alert box.")  ⇐
        }                                            ⇐
</SCRIPT>

</BODY>

</HTML>
```

Now that we've gotten our start with alert boxes, let's proceed to message boxes.

## Using Message Boxes

*Message boxes* are like alert boxes, but they don't display a warning icon. You display message boxes with the VBScript MsgBox subroutine. (There's no JavaScript counterpart.) Let's see this in an example named messages.htm. We start this example with a prompt to the user and a button with the caption "Display message box":

```
<HTML>

<HEAD>
<TITLE>Message box example</TITLE>
</HEAD>

<BODY>

<CENTER>

<H1>Click the button to see a message box...<H1>
<BR>
<BR>
<INPUT TYPE=BUTTON VALUE="Display message box" NAME="DisplayButton">
</CENTER>

</BODY>
         .
         .
         .
```

Next, we write the code that displays the message box when the user clicks the button. To display the message box, we use the VBScript MsgBox subroutine, displaying the message "This is a message box":

```
<HTML>

<HEAD>
<TITLE>Message box example</TITLE>
</HEAD>
```

```
<BODY>
    .
    .
    .
</BODY>

<SCRIPT LANGUAGE=VBScript>
        Sub DisplayButton_OnClick
                MsgBox "This is a message box"                    ⇐
        End Sub
</SCRIPT>
```

Open the Web page now and click the button. When you do, the message box appears, as shown in Figure 8.2. Now we're able to pass information to the user with this useful technique.

**Figure 8.2 Using a message box.**

The code for Figure 8.2, messages.htm, appears in Listing 8.2.

**Listing 8.2 messages.htm**

```
<HTML>

<HEAD>
<TITLE>Message box example</TITLE>
</HEAD>

<BODY>

<CENTER>

<H1>Click the button to see a message box...<H1>
<BR>
<BR>
<INPUT TYPE=BUTTON VALUE="Display message box" NAME="DisplayButton">
</CENTER>

</BODY>

<SCRIPT LANGUAGE=VBScript>
        Sub DisplayButton_OnClick
                MsgBox "This is a message box"
        End Sub
</SCRIPT>
```

We've made progress, already seeing how to work with alert and message boxes. Next, we'll see how to receive some input from the user when we use confirm boxes.

## Using Confirm Boxes

A *confirm box* displays an OK button and a Cancel button, and we can determine which button the user clicked by using the confirm() method. This method returns a value of TRUE if the user has clicked the OK button and FALSE if the user has clicked the Cancel button. Let's put this method to work in an example named confirms.htm. We'll write this example in VBScript first and then in JavaScript.

We begin with a prompt to the user to click a button with the caption "Click to display a confirm box" and a text box in which to display the name of the button the user has clicked:

```
<HTML>

<HEAD>
<TITLE>Confirm box example</TITLE>
</HEAD>

<BODY>

<CENTER>

<H1>Click the button to see a confirm box...</H1>
<BR>
<INPUT TYPE = BUTTON VALUE = "Click to display a confirm box" NAME =
ConfirmButton>
<BR>
<BR>
<INPUT TYPE = TEXT NAME = Textbox SIZE = 30>

</CENTER>

</BODY>
         .
         .
         .
```

When the user does click the button, we use the confirm method to place a confirm box on the screen with the text "Click either button...." We're going to examine the return value of this method, so we place it in an if statement:

```
<HTML>

<HEAD>
<TITLE>Confirm box example</TITLE>
</HEAD>

<BODY>
       .
       .
       .
</BODY>

<SCRIPT LANGUAGE = VBScript>
```

```
Sub ConfirmButton_onClick()
    If (confirm("Click either button...")) Then          ⇐
       .
       .
       .
```

When the user clicks a button, the confirm box closes, and it returns a value of
TRUE or FALSE to our code. If the user clicked the OK button, the confirm
method returns a value of true, so our code indicates that the user clicked the OK
button:

```
<HTML>

<HEAD>
<TITLE>Confirm box example</TITLE>
</HEAD>

<BODY>
   .
   .
   .
</BODY>

<SCRIPT LANGUAGE = VBScript>

    Sub ConfirmButton_onClick()
        If (confirm("Click either button...")) Then
              Textbox.Value = "You clicked the OK button"      ⇐
            .
            .
            .
```

Otherwise, we indicate that the user clicked the Cancel button:

```
<HTML>

<HEAD>
<TITLE>Confirm box example</TITLE>
</HEAD>

<BODY>
```

```
          .
          .
          .
</BODY>

<SCRIPT LANGUAGE = VBScript>

    Sub ConfirmButton_onClick()
        If (confirm("Click either button...")) Then
                Textbox.Value = "You clicked the OK button"
        Else
                Textbox.Value = "You clicked the Cancel button"        ⇐
        End If
    End Sub

</SCRIPT>

</HTML>
```

And that's all we need. Open the page now and click the button to open the confirm box, as shown in Figure 8.3.

You can see our message in the confirm box; click one of the buttons now, and the page will report which button you've clicked, as shown in Figure 8.4. Our confirms.htm example works as planned.

The code for Figure 8.3, confirms.htm, appears in Listing 8.3.

---

**Listing 8.3 confirms.htm**

```
<HTML>

<HEAD>
<TITLE>Confirm box example</TITLE>
</HEAD>

<BODY>

<CENTER>

<H1>Click the button to see a confirm box...</H1>
<BR>
<INPUT TYPE = BUTTON VALUE = "Click to display a confirm box" NAME =
```

*Continued*

---

**Figure 8.3 Displaying a confirm box.**

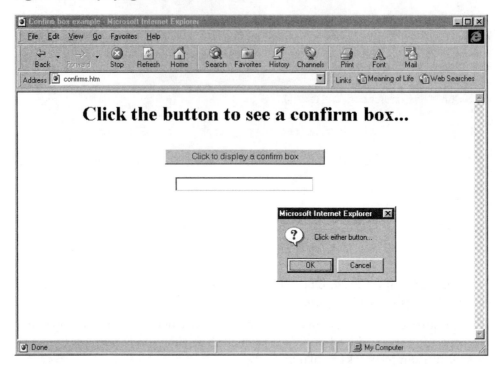

**Listing 8.3 Continued**

```
ConfirmButton>
<BR>
<BR>
<INPUT TYPE = TEXT NAME = Textbox SIZE = 30>

</CENTER>

</BODY>

<SCRIPT LANGUAGE = VBScript>

    Sub ConfirmButton_onClick()
        If (confirm("Click either button...")) Then
                Textbox.Value = "You clicked the OK button"
        Else
                Textbox.Value = "You clicked the Cancel button"
```

**Figure 8.4 The name of the button the user clicked is reported in the confirm box.**

**Listing 8.3 Continued**

```
        End If
    End Sub

</SCRIPT>

</HTML>
```

Netscape Navigator's version of JavaScript supports confirm boxes as well, so we can convert our example into JavaScript. In fact, there's really nothing to it besides changing the language to JavaScript:

```
<HTML>

<HEAD>
<TITLE>Confirm box example</TITLE>
```

*Continued*

**Listing 8.3 Continued**
```
</HEAD>

<BODY>

<FORM name = "form1">
<CENTER>

<H1>Click the button to see a confirm box...</H1>
<BR>
<INPUT TYPE = BUTTON VALUE = "Click to display a confirm box" onClick
= "ConfirmButton_onClick()">
<BR>
<BR>
<INPUT TYPE = TEXT NAME = Textbox SIZE = 30>

</CENTER>
</FORM>

</BODY>

<SCRIPT LANGUAGE = JavaScript>

    function ConfirmButton_onClick()
    {
        if (confirm("Click either button...")) {                        ⇐
                document.form1.Textbox.value = "You clicked the OK
button"
        }

        else {
                document.form1.Textbox.value = "You clicked the
Cancel button"
        }
    }

</SCRIPT>

</HTML>
```

We've gotten some rudimentary input from the user: simple button clicks. However, it's easy to get some text input from the user as well, and we'll look into that next, with input boxes.

# Using Input Boxes

*Input boxes* are supported by the VBScript function inputBox(); there's no JavaScript counterpart besides prompt boxes, which we'll discuss next. The inputBox() function conveniently returns the string that the user typed, so it's easy to use. Let's see this function at work now in a VBScript example named input.htm. We start that page with a button that the user can click to display an input box and a text box in which we'll display the string the user typed:

```
<HTML>

<TITLE>Input example</TITLE>

<BODY>

<CENTER>

<BR>
<H1>Input example</H1>
<INPUT TYPE = TEXT NAME = Textbox SIZE = 20>
<BR>
<BR>
<INPUT TYPE = BUTTON Value = "Show input box" onClick = "ShowInput()">

</CENTER>

</BODY>
    .
    .
    .
```

Next, we set aside a new string, inString, in which to hold the user's input, and then we display the input box. For this example, we'll ask the reader, "Do you enjoy Dynamic HTML?":

```
<HTML>

<TITLE>Input example</TITLE>

<BODY>
    .
    .
    .
```

```
</BODY>

<SCRIPT LANGUAGE = VBScript>

        Dim inString                                                    ⇐

        Sub ShowInput()

                inString = inputBox("Do you enjoy Dynamic HTML?")    ⇐
                .
                .
                .
```

After the user types into the input box and closes that box, we can display what
they've typed, because what they've typed is now stored in inString. If the user has
clicked the Cancel button, inString will be empty, and we indicate that the user
hasn't entered any text:

```
<HTML>

<TITLE>Input example</TITLE>

<BODY>
    .
    .
    .
</BODY>

<SCRIPT LANGUAGE = VBScript>

        Dim inString

        Sub ShowInput()

                inString = inputBox("Do you enjoy Dynamic HTML?")

                If(inString = "") Then                               ⇐
                        Textbox.Value = "You didn't type anything." ⇐
                        .
                        .
                        .
```

On the other hand, if the user has entered text, we can display it in our Web page's text box:

```
<HTML>

<TITLE>Input example</TITLE>

<BODY>
    .
    .
    .
</BODY>

<SCRIPT LANGUAGE = VBScript>

        Dim inString

        Sub ShowInput()

                inString = inputBox("Do you enjoy Dynamic HTML?")

                If(inString = "") Then
                        Textbox.Value = "You didn't type anything."
                Else                                                   ⇐
                        Textbox.Value = "You typed: " & inString       ⇐
                End If                                                 ⇐

        End Sub

</SCRIPT>

</HTML>
```

---

**Listing 8.4 input.htm**

```
<HTML>

<TITLE>Input example</TITLE>

<BODY>

<CENTER>
```

*Continued*

Open this Web page now, and click the button to show the input box. Your screen will look like Figure 8.5. Next, answer the question "Do you like Dynamic HTML?" as you like, and click the OK button.

When you close the input box, your response appears in the Web page's text box, as shown in Figure 8.6. At this point, we're able to read text from the user in our Web pages.

The code for this example, input.htm, appears in Listing 8.4.

## Listing 8.4 Continued

```
<BR>
<H1>Input example</H1>
<INPUT TYPE = TEXT NAME = Textbox SIZE = 20>
<BR>
```

**Figure 8.5 Using an input box.**

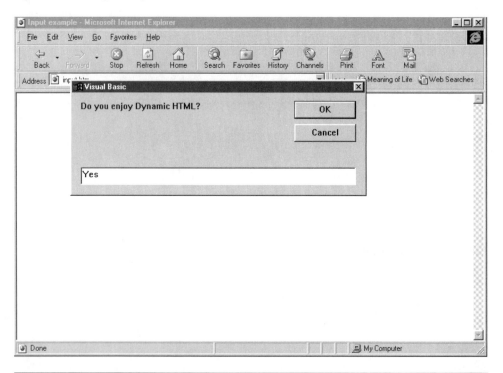

**Figure 8.6 Displaying the text the user has typed into the input box.**

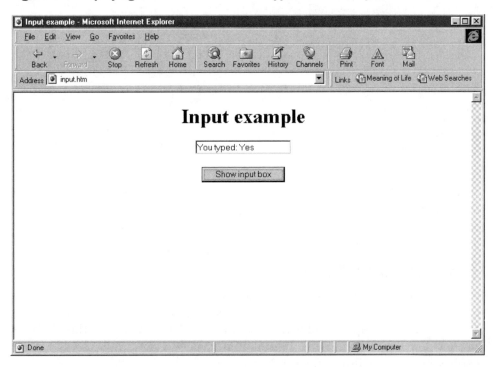

**Listing 8.4 Continued**

```
<BR>
<INPUT TYPE = BUTTON Value = "Show input box" onClick = "ShowInput()">

</CENTER>

</BODY>

<SCRIPT LANGUAGE = VBScript>

        Dim inString

        Sub ShowInput()

                inString = inputBox("Do you enjoy Dynamic HTML?")
```
*Continued*

**Listing 8.4 Continued**

```
                If(inString = "") Then
                        Textbox.Value = "You didn't type anything."
                Else
                        Textbox.Value = "You typed: " & inString
                End If

        End Sub

</SCRIPT>

</HTML>
```

We've seen how to use VBScript input boxes. Both the Internet Explorer and Netscape Navigator window objects support something very like it: the prompt box.

# Using Prompt Boxes

*Prompt boxes* are very similar to input boxes, but they differ a little in appearance, so we'll take a look at them here in a new example named prompter.htm. First, we'll write this example in VBScript, then in JavaScript. We start this example page just like the last one, with a button that displays a prompt to the user and a text box in which to display the user's typed text:

```
<HTML>

<TITLE>Prompt example</TITLE>

<BODY>

<CENTER>

<BR>
<H1>Prompt example</H1>
<INPUT TYPE = TEXT NAME = Textbox SIZE = 20>                           ⇐
<BR>
<BR>
<INPUT TYPE = BUTTON Value = "Show prompt" onClick = "ShowMessage()">⇐

</CENTER>
```

```
</BODY>
    .
    .
    .
```

When the user does click the button in this Web page, our code displays the prompt box with the window object's prompt method, passing it both the question to ask ("Do you enjoy Dynamic HTML?") and a default answer that will appear already typed into the input box. We'll use "Yes" here:

```
<HTML>

<TITLE>Prompt example</TITLE>

<BODY>
    .
    .
    .
</BODY>

<SCRIPT LANGUAGE = VBScript>

        Dim inString

        Sub ShowMessage()

                inString = window.prompt("Do you enjoy Dynamic
HTML?", "Yes")
            .
            .
            .
```

Then we display what the user has typed, as we did in the previous example using the input box:

```
<HTML>

<TITLE>Prompt example</TITLE>

<BODY>
    .
    .
```

```
    .
</BODY>

<SCRIPT LANGUAGE = VBScript>

        Dim inString

        Sub ShowMessage()

                inString = window.prompt("Do you enjoy Dynamic
HTML?", "Yes")

                If(inString = "") Then                          ⇐
                        Textbox.Value = "You didn't type anything."⇐
                Else                                            ⇐
                        Textbox.Value = "You typed: " & inString ⇐
                End If                                          ⇐

        End Sub

</SCRIPT>

</HTML>
```

Now open this page, shown in Figure 8.7, and click the button. You can see the prompt box that we've launched from VBScript; it's the one that mistakenly announces it's a "JavaScript Prompt." That box already displays our question and default answer.

Enter the answer you want and click OK. When you do, our Web page displays your answer, as shown in Figure 8.8. Our prompt box example is a success.

The code for this example, prompter.htm, appears in Listing 8.5.

---

### Listing 8.5 prompter.htm

```
<HTML>

<TITLE>Prompt example</TITLE>
```

**Figure 8.7 Using a Dynamic HTML input box.**

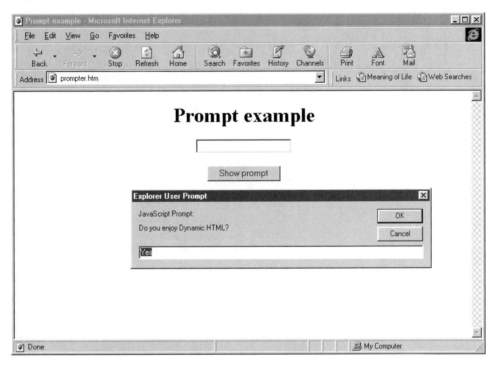

**Listing 8.5 Continued**

```
<BODY>

<CENTER>

<BR>
<H1>Prompt example</H1>
<INPUT TYPE = TEXT NAME = Textbox SIZE = 20>
<BR>
<BR>
<INPUT TYPE = BUTTON Value = "Show prompt" onClick = "ShowMessage()">

</CENTER>

</BODY>
```

*Continued*

**Figure 8.8 Reading input from the user with an input box.**

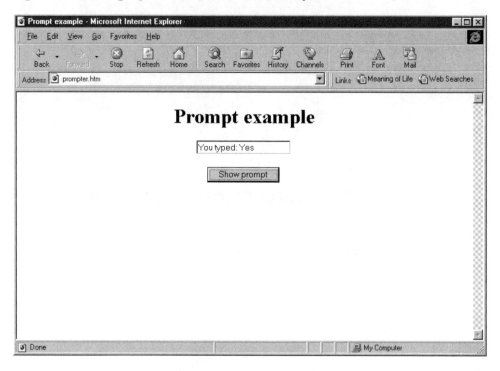

**Listing 8.5 Continued**

```
<SCRIPT LANGUAGE = VBScript>

        Dim inString

        Sub ShowMessage()

                inString = window.prompt("Do you enjoy Dynamic
HTML?", "Yes")

                If(inString = "") Then
                        Textbox.Value = "You didn't type anything."
                Else
                        Textbox.Value = "You typed: " & inString
                End If
```

**Listing 8.5 Continued**

```
        End Sub

</SCRIPT>

</HTML>
```

We can write this same example in JavaScript, which also supports the prompt() method. Again, there's very little to convert, because you use the prompt() method the same way as in VBScript:

```
<HTML>

<TITLE>Prompt example</TITLE>

<BODY>

<CENTER>

<FORM NAME = form1>
<BR>
<H1>Prompt example</H1>
<INPUT TYPE = TEXT NAME = Textbox SIZE = 20>
<BR>
<BR>
<INPUT TYPE = BUTTON Value = "Show prompt" onClick = "ShowMessage()">
</FROM>

</CENTER>

</BODY>

<SCRIPT LANGUAGE = JavaScript>

    var inString

    function ShowMessage()
    {
        inString = window.prompt("Do you enjoy Dynamic HTML?", "Yes")  ⇐

        if (inString == "")
```

*Continued*

**Listing 8.5 Continued**

```
        document.form1.Textbox.value = "You didn't type anything."
    else
        document.form1.Textbox.value = "You typed: " + inString


    }

</SCRIPT>

</HTML>
```

So far, we've used only predefined dialog boxes in our examples: input boxes, alert boxes, and so on. However, we can design our own dialog boxes; in fact, those dialog boxes can simply be a new Web page, written to display the controls we want. To get an idea how this works, let's take a look at how to open a whole new window with a Web page in it at the click of a button.

# Opening Windows

Using the window object's open() method, we can easily open a new copy of the browser with any Web page we want displayed in it. Let's take a look at how that works now in an example named windows.htm. We'll write this example first in VBScript and then in JavaScript.

We start windows.htm with a prompt to the user and a button that has the caption "Show window":

```
<HTML>

<TITLE>Windows</TITLE>

<BODY>

<CENTER>
<BR>
<H1>Click the button to open a new window...</H1>
<BR>
<BR>
<INPUT TYPE = BUTTON Value = "Show window" onClick = "ShowWindow()">
</CENTER>

</BODY>
```

.
.
.

When the user clicks the button, our code opens a new page by simply passing its URL to the open() method. In this case, it opens a new Web page named wnd.htm:

```
<HTML>

<TITLE>Windows</TITLE>

<BODY>
    .
    .
    .
</BODY>

<SCRIPT LANGUAGE = VBScript>

        Sub ShowWindow()                              ⇐
                window.open("wnd.htm")                ⇐
        End Sub                                        ⇐

</SCRIPT>

</HTML>
```

To close a window, you use the close() method.

In general, here's how you use the open() method in Internet Explorer:

```
Window = object.open(URL [, features [, name]])
```

Here, *URL* is the URL of the page you want to open, the optional *features* parameter specifies how to display the window, as shown in Table 8.1, and the optional *name* parameter gives the window a name.

Here's how you use Open() with Netscape Navigator:

```
[windowVar = ][window].open(URL, name, [features])
```

The *URL* parameter specifies the URL of the page to open, *name* is the name of the window, and the *features* parameter lists the features you want in the new window. The possible values for the features parameter appear in Table 8.2. (Separate these values with commas when entering them into the Open() call.)

---

**Table 8.1 Possible Values for the Internet Explorer Open() Parameter Named Features**

| Parameter | Possible Values | Refers to this |
|---|---|---|
| toolbar | yes/no/1/0 | The browser toolbar |
| location | yes/no/1/0 | The input field for entering URLs |
| directories | yes/no/1/0 | Directory buttons |
| status | yes/no/1/0 | Status line at bottom of window |
| menubar | yes/no/1/0 | Menu bar |
| scrollbars | yes/no/1/0 | Enables horizontal and vertical scrollbars |
| resizeable | yes/no/1/0 | Whether resize handles appear at the edge |
| width | pixels | Width of window; defaults to pixels |
| height | pixels | Height of window in pixels |
| top | pixels | Top position in pixels with respect to desktop |
| left | pixels | Left position in pixels with respect to desktop |
| center | yes/no/1/0 | Centered with respect to desktop |
| font | font-family | Font |
| font-size | font-size | Font |
| font-weight | font-weight | Font |
| font-style | font-style | Font |
| edgeStyle | raised/sunken | Style for the window border |
| borderSize | thick/thin | Size of the border around the window |
| helpIcon | yes/no/1/0 | Whether the help icon appears in the title bar |
| minimize | yes/no/1/0 | Whether the Minimize button appears in the title bar |
| maximize | yes/no/1/0 | Whether the Maximize button appears in the title bar |
| systemMenu | yes/no/1/0 | Whether the system menu is available from the border icon |

**Table 8.2 Possible Values for the Netscape Navigator Open() Parameter Named Features**

| Parameter | Possible Values | Refers to this |
|---|---|---|
| toolbar | yes/no/1/0 | The browser toolbar |
| location | yes/no/1/0 | The input field for entering URLs |
| directories | yes/no/1/0 | Directory buttons |
| status | yes/no/1/0 | Status line at bottom of window |
| menubar | yes/no/1/0 | Menu bar |

**Table 8.2 Continued**

| scrollbars | yes/no/1/0 | Enables horizontal and vertical scrollbars |
|---|---|---|
| resizeable | yes/no/1/0 | Whether resize handles appear at the edge |
| width | pixels | Width of window in pixels |
| height | pixels | Height of window in pixels |

Here's the page we'll open in the new copy of the browser, wnd.htm, which simply displays the text "Here's a new window!":

```
<HTML>

<HEAD>
<TITLE>Window example</TITLE>
</HEAD>

<BODY>

<CENTER>
<H1>Here's a new window!</H1>
</CENTER>

</BODY>

</HTML>
```

Open windows.htm now and click the button to open the new window, wnd.htm, as shown in Figure 8.9. You close that new copy of Internet Explorer just as you normally might: with the Close button or with the File menu's Close item. If you want to close the new browser yourself under script control, just save the window object returned by the open() method like this:

```
window1 = window.open("wnd.htm")
```

and use that object's close() method to close it like this:

```
window1.close()
```

Now we're able to open a whole new window that we have designed ourselves.

**Figure 8.9 Opening a new copy of the browser with a new page in it.**

The code for Figure 8.9, windows.htm, appears in Listing 8.6; the code for the window we opened up, wnd.htm, appears in Listing 8.7.

**Listing 8.6 windows.htm**

```
<HTML>

<TITLE>Windows</TITLE>

<BODY>

<CENTER>
<BR>
<H1>Click the button to open a new window...</H1>
<BR>
<BR>
```

**Listing 8.6 Continued**

```
<INPUT TYPE = BUTTON Value = "Show window" onClick = "ShowWindow()">
</CENTER>

</BODY>

<SCRIPT LANGUAGE = VBScript>
        Sub ShowWindow()
                window.open("wnd.htm")
        End Sub
</SCRIPT>

</HTML>
```

**Listing 8.7 wnd.htm**

```
<HTML>
<HEAD>
<TITLE>Window example</TITLE>
</HEAD>

<BODY>

<CENTER>
<H1>Here's a new window!</H1>
</CENTER>

</BODY>

</HTML>
```

In Netscape Navigator, it's the same process, except that we use JavaScript. The conversion to JavaScript is easy:

```
<HTML>

<TITLE>Windows</TITLE>

<BODY>

<FORM>
<CENTER>
<BR>
```

*Continued*

**Listing 8.7 Continued**

```
<H1>Click the button to open a new window...</H1>
<BR>
<BR>
<INPUT TYPE = BUTTON Value = "Show window" onClick = "ShowWindow()">
</CENTER>
</FORM>

</BODY>

<SCRIPT LANGUAGE = JavaScript>
        function ShowWindow()                                    ⇐
        {                                                        ⇐
                window.open("wnd.htm")                           ⇐
        }                                                        ⇐
</SCRIPT>
</HTML>
```

Now we've worked with windows and we're prepared to work with true dialog boxes. Let's explore that topic now. We'll work with Internet Explorer's dialog object in the next two examples. (Netscape doesn't support a dedicated dialog box object yet.)

# Using Dialog Boxes in Internet Explorer

In our next example, targeted to Internet Explorer, we'll let the user pop the following dialog box onto the screen with a prompt to the user, a text box to enter text in, and a button with which to close the dialog box:

When the user types some text into the text box and clicks the Click here after typing text... button, our code will close the dialog box and display the text the user has typed in a text box. Let's take a look at how this works now in a new example, dialogs.htm.

## Preparing to Create a Dialog Box

We start dialogs.htm with a prompt to the user, a button the user can click to display the dialog box, and a text box in which we'll display the text the user typed into the dialog box before closing it:

```
<HTML>

<TITLE>Dialog box example</TITLE>

<BODY>

<CENTER>
<BR>
<H1>Click the button to show the dialog box...</H1>
<BR>
<INPUT TYPE = BUTTON Value = "Show dialog box" NAME = "ShowButton">
<BR>
<BR>
<INPUT TYPE = TEXT NAME = Textbox SIZE = 20>

</CENTER>

</BODY>
    .
    .
    .
```

When the user clicks this button, our code will show our dialog box, which is really a Web page we design. However, instead of being based on a window object, this page will be based on the Internet Explorer *dialog object*. This object has the properties width, height, DialogArguments (to read arguments passed to the dialog box), and ReturnValue (to return values from the dialog box). The dialog object also has one method: close(), to close the box.

We show that dialog box with the window object's showModalDialog() method. (A *modal dialog box* is one that the user must dismiss from the screen before doing anything else in the browser.) In addition, the showModalDialog() method returns a value, and we'll design our dialog box so that the returned value is the text the user has typed into the dialog box. We can display that text in the main Web page's text box:

```
<HTML>

<TITLE>Dialog box example</TITLE>

<BODY>
    .
    .
    .
</BODY>

<SCRIPT LANGUAGE = VBScript>

        Sub ShowButton_OnClick                              ⇐
                TextBox.Value = window.showModalDialog("dlg.htm")   ⇐
        End Sub                                              ⇐

</SCRIPT>

</HTML>
```

You can use the same parameters in the call to showModalDialog() as you use for the Internet Explorer Open() method, as shown in Table 8.1, allowing you to control the size and appearance of your dialog box. That's all we need for the dialogs.htm file, which launches our dialog box, dlg.htm. Let's create dlg.htm now.

## Creating a Dialog Box

This is the dialog box we want to create as dlg.htm:

```
-------------------------------------------
|                                           |
|               Dialog Box                  |
|                                           |
|   Type some text into the text box...     |
|                                           |
```

```
                |      ------------------------------     |
                |      |                            |     |
                |      ------------------------------     |
                |                                         |
                |      ------------------------------     |
                |      |Click here after typing text...|  |
                |      ------------------------------     |
                |                                         |
                ------------------------------------------
```

We create this new dialog box this way, adding the controls we'll need:

```
<HTML>

<BODY>

<CENTER>
<BR>
<BR>
<H1>Dialog Box</H1>
<BR>
Type some text into the text box...
<BR>
<BR>
<INPUT TYPE = TEXT NAME = Textbox SIZE = 20>
<BR>
<BR>
<INPUT TYPE = BUTTON Value = "Click here after typing text..." NAME =
"CloseButton">
</CENTER>

</BODY>
        .
        .
        .
```

The user can type text into the text box and then click the button to close the dialog box. When the user closes the dialog box, we want to pass that text back to the original Web page as the return value from the showModalDialog() method (so that we can display the text the user has typed back in the original Web page). We pass that text back to showModalDialog() by setting the window object's ReturnValue property to that text, and then we close the dialog box with the close() method:

```
<HTML>

<BODY>
    .
    .
    .
</BODY>

<SCRIPT LANGUAGE = VBScript>

        Sub CloseButton_OnClick

                window.ReturnValue = "You typed: " & TextBox.Value  ⇐
                window.Close                                        ⇐

        End Sub
</SCRIPT>

</HTML>
```

That's all we need. Open the dialogs.htm page now, as shown in Figure 8.10.

Now click the button to open the dialog box. As you can see, the dialog box is based on the dialog object, which means the dialog box has no tool bars or menus and cannot be resized.

Type "Hello there!" into the dialog box, as shown in Figure 8.11. Now click the button in the dialog box to close that box. This action transfers the text you've typed back to the original Web page, where it is displayed, as shown in Figure 8.12.

Now we're reading values from the user in our customized dialog boxes. The code for this example, dialogs.htm, appears in Listing 8.8, and the dialog box's code itself appears in Listing 8.9.

---

### Listing 8.8 dialogs.htm

```
<HTML>

<TITLE>Dialog box example</TITLE>

<BODY>

<CENTER>
<BR>
```

---

**Figure 8.10 Preparing to display our dialog box.**

**Listing 8.8 Continued**

```
<H1>Click the button to show the dialog box...</H1>
<BR>
<INPUT TYPE = BUTTON Value = "Show dialog box" NAME = "ShowButton">
<BR>
<BR>
<INPUT TYPE = TEXT NAME = Textbox SIZE = 20>

</CENTER>

</BODY>
<SCRIPT LANGUAGE = VBScript>

        Sub ShowButton_OnClick
                TextBox.Value = window.showModalDialog("dlg.htm")
```

*Continued*

**Figure 8.11 Our new dialog box.**

**Listing 8.8 Continued**

```
        End Sub

</SCRIPT>

</HTML>
```

**Listing 8.9 dlg.htm**

```
<HTML>

<BODY>

<CENTER>
<BR>
```

## Listing 8.9 Continued

```
<BR>
<H1>Dialog Box</H1>
<BR>
Type some text into the text box...
<BR>
<BR>
<INPUT TYPE = TEXT NAME = Textbox SIZE = 20>
<BR>
<BR>
<INPUT TYPE = BUTTON Value = "Click here after typing text..." NAME =
"CloseButton">
</CENTER>

</BODY>
```

*Continued*

**Figure 8.12 Our dialog box reports text the user has typed.**

**Listing 8.9 Continued**

```
<SCRIPT LANGUAGE = VBScript>

        Sub CloseButton_OnClick

                window.ReturnValue = "You typed: " & TextBox.Value
                window.Close

        End Sub

</SCRIPT>
</HTML>
```

So far, then, we've seen how to read values from a dialog box, but what if we want to pass values *to* a dialog box? For example, we might want to initialize a list of options that we display to the user with check boxes in a dialog box. It turns out that we can indeed pass values to dialog boxes, and we'll see how to do that next using Internet Explorer.

# Passing Values with Dialog Boxes in Internet Explorer

Let's say that we have a Web page like this in Internet Explorer, and that we type the text "hello there!" into a text box to send that text to a dialog box:

```
    ------------------------------------------
    |                                        |
    |--------------------------------------  |
    |                                      |  |
    | Sending data to and from a dialog box... |
    |                                      |  |
    |           Type some text here...     |  |
    |           ----------------------     |  |
    |           |hello there!        |     |  |
    |           ----------------------     |  |
    |                                      |  |
    |           --------------------------    |
    |           |Now show the dialog box... | |
    |           --------------------------    |
    |                                      |  |
```

```
|              ---------------------                    |
|              |                   |         |          |
|              ---------------------                    |
|                                                       |
-----------------------------------------------
```

When we click the Now show the dialog box... button, a dialog box opens with
the text we entered into the original Web page:

```
-------------------------------------------
|                                               |
|                  Dialog Box                   |
|                                               |
|        ---------------------                  |
|        |You typed: hello there!|              |
|        ---------------------                  |
|                                               |
|        Now type text here to return...        |
|        ---------------------                  |
|        |                   |                  |
|        ---------------------                  |
|                                               |
|        --------------------------------       |
|        |And click here to close the dialog|   |
|        --------------------------------       |
|                                               |
-------------------------------------------
```

In this way, we've communicated with our dialog box when we open it.

If we wish, we can enter some text into the text box in the dialog box:

```
-------------------------------------------
|                                               |
|                  Dialog Box                   |
|                                               |
|        ---------------------                  |
|        |You typed: hello there!|              |
|        ---------------------                  |
|                                               |
|        Now type text here to return...        |
|        ---------------------                  |
|        |hello again!        |                 |      ⇐
|        ---------------------                  |
|                                               |
```

```
|                                                     |
|    ----------------------------------               |
|    |And click here to close the dialog|             |
|    ----------------------------------               |
|                                                     |
-------------------------------------------
```

Then we click to close the dialog box and see the text we typed into that box
displayed in the original Web page:

```
-----------------------------------------------
|                                               |
|-----------------------------------------------|
|                                               |
| Sending data to and from a dialog box...      |
|                                               |
|            Type some text here...             |
|            ---------------------              |
|            |hello there!         |            |
|            ---------------------              |
|                                               |
|                                               |
|            ---------------------------        |
|            |Now show the dialog box... |      |
|            ---------------------------        |
|                                               |
|                                               |
|            ----------------------             |
|            |You typed: hello again!|          |        <=
|            ----------------------             |
|                                               |
-----------------------------------------------
```

## Passing Parameters to Dialog Boxes

Let's put this example to work now. We start with the Web page we'll need to
launch the dialog box, dlgargs.htm. Note that we pass the text the user entered
into this page's text box to the dialog box in the showModalDialog() method as the
second parameter in that call:

<HTML>

<TITLE>Dialog box with parameters example</TITLE>

<BODY>

```
<CENTER>
<BR>
<H1>Sending data to and from a dialog box...</H1>
Type some text here...
<BR>
<INPUT TYPE = Text NAME = TextBox1 SIZE = 20>
<BR>
<BR>
<INPUT TYPE = BUTTON Value = "Now show the dialog box..." NAME =
"ShowButton">
<BR>
<BR>
<INPUT TYPE = TEXT NAME = Textbox2 SIZE = 20>
</CENTER>

</BODY>

<SCRIPT LANGUAGE = VBScript>

        Sub ShowButton_OnClick
                TextBox2.Value = window.showModalDialog("dlg.htm",
Textbox1.value)                                                           ⇐
        End Sub

</SCRIPT>

</HTML>
```

Now that we've passed text to the dialog box, how do we read it from the dialog box?

## Reading Parameters Passed to Dialog Boxes

In the new dialog box, dlg.htm, we can get the string the user typed with the DialogArguments property. In fact, we'll display the text in that property with a text box when the dialog box first loads:

```
<HTML>

<BODY LANGUAGE = VBSCRIPT onLoad = Page_Initialize>

<CENTER>
```

```
<BR>
<BR>
<H1>Dialog Box</H1>
<BR>
<INPUT TYPE = Text NAME = Textbox1 SIZE = 20>
<BR>
<BR>
Now type text here to return...
<BR>
<INPUT TYPE = TEXT NAME = Textbox2 SIZE = 20>
<BR>
<BR>
<INPUT TYPE = BUTTON Value = "And click here to close the dialog" NAME
= "CloseButton">

</CENTER>

</BODY>

<SCRIPT LANGUAGE = VBScript>

        Sub Page_Initialize
                                                                    ⇐
                TextBox1.Value = "You typed: " & DialogArguments      ⇐
        End Sub                                                       ⇐
          .
          .
          .
```

In this way, we're able to read values passed to us in the call to showModalDialog(). That's all there is to it. When we close the dialog box, we can pass back the text the user has typed, if any, into the dialog box:

```
<HTML>

<BODY LANGUAGE = VBSCRIPT onLoad = Page_Initialize>
    .
    .
    .
</BODY>

<SCRIPT LANGUAGE = VBScript>
```

```
Sub Page_Initialize
        TextBox1.Value = "You typed: " & DialogArguments
End Sub

Sub CloseButton_OnClick                                         ⇐
        window.ReturnValue = "You typed: " & Textbox2.Value ⇐
        close                                                   ⇐
End Sub                                                          ⇐
```

```
</SCRIPT>
```

```
</HTML>
```

And that's it. Open dlgargs.htm in Internet Explorer now and enter some text into the top text box, as shown in Figure 8.13.

Next, click the button in the Web page to open the dialog box. The text we entered in the Web page has been sent on to the dialog box, as shown in Figure 8.14.

Now enter some text into the lower text box in the dialog box and click the button in the dialog box to close it. When you close the dialog box, the text you entered into the dialog box appears in the original Web page, as shown in Figure 8.15. Now we're passing text back and forth between Web pages and dialog boxes!

The code for this example, dlgargs.htm and dlg.htm, appears in Listings 8.10 and 8.11, respectively.

### Listing 8.10 dlgargs.htm

```
<HTML>

<TITLE>Dialog box with parameters example</TITLE>

<BODY>

<CENTER>
<BR>
<H1>Sending data to and from a dialog box...</H1>
Type some text here...
<BR>
<INPUT TYPE = Text NAME = TextBox1 SIZE = 20>
<BR>
```

*Continued*

**Listing 8.10 Continued**

```
<BR>
<INPUT TYPE = BUTTON Value = "Now show the dialog box..." NAME =
"ShowButton">
<BR>
<BR>
<INPUT TYPE = TEXT NAME = Textbox2 SIZE = 20>
</CENTER>

</BODY>

<SCRIPT LANGUAGE = VBScript>

        Sub ShowButton_OnClick
                TextBox2.Value = window.showModalDialog("dlg.htm",
```

**Figure 8.13 Typing text to send to a dialog box.**

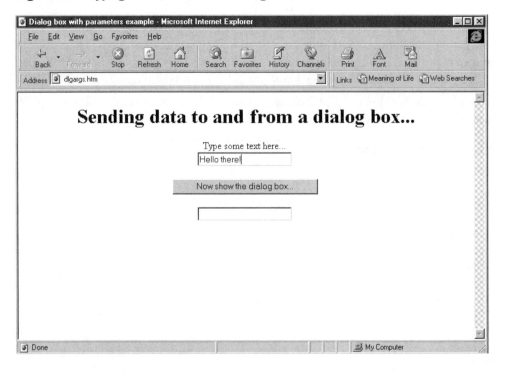

**Figure 8.14 Displaying text sent to a dialog box.**

## Listing 8.10 Continued

```
Textbox1.value)
        End Sub

</SCRIPT>

</HTML>
```

## Listing 8.11 dlg.htm

```
<HTML>

<BODY LANGUAGE = VBSCRIPT onLoad = Page_Initialize>
<CENTER>
<BR>
<BR>
<H1>Dialog Box</H1>
```

*Continued*

**Figure 8.15 Displaying text sent back to us from a dialog box.**

**Listing 8.11 Continued**

```
<BR>
<INPUT TYPE = Text NAME = Textbox1 SIZE = 20>
<BR>
<BR>
Now type text here to return...
<BR>
<INPUT TYPE = TEXT NAME = Textbox2 SIZE = 20>
<BR>
<BR>
<INPUT TYPE = BUTTON Value = "And click here to close the dialog" NAME
= "CloseButton">

</CENTER>
```

**Listing 8.11 Continued**

```
</BODY>

<SCRIPT LANGUAGE = VBScript>

        Sub Page_Initialize
                TextBox1.Value = "You typed: " & DialogArguments
        End Sub

        Sub CloseButton_OnClick
                window.ReturnValue = "You typed: " & Textbox2.Value
                close
        End Sub

</SCRIPT>

</HTML>
```

# What's Ahead

That completes our work on dialog boxes in this chapter. We've seen a great deal about handling various types of dialog boxes here: alert boxes, message boxes, confirm boxes, input boxes, prompt boxes, standard windows, dialog boxes that return values, and now dialog boxes that accept values passed to them. We've made a great deal of progress.

In the next chapter, we'll turn to another powerful technique: seeing how to create Web pages that work offline and with databases. Let's turn to that now.

CHAPTER NINE

# WEB PAGES

*That Work Offline and with Databases*

In this chapter, we'll take a look at an advanced topic: using the Internet Explorer tabular data control. That sounds like pretty dry stuff, until you find out what it can do. Using the data control, you can *bind* data to a Web page and so avoid the necessity of multiple downloads as the user peruses a database or set of pages. All the needed data can be downloaded at once, and instead of having to refer back to the server, your Web page can work with the data you bind to it, sorting, selectively displaying, and filtering that data.

This is one of Microsoft's first efforts to address a serious problem in working with the Web: speed. If the data resides on a user's machine already and you can use the data control to manipulate it, there is no need to refer back to the server. In this way, the tabular data control is a major part of Microsoft's conception of Dynamic HTML.

We'll see three aspects of data control in this chapter that will let us work with bound data: sorting data, moving through a database's records, and filtering data (that is, searching for data that meets a particular criterion). These are all powerful techniques, and we'll start at once by seeing how to bind and sort data.

## Binding and Sorting Data

In our first example, we'll bind a database of student grades to a Web page using the data control, where we display the students' first names, last names, ID numbers, and scores, displaying that data in a table:

```
--------------------------------------------------------------
|------------------------------------------------------------|
|                                                            |
|   -----------------------------------------------------    |
|   | First Name  |  Last Name  |   ID    |  Score  |   |    |
|   |----------------------------------------------------|   |
|   |   Edward    |  Appleton   |   16    |  98.3   |   |    |
|   |   Susan     |  Mazula     |   13    |  78.6   |   |    |
|   |   Thomas    |  Orange     |   11    |  83.3   |   |    |
|   |   Carol     |  Smith      |   10    |  56.4   |   |    |
|   |   Bertie    |  Maples     |   18    |  28     |   |    |
|   |   Nancy     |  Beer       |   19    |  100    |   |    |
|   |   Victor    |  Starch     |   12    |  72.1   |   |    |
|   |   Paul      |  Prosser    |   15    |  48.3   |   |    |
|   |   Lars      |  Stoker     |   14    |  88.8   |   |    |
|   -----------------------------------------------------    |
|                                                            |
--------------------------------------------------------------
```

When the user clicks a heading in the table, such as First Name, Last Name, or ID, the table will sort itself so the data in the matching column is in ascending order. In this way, we'll not only bind the data to a Web page, but also manipulate it. Let's take a look at how this works, using the data control. Here's how you use that control:

```
<OBJECT ID=object
CLASSID = "clsid:333C7BC4-460F-11D0-BC04-0080C7055A83">
    [<PARAM NAME=property VALUE=setting>]
</OBJECT>
```

The possible values for *property* appear in Table 9.1, and the *setting* parameter varies depending on the property, as we'll see.

## Table 9.1 Property Values for the Internet Explorer Data Control

| Property | Means |
| --- | --- |
| AppendData | Specifies whether new data is appended or replaces existing data |
| CharSet | Identifies the character set of the data file |
| DataURL | Specifies the location of the data file |
| EscapeChar | Specifies the character used to escape special characters |
| FieldDelim | Specifies the character used to mark the end of data fields |

**Table 9.1 Continued**

| Property | Means |
|---|---|
| Filter | Specifies the criteria to use for filtering the data |
| Language | Specifies the language of data file, including numerical and date formats |
| RowDelim | Specifies the character used to mark the end of each row |
| SortColumn | Identifies the columns to be sorted, and ascending or descending sort order |
| TextQualifier | Specifies the optional character that surrounds a field |
| UseHeader | Specifies whether or not the first line of the data file contains header information |

We'll need a data file to bind to our Web page, and we'll call that file grades.txt. This file will hold all the data we will bind to our Web page. We start that file with the name we'll give to each column (also called a *data field*): FirstName, LastName, ID, and Score. The default type of data is STRING, and if you want to store a different type of data, you should indicate its type, such as INT or FLOAT:

```
FirstName,LastName, ID:INT,        Score:FLOAT
```

Next, we add the data that we'll display in each column of the table:

```
FirstName,LastName, ID:INT,        Score:FLOAT Edward,Appleton,     16,
98.3                                                                      ⇐

Susan,Mazula,       13,  78.6                                             ⇐
Thomas,Orange,      11,  83.3                                             ⇐
Carol,Smith,        10,  56.4                                             ⇐
Bertie,Maples,      18,  28.0                                             ⇐
Nancy,Beer,         19,  100.0                                            ⇐
Victor,Starch,      12,  72.1                                             ⇐
Paul,Prosser,       15,  48.3                                             ⇐
Lars,Stoker,        14,  88.8                                             ⇐
```

## Binding Data to a Web Page

Now let's see how to bind this data to a Web page. Let's call this example sorter.htm, and we start it the usual way:

```
<HTML>

<HEAD>
<TITLE>Repeated table data binding example</TITLE>
</HEAD>


<BODY>

<CENTER>
<H1>Repeated table data binding example</H1>
    .
    .
    .
```

Next, we add a data control, which we name gradelist, connecting our grades.txt file to it this way (you can use any URL for the data file, of course):

```
<HTML>

<HEAD>
<TITLE>Repeated table data binding example</TITLE>
</HEAD>


<BODY>

<CENTER>
<H1>Repeated table data binding example</H1>

<OBJECT ID = "gradelist"
CLASSID = "clsid:333C7BC4-460F-11D0-BC04-0080C7055A83"
BORDER="0" WIDTH="0" HEIGHT="0">                                    ⇐
    <PARAM NAME = "DataURL" VALUE = "grades.txt">                   ⇐
    <PARAM NAME = "UseHeader" VALUE = "True">                       ⇐
</OBJECT>
    .
    .
    .
```

We're ready to bind our data to a table.

## Connecting Data to a Table

When you bind a database like grades.txt to a table in Internet Explorer, you use the DATASRC attribute; when you connect individual fields in a database to cells in such a table, you use the DATAFLD attribute. In addition, the header of the table (which you create with the <THEAD> tag) is active, and in this example, we'll let the user click a column header to sort the table. (For example, when the user clicks the ID column header, the table will be sorted by ID value.) We won't need to set up a row in the table body for each row in our grades.txt data, because that's handled automatically when you bind data to a table.

Let's see how this example looks in code, where we connect grades.txt to the table and set up a header for that table this way:

```
<HTML>

<HEAD>
<TITLE>Repeated table data binding example</TITLE>
</HEAD>


<BODY>

<CENTER>
<H1>Repeated table data binding example</H1>

<OBJECT ID = "gradelist"
CLASSID = "clsid:333C7BC4-460F-11D0-BC04-0080C7055A83"
BORDER="0" WIDTH="0" HEIGHT="0">
    <PARAM NAME = "DataURL" VALUE = "grades.txt">
    <PARAM NAME = "UseHeader" VALUE = "True">
</OBJECT>

Click the Table headers to resort the table...
<BR>
<BR>

<TABLE BORDER DATASRC = "#gradelist">            ⇐

<THEAD>                                          ⇐
<TR>                                             ⇐
        <TD><B><U><DIV ID = FirstName>First Name</DIV></U></B></TD>   ⇐
```

```
          <TD><B><U><DIV ID = LastName>Last Name</DIV></U></B></TD>     ⇐
          <TD><B><U><DIV ID = ID>ID</DIV></U></B></TD>                   ⇐
          <TD><B><U><DIV ID = Score>Score</DIV></U></B></TD>            ⇐
</THEAD>                                                                 ⇐
</TR>                                                                    ⇐
    .
    .
    .
```

In addition, we set up the table body by defining just one row, but connecting each cell in that row to a field (like FirstName, LastName, and so on) in grades.txt with the DATAFLD attribute:

```
<HTML>

<HEAD>
<TITLE>Repeated table data binding example</TITLE>
</HEAD>


<BODY>

<CENTER>
<H1>Repeated table data binding example</H1>

<OBJECT ID = "gradelist"
CLASSID = "clsid:333C7BC4-460F-11D0-BC04-0080C7055A83"
BORDER="0" WIDTH="0" HEIGHT="0">
    <PARAM NAME = "DataURL" VALUE = "grades.txt">
    <PARAM NAME = "UseHeader" VALUE = "True">
</OBJECT>

Click the Table headers to resort the table...
<BR>
<BR>

<TABLE BORDER DATASRC = "#gradelist">

<THEAD>
<TR>
        <TD><B><U><DIV ID = FirstName>First Name</DIV></U></B></TD>
        <TD><B><U><DIV ID = LastName>Last Name</DIV></U></B></TD>
```

```
        <TD><B><U><DIV ID = ID>ID</DIV></U></B></TD>
        <TD><B><U><DIV ID = Score>Score</DIV></U></B></TD>
</THEAD>
</TR>

<TBODY>
<TR>                                                                    ⇐
        <TD><DIV DATAFLD = "FirstName"></DIV></TD>                      ⇐
        <TD><DIV DATAFLD = "LastName"></DIV></TD>                       ⇐
        <TD><DIV DATAFLD = "ID"></DIV></TD>                             ⇐
        <TD><DIV DATAFLD = "Score"></DIV></TD>                          ⇐
</TR>                                                                   ⇐
</TBODY>                                                                ⇐
</TABLE>                                                                ⇐

</CENTER>
```

We've connected grades.txt to the table. The data control will add rows to our table as needed.

The next step is to sort the table by columns when the user clicks a column header. We start by setting up a subroutine for the first column header's click event, FirstName_ onClick():

```
<SCRIPT LANGUAGE = "VBSCRIPT">

Sub FirstName_onClick()

    .
    .
    .
```

To sort the table by the data in the first column, we use our data control's SortColumn property and then its Reset() method. We've named the data control gradelist, so sorting the database on the data in the first column looks like this:

```
<SCRIPT LANGUAGE = "VBSCRIPT">

Sub FirstName_onClick()

  gradelist.SortColumn = "FirstName"                                   ⇐
  gradelist.Reset()⇐

END Sub
    .
```

.

.

We can do the same for the other columns, allowing the user to sort based on those columns as well:

```
<SCRIPT LANGUAGE = "VBSCRIPT">

Sub LastName_onClick()

   gradelist.SortColumn = "LastName"
   gradelist.Reset()

END Sub

Sub ID_onClick()

   gradelist.SortColumn = "ID"
   gradelist.Reset()

END Sub

Sub Score_onClick()

   gradelist.SortColumn = "Score"
   gradelist.Reset()

END Sub

</SCRIPT>

</BODY>

</HTML>
```

That's all it takes. Our sorter example is complete. Open it now, then click one of the column heads, such as Last Name. As you can see in Figure 9.1, the table sorts itself based on that column. Now we've bound data to a Web page and sorted it. Our sorter.htm example is a success.

The code for Figure 9.1's example, sorter.htm, appears in Listing 9.1.

## Figure 9.1 Sorting a database in a Web page.

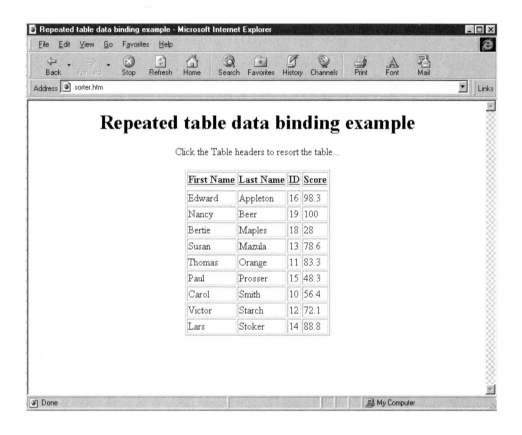

## Listing 9.1 sorter.htm

```
<HTML>

<HEAD>
<TITLE>Repeated table data binding example</TITLE>
</HEAD>


<BODY>
```

*Continued*

**Listing 9.1 Continued**

```
<CENTER>
<H1>Repeated table data binding example</H1>

<OBJECT ID = "gradelist"
CLASSID = "clsid:333C7BC4-460F-11D0-BC04-0080C7055A83"
BORDER="0" WIDTH="0" HEIGHT="0">
    <PARAM NAME = "DataURL" VALUE = "grades.txt">
    <PARAM NAME = "UseHeader" VALUE = "True">
</OBJECT>

Click the Table headers to resort the table...
<BR>
<BR>

<TABLE BORDER DATASRC = "#gradelist">

<THEAD>
<TR>
        <TD><B><U><DIV ID = FirstName>First Name</DIV></U></B></TD>
        <TD><B><U><DIV ID = LastName>Last Name</DIV></U></B></TD>
        <TD><B><U><DIV ID = ID>ID</DIV></U></B></TD>
        <TD><B><U><DIV ID = Score>Score</DIV></U></B></TD>
</THEAD>
</TR>

<TBODY>
<TR>
        <TD><DIV DATAFLD = "FirstName"></DIV></TD>
        <TD><DIV DATAFLD = "LastName"></DIV></TD>
        <TD><DIV DATAFLD = "ID"></DIV></TD>
        <TD><DIV DATAFLD = "Score"></DIV></TD>
</TR>
</TBODY>
</TABLE>

</CENTER>


<SCRIPT LANGUAGE = "VBSCRIPT">

Sub FirstName_onClick()
```

**Listing 9.1 Continued**

```
  gradelist.SortColumn = "FirstName"
  gradelist.Reset()

END Sub

Sub LastName_onClick()

  gradelist.SortColumn = "LastName"
  gradelist.Reset()

END Sub

Sub ID_onClick()

  gradelist.SortColumn = "ID"
  gradelist.Reset()

END Sub

Sub Score_onClick()

  gradelist.SortColumn = "Score"
  gradelist.Reset()

END Sub

</SCRIPT>

</BODY>

</HTML>
```

Now we've gotten an introduction to working with bound data. Let's continue on now to see how to move through a database full of records.

# Binding a Database

We will use our grades.txt file as a database in this next example:

```
FirstName,LastName,  ID:INT,        Score:FLOAT
Edward,Appleton,     16,            98.3
Susan,Mazula,        13,            78.6
```

```
Thomas,Orange,         11,            83.3
Carol,Smith,           10,            56.4
Bertie,Maples,         18,            28.0
Nancy,Beer,            19,            100.0
Victor,Starch,         12,            72.1
Paul,Prosser,          15,            48.3
Lars,Stoker,           14,            88.8
```

Here, we'll treat each row as a record in our database, and we'll display all the data from a particular record in a Web page:

```
  -------------------------------------------------------------
|                                                               |
|-------------------------------------------------------------- |
|                                                               |
|                         -------------                         |
|           First Name: |  Edward     |                         |
|                         -------------                         |
|                                                               |
|                         -------------                         |
|           Last Name:  |  Appleton   |                         |
|                         -------------                         |
|                                                               |
|                         -------------                         |
|                  ID:  |  16         |                         |
|                         -------------                         |
|                                                               |
|                         -------------                         |
|              Score:   |  98.3       |                         |
|                         -------------                         |
|                                                               |
|           ----------     -------------                        |
|         |  <Back   |   | Forward>   |                         |
|           ----------     -------------                        |
|                                                               |
  -------------------------------------------------------------
```

When the user clicks the Forward button, the code will move to the next record in the database (the Susan Mzula record). When the user clicks the Back button, the code will move back one record. In this way, we'll let the user move through our bound database simply by clicking buttons.

Let's start this database example, which we'll call data.htm:

```
<HTML>

<HEAD>
<TITLE>Current record data binding</TITLE>
</HEAD>


<BODY>

<CENTER>

<H1>Current record binding...</H1>
      .
      .
      .
```

Next, we add a data control we call gradelist and connect it to grades.txt:

```
<HTML>

<HEAD>
<TITLE>Current record data binding</TITLE>
</HEAD>


<BODY>

<CENTER>

<H1>Current record binding...</H1>

Click the buttons to move through the database...
<BR>
<BR>

<OBJECT ID = "gradelist"
        CLASSID = "clsid:333C7BC4-460F-11D0-BC04-0080C7055A83"
        BORDER = "0" WIDTH = "0" HEIGHT = "0">            ⇐
  <PARAM NAME = "DataURL" VALUE = "grades.txt">           ⇐
  <PARAM NAME = "UseHeader" VALUE = "True">               ⇐
</OBJECT>
      .
```

## Constructing a Database Table

We will construct our database-displaying table now. Our table will consist of four rows, one for each data field: FirstName, LastName, ID, and Score. Each row will have two columns: one for the data in the current record and one for a label for that data.

Let's see how this works. We start with the first row in our table, which holds the label "First Name:" and displays the data in the FirstName field of the current record in the database. To reach the data in the FirstName field of the current record, we use the DATAFLD attribute, setting it to "FirstName":

```
<HTML>

<HEAD>
<TITLE>Current record data binding</TITLE>
</HEAD>
     .
     .
     .

<TABLE ALIGN = CENTER>
<TR>
<TD ALIGN = RIGHT><LABEL FOR = FirstName>First Name: </LABEL></TD>      ⇐
<TD ALIGN = LEFT><INPUT id = FirstName TYPE = text DATASRC =
#gradelist DATAFLD = "FirstName"></TD>                                  ⇐
</TR>
     .
     .
     .
```

In this way, we are able to tie a particular cell in a table to a particular field in a database. We are able to do the same for the other cells in the table:

```
<HTML>

<HEAD>
<TITLE>Current record data binding</TITLE>
</HEAD>
     .
     .
```

```
        .
<TR>
<TD ALIGN = RIGHT><LABEL FOR = LastName>Last Name: </LABEL></TD>
<TD ALIGN = LEFT><INPUT id = LastName TYPE = text DATASRC = #gradelist
DATAFLD = "LastName"></TD>
</TR>

<TR>
<TD ALIGN = RIGHT><LABEL FOR = ID>ID: </LABEL></TD>
<TD ALIGN = LEFT><INPUT id = ID TYPE = text DATASRC = #gradelist
DATAFLD = "ID"></TD>
</TR>

<TR>
<TD ALIGN = RIGHT><LABEL FOR = Score>Score: </LABEL></TD>
<TD ALIGN = LEFT><INPUT id = Score TYPE = text DATASRC = #gradelist
DATAFLD = "Score"></TD>
</TR>
</TABLE>

<BR>
```

This completes our table. Next, we will make active the buttons that let the user navigate through the database.

## Navigating in a Database

We add the two navigation buttons, Back and Forward, to the Web page:

```
<HTML>

<HEAD>
<TITLE>Current record data binding</TITLE>
</HEAD>
        .
        .
        .
<TR>
<TD ALIGN = RIGHT><LABEL FOR = LastName>Last Name: </LABEL></TD>
<TD ALIGN = LEFT><INPUT id = LastName TYPE = text DATASRC = #gradelist
DATAFLD = "LastName"></TD>
</TR>

<TR>
```

```
<TD ALIGN = RIGHT><LABEL FOR = ID>ID: </LABEL></TD>
<TD ALIGN = LEFT><INPUT id = ID TYPE = text DATASRC = #gradelist
DATAFLD = "ID"></TD>
</TR>

<TR>
<TD ALIGN = RIGHT><LABEL FOR = Score>Score: </LABEL></TD>
<TD ALIGN = LEFT><INPUT id = Score TYPE = text DATASRC = #gradelist
DATAFLD = "Score"></TD>
</TR>
</TABLE>

<BR>

<TABLE ALIGN = CENTER>
  <TR>
    <TD><INPUT TYPE = BUTTON ID = back VALUE =    " < Back  "></TD>⇐
    <TD><INPUT TYPE = BUTTON ID = forward VALUE = "Forward >"></TD> ⇐
  </TR>
</TABLE>
```

Now our buttons are ready to go, and we can connect them to code to make them work. We'll use the gradelist control's recordset object for that. For example, to move to the previous record, we use the recordset object's MovePrevious() method:

```
<SCRIPT LANGUAGE = VBSCRIPT>

Sub back_onClick()

    gradelist.recordset.MovePrevious                                      ⇐

End Sub
```

However, we should not try to move back before the beginning of the database. We can check our position in the database with the AbsolutePosition property and make sure that we don't try to move before the beginning of the database:

```
<SCRIPT LANGUAGE = VBSCRIPT>

Sub back_onClick()

  If gradelist.recordset.AbsolutePosition > 1 then                        ⇐
```

```
      gradelist.recordset.MovePrevious
   End If                                                           ⇐

End Sub
```

In the same way, we use the MoveNext() method to move to the next database record when the user clicks the Forward button:

```
Sub forward_onClick()

      gradelist.recordset.MoveNext                                  ⇐

End Sub
```

We should also make sure we do not try to move past the end of the database. We check that by comparing our present position to the total number of records in the database, which we find from the RecordCount property. If we're about to go past the end of the database, we cancel the operation:

```
Sub forward_onClick()

  If gradelist.recordset.AbsolutePosition <
gradelist.recordset.RecordCount then                                ⇐
      gradelist.recordset.MoveNext
   End If                                                           ⇐

End Sub
```

That's all we need. Open the Web page now in Internet Explorer, shown in Figure 9.2. When you click the Forward and Back buttons in the Web page, the data in the table's cells is automatically updated to display the data for the new current record. Our database navigation example is a success.

The code for Figure 9.2's example, data.htm, appears in Listing 9.2.

---

**Listing 9.2 data.htm**

```
<HTML>

<HEAD>
<TITLE>Current record data binding</TITLE>
</HEAD>


<BODY>                                                    Continued
```

---

**Figure 9.2 Navigating through a database in a Web page.**

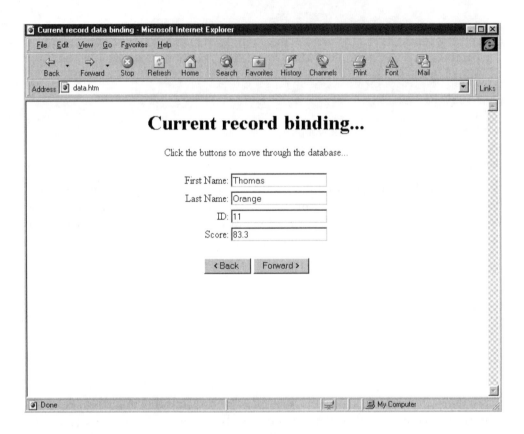

**Listing 9.2 Continued**

```
<CENTER>

<H1>Current record binding...</H1>

Click the buttons to move through the database...
<BR>
<BR>

<OBJECT ID = "gradelist"
        CLASSID = "clsid:333C7BC4-460F-11D0-BC04-0080C7055A83"
```

**Listing 9.2 Continued**

```
          BORDER = "0" WIDTH = "0" HEIGHT = "0">
  <PARAM NAME = "DataURL" VALUE = "grades.txt">
  <PARAM NAME = "UseHeader" VALUE = "True">
</OBJECT>

<TABLE ALIGN = CENTER>
<TR>
<TD ALIGN = RIGHT><LABEL FOR = FirstName>First Name: </LABEL></TD>
<TD ALIGN = LEFT><INPUT id = FirstName TYPE = text DATASRC =
#gradelist DATAFLD = "FirstName"></TD>
</TR>

<TR>
<TD ALIGN = RIGHT><LABEL FOR = LastName>Last Name: </LABEL></TD>
<TD ALIGN = LEFT><INPUT id = LastName TYPE = text DATASRC = #gradelist
DATAFLD = "LastName"></TD>
</TR>

<TR>
<TD ALIGN = RIGHT><LABEL FOR = ID>ID: </LABEL></TD>
<TD ALIGN = LEFT><INPUT id = ID TYPE = text DATASRC = #gradelist
DATAFLD = "ID"></TD>
</TR>

<TR>
<TD ALIGN = RIGHT><LABEL FOR = Score>Score: </LABEL></TD>
<TD ALIGN = LEFT><INPUT id = Score TYPE = text DATASRC = #gradelist
DATAFLD = "Score"></TD>
</TR>
</TABLE>

<BR>
<TABLE ALIGN = CENTER>
  <TR>
    <TD><INPUT TYPE = BUTTON ID = back VALUE =    " < Back  "></TD>
    <TD><INPUT TYPE = BUTTON ID = forward VALUE = "Forward >"></TD>
  </TR>
</TABLE>

</CENTER>
```

*Continued*

**Listing 9.2 Continued**

```
<SCRIPT LANGUAGE = VBSCRIPT>

Sub back_onClick()

  If gradelist.recordset.AbsolutePosition > 1 then
    gradelist.recordset.MovePrevious
  End If

End Sub

Sub forward_onClick()

  If gradelist.recordset.AbsolutePosition <
gradelist.recordset.RecordCount then
    gradelist.recordset.MoveNext
  End If

End Sub

</SCRIPT>

</BODY>

</HTML>
```

Now we've come a long way with data binding—but there's more to come. Our next and last exploration of data binding will concern data *filtering*, one of the capabilities of database handling. When you filter your data according to a particular criterion, you create a subset of all the data that meets that criterion. Let's look into this now.

# Filtering Bound Data

Let's say that we have a large database of information on various types of pets and that we want to filter it as the user requires. For example, if the user clicks a radio button marked Dogs in one frame, our page will display the data from the database covering dogs in a second frame:

```
  --------------------------------------------------------------
 |                                                              |
 |------------------------------------------------------------- |
 | (*) Dogs                                                     |
```

```
| ( ) Cats                                                  |
| ( ) Birds                                                 |
|-----------------------------------------------------------|
| Here's the data you wanted...                             |
| DOGS                                                      |
| Dogs make nice pets.                                      |
|                                                           |
|                                                           |
|                                                           |
|                                                           |
|                                                           |
|                                                           |
|                                                           |
 -----------------------------------------------------------
```

If the user clicks the radio button marked Birds, the code filters the database and the page displays the data on birds:

```
 -----------------------------------------------------------
|                                                           |
|-----------------------------------------------------------|
| ( ) Dogs                                                  |
| ( ) Cats                                                  |
| (*) Birds                                                 |
|-----------------------------------------------------------|
| Here's the data you wanted...                             |
| BIRDS                                                     |
| Birds make nice musical pets.                             |
|                                                           |
|                                                           |
|                                                           |
|                                                           |
|                                                           |
|                                                           |
 -----------------------------------------------------------
```

Let's create this example, binding.htm, now. We'll need two frames in binding.htm, one for the radio buttons and one for a table holding the data we've filtered from the database. We create those two frames this way, filling the first frame with a page named header.htm and the second frame, which we'll call dataFrame and in which we'll display data about various types of pets, with a page named petlist.htm:

```
<HTML>

<HEAD>
  <TITLE>Data binding example...</TITLE>
</HEAD>

<FRAMESET ROWS = "30%,70%">                                      ⇐
  <FRAME SRC = "header.htm">                                     ⇐
  <FRAME SRC = "petlist.htm" NAME = "dataFrame">                 ⇐
</FRAMESET>                                                      ⇐
</HTML>
```

That's it for binding.htm. Now we will create the data file with the data about various types of pets, pets.txt, and the two pages we'll display in the two frames, header.htm (which holds the radio buttons) and petlist.htm (which will display the data we filter from the database about various pet types). We'll start with the data file, pets.txt.

## Creating Our Filtered Data File

We intend to have three categories of data we can filter from our data file: dogs, cats, and birds. We set up those categories, giving them the group name "category" this way in the database file, pets.txt:

```
category

dogs
cats
birds
```

Next, let's add a title for each category that we can display when we filter our data. We'll call this next field "title":

```
category,title

dogs,<B>DOGS</B>
cats,<B>CATS</B>
birds,<B>BIRDS</B>
```

(The <B> and </B> here are the standard HTML for bolding text.)

Finally, we include the description of each pet in a new field, "description":

```
category,title,description

dogs,<B>DOGS</B>,Dogs make nice pets.
```

```
cats,<B>CATS</B>,Cats can be nice sometimes.
birds,<B>BIRDS</B>,Birds are nice musical pets.
```

Now we'll be able to filter our pets.txt file based on category, title, or description (although we'll stick to filtering the data by category here). When the user clicks the Dogs radio button, the code will filter out the record that has the category "dogs" and the page will display that record. When the user clicks the Cats radio button, the code will filter out the cats record and the page will display that, and so on.

## Creating the Data Control

Let's continue now by creating the data control, named petdata, we'll need. We'll connect it to pets.txt. We place the data control in the petlist.htm file, binding it to pets.txt:

```
<HTML>

<BODY>

<OBJECT ID = "petdata" WIDTH = 0 HEIGHT = 0
    CLASSID = "CLSID:333C7BC4-460F-11D0-BC04-0080C7055A83">          ⇐

      <PARAM NAME = "UseHeader" VALUE = "True">                     ⇐
      <PARAM NAME = "DataURL" VALUE = "pets.txt">                   ⇐
      .
      .
      .
```

We also indicate that we intend to filter our data on a particular column. When the Web page first appears, we want our code to filter our database for the record concerning dogs, using the Filter parameter:

```
<HTML>

<BODY>

<OBJECT ID = "petdata" WIDTH = 0 HEIGHT = 0
    CLASSID = "CLSID:333C7BC4-460F-11D0-BC04-0080C7055A83">
      <PARAM NAME = "UseHeader" VALUE = "True">
      <PARAM NAME = "DataURL" VALUE = "pets.txt">
      <PARAM NAME = "Filter" VALUE = "category=dogs">               ⇐

</OBJECT>
```

.
.
.

At this point, then, our data control petdata holds the record on dogs, and we can display that data in a table. To do that, we connect a new table to that data control in petlist.htm:

```
<HTML>

<BODY>

<OBJECT ID = "petdata" WIDTH = 0 HEIGHT = 0
    CLASSID = "CLSID:333C7BC4-460F-11D0-BC04-0080C7055A83">

    <PARAM NAME = "Filter" VALUE = "category=dogs">
    <PARAM NAME = "UseHeader" VALUE = "True">
    <PARAM NAME = "DataURL" VALUE = "pets.txt">

</OBJECT>

<TABLE DATASRC = "#petdata">                              ⇐
    .
    .
    .
```

A bound table needs a header and a body, so we create the table header with the text, "Here's the data you wanted . . .":

```
<HTML>

<BODY>

<OBJECT ID = "petdata" WIDTH = 0 HEIGHT = 0
    CLASSID = "CLSID:333C7BC4-460F-11D0-BC04-0080C7055A83">
    <PARAM NAME = "Filter" VALUE = "category=dogs">
    <PARAM NAME = "UseHeader" VALUE = "True">
    <PARAM NAME = "DataURL" VALUE = "pets.txt">

</OBJECT>

<TABLE DATASRC = "#petdata">
```

```
<THEAD>                                                      ⇐
<TD ALIGN = LEFT VALIGN = BOTTOM>                            ⇐
<U>Here's the data you wanted...</U>                         ⇐
</TD>                                                        ⇐
</THEAD>                                                     ⇐
    .
    .
    .
```

Next, we create the table body, tying the cells there to the title and description
fields we've placed in our pets.txt file. Because we have used the <B> and </B>
tags in the title record, we format the cells as HTML to be able to use HTML tags
with the DATAFORMATAS attribute:

```
<HTML>

<BODY>

<OBJECT ID = "petdata" WIDTH = 0 HEIGHT = 0
    CLASSID = "CLSID:333C7BC4-460F-11D0-BC04-0080C7055A83">
      <PARAM NAME = "FilterValue" VALUE = "category=dogs">
      <PARAM NAME = "UseHeader" VALUE = "True">
      <PARAM NAME = "DataURL" VALUE = "pets.txt">

</OBJECT>

<TABLE DATASRC = "#petdata">

    <THEAD>
    <TD ALIGN = LEFT VALIGN = BOTTOM>
    <U>Here's the data you wanted...</U>
    </TD>
    </THEAD>

    <TBODY>                                                  ⇐
    <TD ALIGN = LEFT VALIGN = TOP>                           ⇐
    <DIV DATAFLD = "title" DATAFORMATAS = html></DIV><BR>    ⇐
    <DIV DATAFLD = "description" DATAFORMATAS = html></DIV>  ⇐
    </TD>                                                    ⇐
    </TBODY>                                                 ⇐

</TABLE>
```

```
</BODY>

</HTML>
```

Now we've created our data control and bound it to a table, so that table will display the current record from the control. Let's continue now with the header.htm file; this is the file that will display the radio buttons and hold the code that will filter the database.

## Creating the Header File

We start header.htm with the radio buttons, one for each category: dogs, cats, and birds, giving them the IDs "dogs," "cats," and "birds." Note that because we start off displaying data about dogs, we make sure that the correct radio button is checked initially:

```
<HTML>

<HEAD>
<TITLE>Data binding and filtering...</TITLE>
</HEAD>

<BODY>


<DIV ID = RADIOS ALIGN = LEFT>

    <INPUT TYPE = RADIO NAME = category ID = dogs  onClick =
radioClick() CHECKED><B>Dogs</B><BR>                              ⇐
    <INPUT TYPE = RADIO NAME = category ID = cats  onClick =
radioClick() ><B>Cats</B><BR>                                    ⇐
    <INPUT TYPE = RADIO NAME = category ID = birds onClick =
radioClick() ><B>Birds</B><BR>                                   ⇐
    .
    .
    .
```

The final step is to filter the database according to the button the user has clicked. We will write the code to filter the database in JavaScript, not VBScript, because somewhere between Internet Explorer 4.0 Preview versions 1 and 2, VBScript inexplicably lost the ability to be able to reach data controls in frames other than the current one (and from the header's frame, we'll have to reach the data control in the petlist frame we've named dataFrame).

We've set up the radio buttons so that when the user clicks a radio button, Internet Explorer will call the JavaScript function radioClick(), so we add that function now:

```
<HTML>

<HEAD>
<TITLE>Data binding and filtering...</TITLE>
</HEAD>

<BODY>

<DIV ID = RADIOS ALIGN = LEFT>

    <INPUT TYPE = RADIO NAME = category ID = dogs  onClick =
radioClick() CHECKED><B>Dogs</B><BR>
    <INPUT TYPE = RADIO NAME = category ID = cats  onClick =
radioClick() ><B>Cats</B><BR>
    <INPUT TYPE = RADIO NAME = category ID = birds onClick =
radioClick() ><B>Birds</B><BR>

</DIV>

<SCRIPT LANGUAGE = JAVASCRIPT>
    function radioClick()                                    ⇐
    {
    .
    .
    .
    }                                                        ⇐
</SCRIPT>
    .
    .
    .
```

When the user clicks a radio button, we want to set the filter of the data control to match—for example, if the user clicks the radio button labeled birds, we should set the data control's Filter property to "category=birds." We've set the ID of each radio button to match its name: The ID of the cats button is "cats," the ID of the birds button is "birds," and so on. This means that we can simply create a new string to place in the Filter property like this, using the ID of the control that caused the event:

---

```
<HTML>

<HEAD>
<TITLE>Data binding and filtering...</TITLE>
</HEAD>
        .
        .
        .

<SCRIPT LANGUAGE = JAVASCRIPT>
    function radioClick()
    {
        var newFilter = "category=\"" + window.event.srcElement.id +
"\"";                                                                   ⇐
        .
        .
        .
```

However, the actual data control is in another frame, the one with the list of pet information. We've named that frame dataFrame in the main Web page, binding.htm:

```
<HTML>

<HEAD>
    <TITLE>Data binding example...</TITLE>
</HEAD>

<FRAMESET ROWS = "30%,70%">
    <FRAME SRC = "header.htm">
    <FRAME SRC = "petlist.htm" NAME = "dataFrame">                      ⇐
</FRAMESET>
</HTML>
```

We can reach the data control in the dataFrame frame by first finding the parent window of our frame and then finding the data control—which we've named petdata—in the dataFrame control. When we've found that control, we can set its Filter property to the new filter string this way:

```
<HTML>

<HEAD>
<TITLE>Data binding and filtering...</TITLE>
</HEAD>
```

```
      .
      .
      .
<SCRIPT LANGUAGE = JAVASCRIPT>
    function radioClick()
    {
        var newFilter = "category=\"" + window.event.srcElement.id +
"\"";

        window.parent.dataFrame.petdata.Filter = newFilter;        ⇐
        .
        .
        .
```

All that remains is to make sure the data control displays the new data (as filtered from the pets.txt file), and we do that by *refreshing* that control with its refresh() method:

```
<HTML>

<HEAD>
<TITLE>Data binding and filtering...</TITLE>
</HEAD>
    .
    .
    .
<SCRIPT LANGUAGE = JAVASCRIPT>
    function radioClick()
    {
        var newFilter = "category=\"" + window.event.srcElement.id +
"\"";

        window.parent.dataFrame.petdata.Filter = newFilter;
        window.parent.dataFrame.petdata.Reset();                   ⇐
    }
</SCRIPT>

</BODY>

</HTML>
```

And that's all there is to it. Now open the page in Internet Explorer; it will resemble Figure 9.3.

As you can see in Figure 9.3, the Web page starts by displaying the data we've put in our database for dogs. When you click the radio button marked

## Figure 9.3 Getting ready to filter data in a database.

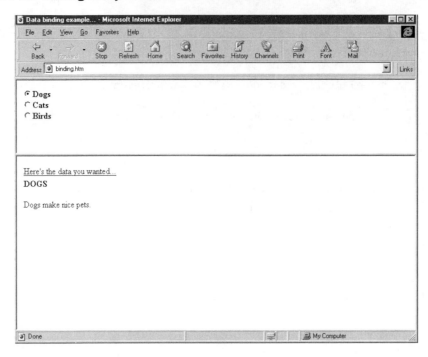

Birds, however, the data for birds is filtered from the database and displayed, as shown in Figure 9.4. Our filtering example works as planned. Now we're filtering the data we want out of a database.

The code for this example appears in Listing 9.3, binding.htm; Listing 9.4, header.htm; Listing 9.5, pets.txt; and Listing 9.6, petlist.htm.

## Listing 9.3 binding.htm

```
<HTML>

<HEAD>
  <TITLE>Data binding example...</TITLE>
</HEAD>

<FRAMESET ROWS = "30%,70%">
  <FRAME SRC = "header.htm">
```

**Figure 9.4 Filtering data in a database.**

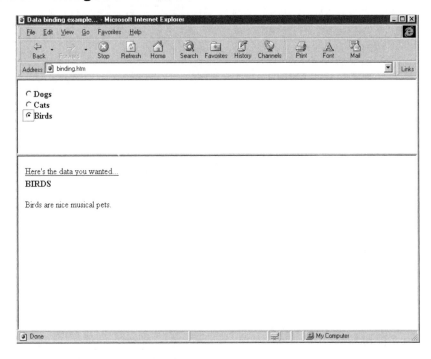

```
   <FRAME SRC = "petlist.htm" NAME = "dataFrame">
</FRAMESET>
</HTML>
```

## Listing 9.4 header.htm

```
<HTML>

<HEAD>
<TITLE>Data binding and filtering...</TITLE>
</HEAD>

<BODY>

<DIV ID = RADIOS ALIGN = LEFT>

    <INPUT TYPE = RADIO NAME = category ID = dogs  onClick =
radioClick() CHECKED><B>Dogs</B><BR>
```

*Continued*

**Listing 9.4 Continued**

```
    <INPUT TYPE = RADIO NAME = category ID = cats  onClick =
radioClick() ><B>Cats</B><BR>
    <INPUT TYPE = RADIO NAME = category ID = birds onClick =
radioClick() ><B>Birds</B><BR>

</DIV>

<SCRIPT LANGUAGE = JAVASCRIPT>
    function radioClick()
    {
       var newFilter = "category=\"" + window.event.srcElement.id +
"\"";
       window.parent.dataFrame.petdata.Filter = newFilter;
       window.parent.dataFrame.petdata.Reset();
    }
</SCRIPT>

</BODY>

</HTML>
```

**Listing 9.5 pets.txt**

```
category,title,description

dogs,<B>DOGS</B>,Dogs make nice pets.
cats,<B>CATS</B>,Cats can be nice sometimes.
birds,<B>BIRDS</B>,Birds are nice musical pets.
```

**Listing 9.6 petlist.htm**

```
<HTML>

<BODY>

<OBJECT ID = "petdata" WIDTH = 0 HEIGHT = 0
   CLASSID = "CLSID:333C7BC4-460F-11D0-BC04-0080C7055A83">
    <PARAM NAME = "Filter" VALUE = "category=dogs">
    <PARAM NAME = "UseHeader" VALUE = "True">
    <PARAM NAME = "DataURL" VALUE = "pets.txt">

</OBJECT>
```

```
<TABLE DATASRC = "#petdata">

    <THEAD>
    <TD ALIGN = LEFT VALIGN = BOTTOM>
    <U>Here's the data you wanted...</U>
    </TD>
    </THEAD>

    <TBODY>
    <TD ALIGN = LEFT VALIGN = TOP>
    <DIV DATAFLD = "title" DATAFORMATAS = html></DIV><BR>
    <DIV DATAFLD = "description" DATAFORMATAS = html></DIV>
    </TD>
    </TBODY>

</TABLE>

</BODY>

</HTML>
```

## And That's It

That's it for our filtering example—and that's it for this book. We've come far in this book, from simple HTML to rewriting Web pages on the fly, from style sheets to dynamic fonts, from using the keyboard directly to making all HTML tags active, from new graphics effects to dynamic animation, from dialog boxes to data binding. All that remains now is to put all this power to work. Happy programming!

# THE SAMPLES ON
## *The Web Site*

All the examples for this book are on the Web site. You can download the examples zipped in the file named code.zip or look at the examples individually in your browser by clicking the appropriate link. (Each link corresponds to a Web page from the book.) If you download code.zip and unzip it, a new directory will be created for each example, and each directory will contain the code for that example. To see an example at work, just open the .htm file (located in the directory with the same name as the example) in your browser.

Note that some of the examples work only with Internet Explorer and some only with Netscape Navigator, as indicated in the book. If the page uses a script, that script is written in VBScript for Internet Explorer and in JavaScript for Netscape Navigator. For example, the VBScript version of the BODY example is body.htm, and the JavaScript version is bodyj.htm. Many of the examples on the Web site are written in both VBScript and JavaScript.

Here are the examples and what they do:

| Example | What it does |
| --- | --- |
| ACTIVELM | Example showing how to determine which element in a Web page has the focus |
| AIRPORT | Rewrites a page in a frame on the fly depending on the user's selection |
| ALERTS | How to use alert boxes |
| ANIMATE | An animation example moving and rotating arbitrary colored shapes |
| ANIMATE2 | An animation example using layers |

| Example | What it does |
| --- | --- |
| BINDING | Example showing how to use data binding, avoiding the need for multiple downloads from the server |
| BODY | How to change attributes of the <BODY> tag; the example changes the body's tool tip text |
| BROWSER | Determines what browser you are using and version of that browser |
| BUTTONS | How to use buttons in a script |
| CHECKS | How to use check boxes in a script |
| CLASSES | Example showing how to use style sheet classes |
| CONFIRMS | How to use a confirm dialog box |
| DATA | How to connect a database to a Web page and navigate through it |
| DEPART | Web page that rewrites itself depending on the time of day |
| DIALOGS | Dialog box example; the text you type into the dialog box is passed back to the original page |
| DIV | Example setting the style attributes of text in a <DIV> |
| DLGARGS | Dialog box example; this example both passes parameters to a dialog box and returns parameters from a dialog box |
| DRAGDROP | How to drag and drop using layers |
| DYNAM | Rewriting a Web page on the fly |
| FADER | An example in which text fades out when you click a button |
| FILTERS | How to use filters for many effects, such as wave, shadow, and more |
| FONT | How to use the <FONT> tag to change text size |
| GRAPHICS | How to use the structured graphics control to draw in a Web page |
| H1 | Example showing how to use the attributes of the <H1> tag |
| HILIGHT | Expanding and coloring text as the mouse passes over it |
| HILINK | Highlighting hyperlinks as the mouse passes over them |
| HSTYLES | Setting <Hn> tags' styles |
| HTML | Review example of basic HTML tags |
| HTMLTAG | Setting attributes of the <HTML> tag |
| IMG | Changing an image on the fly using the <IMG> tag |

| Example | What it does |
|---|---|
| INIT | How to initialize a Web page |
| INPUT | An example showing how to use input boxes |
| KEYS | Example showing how to read keys from the keyboard in a Web page script |
| LAYERS | How to use layers in a Web page |
| LOADER | Web page that loads one or another image depending on what the user requires at run time |
| MESSAGES | How to use message boxes |
| MOUSER | Example showing how to keep track of the mouse as it moves and the user clicks it |
| MOVER | How to use the path control to move an image along a pre-set path |
| OVERLAP | How to overlap text in a Web page |
| PROMPTER | Using prompt boxes |
| RADIOS | How to use radio buttons in a Web page |
| RANGER | Using text ranges; replacing text on the fly |
| RESIZER | Resizing a text box on the fly |
| SELECT | Example showing how to use select controls in a Web page |
| SELECTIT | Click the button to select (highlight) everything in this Web page |
| SELECTS | Causing the page to tell the user what text he or she has selected with the mouse |
| SETBORD | Sets the border width of a table on command |
| SORTER | Sorts a database connected to a Web page |
| STYLES | Example showing how to use style sheets |
| TEXTBOX | How to use text boxes |
| WINDOWS | Example showing how to open and use another window |
| WRITER | How to rewrite a page's entire HTML content |

Happy programming!

# INDEX